Of Time and the Artist

[handwritten annotation: This is a deep & pregnant theme. Does it get anywhere? This whole passage on the Boston Irish is fine –]

thought of the wild, extravagant and liberal creatures of his childhood
—of Mr. Fogarty, Tim Donovan, and the MacReadys—it seemed to
him that they belonged to a grander and completely different race; or
perhaps, he thought, the glory of earth and air and sky there had kept
them ripe and sweet as they always were, while their brothers here had
withered upon the rootless pavements, soured and sickened in the savage tumult of the streets, grown hard and dead and ugly in the barren
land.

The only person near him in the house, and the only person there the
boy saw with any regularity was a Chinese student named Wang: he
had the room next to him—in fact he had the two next rooms, for he
was immensely rich, the son of a man in the mandarin class who gov-
erned one of the Chinese provinces.

. But his habits and conduct were in marked contrast to those of the
average Oriental who attends an American university. These others,
studious seekers after knowledge, had come to work. Mr. Wang, a lazy
and good-humored wastrel with more money than he could spend, had
come to play. And play he did, with a whole-hearted devotion to pleasure that was worthy of a better purpose. His pleasures were for the most
part simple, but they were also costly, running to flowered silk dressing
gowns, expensively tailored clothes cut in a rakish Broadway style, silk
shirts, five-pound boxes of chocolate creams, of which he was inordi-
nately fond, week-end trips to New York, stupendous banquets at an
expensive Chinese restaurant in Boston, phonograph records, of which
he had a great many, and the companionship of "nice flat girls"—by this
he meant to say his women should be "fat," which apparently was the
primary requisite for voluptuous pulchritude.

Mr. Wang himself was just a fat, stupid, indolent, and good-hearted
child: his two big rooms in the rear of the Murphy establishment were
lavishly furnished with carved teak-wood, magnificent screens, fat
divans, couches, and chests. The rooms were always lighted with the
glow of dim and sensual lamps, there was always an odor of sandal-
wood and incense, and from time to time one heard Mr. Wang's shrill
sudden scream of childish laughter. He had two cronies, young Chinese
who seemed as idle, wealthy, and pleasure-loving as himself; they came
to his rooms every night, and then one could hear them jabbering and
chattering away in their strange speech, and sometimes silence, low
eager whisperings, and then screams of laughter.

Page 166 from Bernard DeVoto's copy of the second printing of Of Time and
the River, *annotated by DeVoto. Printed by permission of the Department of
Special Collections and University Archives, Stanford University. Annotation reads:
"This is a deep and pregnant theme. Does it get anywhere? This whole passage on
the Boston Irish is fine – ".*

Carol Ingalls Johnston

Of Time and the Artist

Thomas Wolfe, His Novels, and the Critics

CAMDEN HOUSE

Copyright © 1996 by
CAMDEN HOUSE, INC.

Published by Camden House, Inc.
Drawer 2025
Columbia, SC 29202 USA

Printed on acid-free paper.
Binding materials are chosen for strength and
durability.

ISBN:1-57113-067-5

Library of Congress Cataloging-in-Publication Data

Johnston, Carol Ingalls, 1948-
    Of time and the artist : Thomas Wolfe, his novels, and the critics
    / Carol Ingalls Johnston.
        p.   cm. -- (Studies in English and American literature, linguistics,
and culture)
    Includes bibliographical references and index.
    ISBN 1-57113-067-5 (alk. paper)
    1. Wolfe, Thomas, 1900-1938--Criticism and interpretation-
-History. 2. American fiction--History and criticism--Theory, etc.
3. Criticism--United States--History--20th century.   I. Title.
II. Series : Studies in English and American literature, linguistics,
 and culture (Unnumbered)
PS3545.0337Z74   1995
813'.52--dc20   95-367
                                                     CIP

Acknowledgments

I would like to thank my readers, John Idol, Jr., Professor Emeritus, Clemson University; Julian Mason, Professor Emeritus, The University of North Carolina-Charlotte; Donna White, Assistant Professor, Clemson University, and my Camden House editors, Benjamin Franklin V and James Hardin, as well as the Camden House staff for the time, effort, and energy they have expended in helping improve the quality of this text. The strengths of this book are the results of their labors; the weaknesses are my own.

In addition, I want to thank the members of The Thomas Wolfe Society (especially Mort Teicher, Suzanne Stutmann, and Mary Aswell Doll) for providing me with partial funding for this project by means of a William B. Wisdom Grant in Aid of Research. I am particularly grateful to Adelaide Wisdom Benjamin for her generous funding of that award. I would also like to express my thanks to Duane Schneider and Ted Mitchell for their encouragement of this text in its early stages and to the following librarians: Alice Cotten, Reference Historian, the North Carolina Collection at the University of North Carolina-Chapel Hill; Phillip Banks, the Pack Memorial Library in Asheville; and Leslie A. Morris, Curator of Manuscripts, Houghton Library, Harvard University. At the Cooper Library at Clemson University, I wish to thank the following members of the inter-library loan staff who worked overtime to help me prepare this book: Betty Cook, Alan Knight, Victoria Hamilton, Tracy James, and Marian Withington.

Few English Departments are as nurturing of scholarship as the Department at Clemson University. To the faculty and staff of that program, especially to Frank Day, Kevin Dettmar, Sylvia Titus, Beth Daniell, and Martin Jacobi, I am particularly grateful. In addition I am grateful for the support of the Dean of the College of Architecture, Arts, and the Humanities, James F. Barker. Brian Konopka and Matt Turner worked on this text as my graduate assistants during the summer of 1995. William Adams copyedited this text and Pascale Jarlman and Sharon Beckett prepared translations of a number of the German reviews of Wolfe's novels used in this text. I thank them all for their assistance.

Among my friends and neighbors there are many without whose help this book would never have been written, among these are the Bagtases (Betty, Manny, Emily, Randy, Danny, Jeanette, and Tony); the Culbersons (Jean, Ken, and Chas); the Calhouns (Dick and Doris); the Lashbrooks (Shayna, Patrick, Lillian, and Correll); the Lybrands (Vicki, Meridyth, and John); the McCormicks (Rob, Linda, Zach and Daphny); the Vines (Margo, Dwight, Laura, David, and Mark); the Wilsons (Janice, Rick, and Makenzie); Jim Ingalls; Jim Clark; and Bonnie Ferrell.

Permissions

Excerpts from *Look Homeward, Angel* reprinted with the permission of Scribner, a Division of Simon & Schuster, Inc. Copyright 1929 Charles Scribner's Sons; copyright renewed © 1957 Edward C. Aswell, Administrator, C.T.A., of the Estate of Thomas Wolfe and/or Fred W. Wolfe. Excerpts from *Of Time and the River* reprinted with the permission of Scribner, a Division of Simon & Schuster, Inc. Copyright 1935 Charles Scribner's Sons; copyright renewed © 1963 Paul Gitlin, Administrator, C.T.A. Excerpts from *The Letters of Thomas Wolfe* edited by Elizabeth Nowell. Copyright 1956 Edward C. Aswell, Administrator, C.T.A., of the Estate of Thomas Wolfe; copyright renewed © 1984 Paul Gitlin, Administrator of the Estate of Thomas Wolfe. Excerpts from *You Can't Go Home Again* reprinted by permission of HarperCollins Publishers, Inc. Copyright 1934, 1937, 1938, 1939, 1940 by Maxwell Perkins as Executor of the Estate of Thomas Wolfe. Copyright renewed © 1968 by Paul Gitlin. Excerpts from *The Notebooks of Thomas Wolfe*, edited by Richard S. Kennedy and Paschal Reeves, with permission of The University of North Carolina Press copyright © 1970. Excerpts from the Nowell-Fisher Correspondence, CW2 Series, Thomas Wolfe Collection, North Carolina Collection, University of North Carolina Library, Chapel Hill, North Carolina, printed with permission of Robert G. Anthony, Jr., Curator, and Clara Perkins Stites. Excerpts from translation of the German reviews by Ullrich Sonnemann, Hermann Linden, Ludwig Winder, Kurt Münzer, and A. E. Günther (*AC9.w 8327.L999g Box 1) printed by permission of the Houghton Library, Harvard University, Leslie A. Morris, Curator of Manuscripts. Excerpts from Bernard DeVoto's copy of Thomas Wolfe's *Of Time and the River* printed by permission of Avis DeVoto. The author additionally wishes to thank John S. Phillipson and Aldo P. Magi, editors of *The Thomas Wolfe Review*, for providing her with permission to reprint in rewritten form excerpts from her essay, "The Critical Reception of *Of Time and the River*," which originally appeared in the Spring 1987 issue of that journal, and H. G. Jones, editor, *Thomas Wolfe at Eighty-seven* (Chapel Hill: North Caroliniana Society and the North Carolina Collection, 1988) for permission to reprint in a rewritten form excerpts from her essay "Thomas Wolfe: Detailing a Literary Career" which originally appeared in that volume.

This book was written for Mom, Dad, Betty, and Cathy

— You are the wind beneath my wings . . . .

Contents

chauffeur and motor car, a place at Marblehead, and several thousand
shares of Boston and Maine.

And so it went, all up and down the line, at one of Miss Potter's
Friday afternoons. There, in her house, you could be sure that if the
lion and the lamb did not lie down together their hostess would seat
them in such close proximity to each other that the ensuing slaughter
would be made as easy, swift, and unadorned as possible.

And as the sound of snarl and curse grew louder in the clamorous
tumult of these Friday afternoons, as the face grew livid with its hate,
as the eye began to glitter, and the vein to swell upon the temple, Miss
Potter would look about her with triumphant satisfaction, seeing that
her work was good, thinking with delight:

"How stimulating! How fine it is to see so many interesting people
together—people who are really doing things! To see the flash and
play of wit, to watch the clash of brilliant intellects, to think of all these
fine young men and women have in common, and of the mutual benefits they will derive from contact with one another!—ah-ha! What a
delightful thing to see—but who is this that just came—" she would
mutter, peering toward the door, for she was very near-sighted--"who?
Who?—O-oh! Professor Lawes of the Art Department—oh, Professor
Lawes, I'm so glad you could come. We have the most *interesting*
young man here today—Mr. Wilder, who painted that picture every
one's talking about—"Portrait of a Nude Falling Upon Her Neck in a
Wet Bathroom"— Mr. Wilder, this is Doctor Lawes, the author of
Sanity and Tradition in the Renaissance—I know you're going to find
so much in common."

And having done her duty, she would wheeze heavily away, looking
around with her strange fixed grin and bulging eyes to see if she had
left anything or anyone undone or whether there was still hope of
some new riot, chaos, brawl, or bitter argument.

And yet there was a kind of wisdom in her too, that few who came
there to her house suspected: a kind of shrewdness in the fixed bulging
stare of her old eyes that sometimes saw more than the others knew.
Perhaps it was only a kind of instinct of the old woman's warm humanity that made her speak to the fragile little man with burning eyes more
gently than she spoke to others, to seat him on her right hand at the
dinner table, and to say from time to time: "Give Mr. Ten Eyck some
more of that roast beef. Oh, Mr. Ten Eyck, *do*—you've hardly eaten
anything."

Page 291 from Bernard DeVoto's copy of the second printing of Of Time and
the River, *annotated by DeVoto. Printed by permission of the Department of
Special Collections and University Archives, Stanford University. Annotation at the
top of the page reads:"He shouldn't try satire". Annotation in right-hand margin
reads "Worse than Lewis's worst".*

Introduction

> *As some day it may happen that a victim must be found,*
> *I've got a little list — I've got a little list*
> *Of social offenders who might well be underground,*
> *And who never would be missed — who never would be missed!*

THE REFRAIN IS from Ko-Ko's song in *The Mikado* and the words are Sir William Gilbert's, but the sentiment is all Thomas Wolfe's. In his 7 September 1936 pocket notebook entry, Wolfe writes "A LITTLE LIST" on which he includes the names of people destined for satirical treatment (*Notebooks* 830). Two of these, Henry Seidel Canby and Edwin Berry Burgum, were critics who had negatively responded to Wolfe's second novel, *Of Time and the River*. Canby, whose review of *Of Time and the River*, "The River of Youth," revolves about a rhetorical question ("Have you ever tried to review the Encyclopedia Britannica?") and a predilection for the word *impotent*, is served up by Wolfe to the reading public in *The Hills Beyond* as Dr. Hugo Twelvetrees Turner, "the nation's leading critical practitioner of middle-of-the-roadism," (150). Burgum, Wolfe's colleague at Washington Square who had evidently denounced *Of Time and the River* as an example of the worst in the bourgeois novel and as a preface to the rise of fascism,[1] receives similar treatment in Wolfe's *You Can't Go Home Again*: "There was Spurgeon from the teaching days at the School for Utility Cultures — good Spurgeon — Chester Spurgeon of the Ph.D. — Spurgeon of 'the great tradition' . . . who wrote hon-eyed flatteries of Thornton Wilder and his *Bridge* . . . . Where now, brave intellect, by passion uninflamed? Spurgeon of the flashing mind, by emotion unimpulsed, is now a devoted leader of the intellectual Communists." Wolfe continues, referring the reader to Spurgeon's recent article, "Mr. Wilder's Piffle" in *The New Masses*: "Hail, Comrade Spurgeon — and most heartily, my bright-eyed Intellectual, farewell!" (410).[2]

---

[1] See Betty Thompson, "Thomas Wolfe: Two Decades of Criticism," *The South Atlantic Quarterly*, 49 (July 1950), 378–379.

[2] Like many of the names chosen by Wolfe for his characters, Chester Spurgeon is a play on sounds or words which Wolfe wanted the reader to associate with that character. For Burgum, who Wolfe felt had maligned him, he chose a name that sounds like *cast aspersions*.

Had he not been given the name of Wolfe at birth by his stonecutter father, this young writer would certainly have had to invent it, for all the words that we use to refer to the wolf refer to this namesake: he was rapacious, hungry, greedy for success and fame, an alienated and a lonely wanderer, prowling – uncommonly generous and gentle when he was well treated, angry and violent when he felt betrayed. Maxwell Perkins, who knew of Wolfe's predilection for striding through the streets of Brooklyn late at night, muttering to himself, referred to him as the "lone wolfe" (*Max Perkins* 161). Wolfe lived the American dream: poor, uncultured backwoods Wolfe, springing into the history of American culture on the basis of his genius alone. His life is the stuff of legends; and like the nineteenth-century writer Louisa May Alcott, whose thinly veiled self-description in *Little Women* has provided generations of young women with a model of *woman as writer*, so Thomas Wolfe has provided six and a half decades of young American writers with a model of the *young man as novelist*. Whom hasn't he influenced? Where would James Agee and James Jones, Jack Kerouac and Herman Wouk, David Madden, and Ross Lockridge have found their protagonists had there never been a Wolfe?

Of Time and the Artist: Thomas Wolfe, His Novels, and the Critics explores the relationship between Wolfe and his critics – a dynamic dialog in which the stakes, at first a young author's literary reputation and his ability to support himself as an artist and later the needs of his estate to maintain its value, were high. Wolfe's energies were pitted against the fashionable critical theorists of the twenties and thirties, Humanists and Agrarians, Marxists and Freudians, as much as they were pitted against the Genteel Tradition of the earlier century. Wolfe functioned outside of this debate – his work was welcomed by many, but it was as frequently attacked by all of the groups within the critical community. Fighting for the opportunity to write and publish, which for Wolfe meant fighting for his life, he dealt with his critics accordingly, often using his fiction as a means of responding to them. This text deals not only with the critical community in which Wolfe's work has been evaluated over the past sixty-five years, but with the depressions that Wolfe endured after reading the English reviews of *Look Homeward, Angel* and the critical attacks on *Of Time and the River*, as well as with his responses to his critics in his correspondence, notebooks, and fiction. In the process of detailing Wolfe's relationship to his critics, *Of Time and the Artist* will document the importance of Thomas Wolfe in the American literary community of the thirties and forties and define the manner in which his literary presence has profoundly affected the critical and literary marketplace in twentieth-century America.

The Writer and His Critics

Discussions focusing on the theme of the growth of the artist in a hostile environment in Wolfe's novels are commonplace in Wolfe studies, but almost nothing has been written on a central element in that theme: the relationship between the artist and his critics as it is depicted in Wolfe's fiction. Wolfe's four semi-autobiographical novels, *Look Homeward, Angel* (1929), *Of Time and the River* (1935), *The Web and the Rock* (1939), and *You Can't Go Home Again* (1940), form the core of his enormous literary canon. Although they differ in many respects, they share a common theme: the conflict between the vitality of the artists (the Eugene Gants and the George Webbers) and the pretensions of the recognized carriers of culture in American society (intellectuals, academics, and critics).

At home with the common people – middle-class Southerners, salesmen, and landlords – and with the oral tradition of the South, Wolfe and his protagonists are uniquely conscious of the gap between their culture (the culture of baseball, politics, local gossip, and the storyteller) and the more self-conscious *culture* of the intellectuals and critics in Boston, New York, and London. In his depictions of the North State Fitting School and Eugene Gant's pulp-fiction daydreams in *Look Homeward, Angel*, his dramatizations of the School of Utility Cultures and the intellectuals at Harvard in *Of Time and the River*, his attacks on the pretentious Jerry Alsop and on the Marxists and the Agrarians in *The Web and the Rock*, and his sociological commentary on the party at the Jack's and references to Eliot's "The Hollow Men" in *You Can't Go Home Again*, Wolfe contrasts his protagonists to the cultivated but sterile intellectuals of the North and to the refined, but often spineless and brainless, young gentlemen of the "New Confederacy." For Wolfe, the response of the critical community to his writing was not only an important part of his professional life – a variable that determined his ability to continue as an artist – but a major theme in the fiction he produced.

Despite his championing of the energy of the middle class and the oral tradition of storytelling, Wolfe was a consummate writer in the Romantic tradition of Emerson, Whitman, and Melville. In addition, he was among the best educated of the major writers of his generation. He received formal training in the writing programs at two major universities, the University of North Carolina at Chapel Hill and Harvard, from which he received an AB and an MA, respectively. His powers of characterization, the strength of his humor, his remarkable rhetorical flourishes, and his willingness to experiment with language and form in an attempt to find a means of translating human consciousness to the printed page enabled him to energize the age-old story of the maturation of the young artist in his conflicts with society and to transform it into something new. His powerful descriptive passages, his dithyrambs, and his climactic sentence structures stood in direct contrast to the short, pithy phrasing of contemporary novelists like Hemingway or Stein, practitioners of the art of literary restraint. Of all the modern novelists of the first half of this century, with the possible exception of Fitzgerald, Wolfe alone seemed to be spinning out the web of fiction – at the same time that his contemporaries were intent on reeling it in.

As a result Wolfe (unlike Dreiser, who wrote "dull" fiction because he believed it an accurate reflection of a life that was dull, and unlike Anderson, whose fiction reads more like a plot summary than a novel) was able to provide his readers with a rich and intricate text that touched them simultaneously on several levels and with an elaborate and sensuous prose poetry that was anything but unsophisticated. That prose style incorporated the homely and exaggerated characters and actions characteristic of the regional Southern storyteller, but it embedded that tradition in the rhetorically powerful language of American and English Romanticism and the stream of consciousness of the new Realism.

Because so much of his writing is autobiographical and based on the perspective of the maturing writer, that is, on the tension produced by the double vision of the narrator in his fiction, Wolfe was more vulnerable to the critics than were many of his contemporaries. The reader encounters in the narratives of these texts both the voice of the young unpublished writer (in the process of living that life that will provide him with the subject matter for his novels) and the voice of the older, more mature, and established writer who is telling the story. The visions of Eugene Gant and George Webber, which are in so many ways different not only from the established views of the communities in which they were born but also from the views of the communities in which they are educated and work, become authoritative only in light of the readers' recognition that these young men will become *true* artists, the authors of the very novels in which they appear.[3] For Wolfe a negative critical response to one of his novels, or even a luke-warm critical response to one of his novels, endangered not only his literary career but the important narrative tension produced by this self-referential element in his texts, the paradigm of his literary world. If in the final analysis Eugene Gant and George Webber produce nothing better than mediocre art, the value of their unique perspectives becomes limited and the text of the novels written by Thomas Wolfe no longer sustain but, instead, parody the author's intent.

[3]See Margaret Mills Harper, *The Aristocracy of Art in Joyce and Wolfe* (Baton Rouge and London: Louisiana S U P, 1990), for an extended discussion of Wolfe's double vision.

Throughout *Of Time and the Artist*, I have made every effort to convey the excitement of the literary debate surrounding Thomas Wolfe and his literary canon. So much criticism of Wolfe and criticism of Wolfe criticism has been written, with interpretation and evaluation piled on interpretation and evaluation, that it can be overwhelming. The interaction of art and criticism is not linear – it is multidimensional – with literature and critical study being joined by the same kind of web with which Wolfe connected the individual and society in *The Web and the Rock*. For instance, the hero of *Look Homeward, Angel*, Eugene Gant (the subject of hundreds of pages of critical interpretation and the inveterate experiencer of reality and obsessed reader of books) could never have been fashioned by Wolfe without his exposure as an undergraduate at Chapel Hill to the critical theory of Frederich Koch or to the two major American critics, George Pierce Baker and John Livingston Lowes, at Harvard. Koch's Carolina Playmakers and Baker's 47 Workshop stressed the importance of personal experience at the core of the dramatic process, and by teaching the art of the playwright emphasized the value of the creative imagination over the analytical; Lowes's class on the Romantics (taught while he was completing his epic study of Coleridge, *The Road to Xanadu*) identified for Wolfe the process by which this creative imagination functioned, the synthesis of enormous and diverse reading. The critical community and its theory was thus as important in fathering the hero of Wolfe's first novel as it was responsible for evaluating that novel after its publication. If, as so many of Wolfe's interpreters have suggested, the search for the father was Wolfe's preeminent theme, the young artist found that literary *father* in his critics and editors.

Thomas Wolfe writes in his 1936 manifesto, *The Story of a Novel*, that "there is no such thing as an artistic vacuum" (25–26). *Of Time and the Artist* is based on that thesis; its premise is that literature and criticism nourish each other and each in turn nourishes and is nourished by society. The final work produced by the artist, although often marketed as the product of a single individual, is often as much the product of the pressures placed on that writer by the social and critical community he inhabits as it is the product of his unique experience. The focus of *Of Time and the Artist* is not on Thomas Wolfe the man or Thomas Wolfe the writer, but on Thomas Wolfe as a member of the literary community and the spirited dialog that has persisted between his writing and that community for the past sixty-five years.

The Critical Community

In critical terms Thomas Wolfe has at least three distinct reputations: the response of the contemporary book reviewers (generally published in newspapers and magazines); the response of the contemporary literary and academic community (generally published in literary journals); and the retrospective evaluations of his achievement by later literary historians, critics, and scholars. This study deals with all three – taking as its structure the idea of "the pebble and the pool" that Wolfe describes in early manuscript versions of *The Web and the Rock*. "One," Wolfe writes, "drops the pebble in the pool . . . but instead of pebble and pool simply in personal terms of pebble and pool, one gets a widening ever-enlarging picture of the whole thing – the pebble becomes important, if important at all, only in terms of this general and constant pattern of which it is the temporary and accidental stimulus . . . the pebble, if you like, is only a means to this end" (*Notebooks* 941). For the purposes of this book, Wolfe's writing is the pebble and the pattern (his influence on American literary history) is made by the ripples moving outward like a series of concentric circles: the critical assessments of his work by reviewers, contemporary critics, and later critics and scholars – American, English, and German – that has since 1929 enriched the literary scene.

Readers of this volume may be surprised to find that it includes editions, anthologies, and book collections as part of the critical tradition. For the purposes of this study, criticism refers to the work of any individual or group, critic or scholar (including textual critics and editors), which serves as an intermediary between the author and the audience, explaining explicitly in essays and books or implicitly in editorial decisions and selections the importance a writer's work has for their generation. However, in the process of studying Wolfe's critics in this volume, it will become obvious that few of them stuck narrowly to this task; but that for most the process of criticizing a specific work became, as H. L. Mencken notes in his "A Footnote on Criticism," a means of working with the materials of life itself.[4]

It can be argued that Wolfe's anthology appearances are for many their first, and for some their only, introduction to the writings of this author. The decision of anthology editors to include an excerpt from a novel or a short story by Wolfe, accompanied by a brief historical/analytical introduction, in the long run may have a greater influence on Wolfe's reputation in the general community than do the major critical and scholarly works which are generally read only within the academic

---

[4] *Prejudices: Third Series* (New York: Farrar, Straus and Giroux, 1977), 87.

and literary communities. Similarly, within the academic community the number of and nature of dissertations produced on Wolfe reflect the health and nature of his reputation at any given time. Over the past sixty-five years, Wolfe has made over three hundred anthology appearances and been the subject of more than one hundred dissertations.

Collectors of Wolfe's work have also displayed critical judgement: among the best have been the private collector William B. Wisdom, whose Wolfe collection, at first housed in the family attic in New Orleans, later found a home at the Houghton; Myra Champion who indefatigably surveyed the leading figures of Wolfe's day to elicit commentary on their early responses to Wolfe and who framed the Wolfe Collection at the Pack Memorial Library in Asheville; Mary Lindsay Thornton, William S. Powell, H. G. Jones, Robert G. Anthony, Jr., and Jerry and Alice Cotten who have nurtured the Wolfe collection at the North Carolina Collection at Chapel Hill; Eve Braden and William Hatchett; and Aldo Magi, whose private collection in Sandusky, Ohio, has provided many a young scholar with a starting point for research.

Wolfe's fiction and life have also been the inspiration for other writers. In addition to Ketti Frings's 1958 Pulitzer Prize-winning adaptation of *Look Homeward, Angel* for the stage, more than fifty poems have been written either addressed to or depicting some element of Wolfe's work or life; at least three published novels (two by Aline Bernstein, *The Journey Down* [1938] and *Three Blue Suits* [1957], and one by Herman Wouk, *Youngblood Hawke* [1962]) deal with a Wolfe-like character; and there are, in addition, short stories by Ray Bradbury and David Madden, musical scores, radio and television programs, recordings, and theatrical presentations which in a variety of ways focus the attention of the general public on elements in Wolfe's life and fiction.

1: Pros and Cons – An Overview of Wolfe Studies

THE QUALITY AND nature of Wolfe's writing has been heavily debated since he first burst upon the American literary community in 1929 with the publication of *Look Homeward, Angel*. His literary canon has been the subject of more than five hundred reviews, an additional six hundred critical essays, and over eighty books. Many of these will be dealt with in this volume. The truth is that despite his productivity, more has been written about Thomas Wolfe than was ever written by him.

The purpose of this chapter is to discuss (in more-general terms than the chronologically structured narratives of chapters two through eight of this book allow) those major critics and major critical studies which, over the past sixty-five years, have defined and redefined Wolfe's presence in the literary community and to suggest the range of and distinction between *responsible* and *irresponsible* critical approaches to the analysis and evaluation of Wolfe's work.

Defining Critics and Studies

Over the past sixty-five years, a number of major critics and major critical studies have been responsible for shaping the study of Thomas Wolfe. In this category, at least eighteen critics should be singled out for discussion: Herbert J. Muller, the Purdue professor with whom Wolfe stayed while he delivered his Purdue Speech in 1938 and whose 1947 study, *Thomas Wolfe*, is the earliest and remains among the best of the full-length studies of Wolfe's writing; Pamela Hansford Johnson (British novelist and wife of C. P. Snow), whose 1947 *Thomas Wolfe: A Critical Study* (later retitled *Hungry Gulliver*) was the first full-length English study of Wolfe's writing; Richard Walser, whose 1953 study, *The Enigma of Thomas Wolfe*, was the first published collection of the responses of reviewers and critics to Wolfe's writing; Louis D. Rubin, Jr., who in his *Thomas Wolfe: The Weather of His Youth* (1955) examines the major themes and formative forces in Wolfe's four novels; Floyd C. Watkins, whose *Thomas Wolfe's Characters: Portraits from Life* (1957) identifies the Asheville citizens in Wolfe's novels; Richard S. Kennedy, whose monumental *The Window of Memory: The Literary Career of Thomas Wolfe* (1962) jump-started textual study of Wolfe in the sixties and remains, in the nineties, the single most-articulate study of Wolfe's manuscript material and method of composition; Paschal Reeves, whose *Thomas Wolfe's Albatross* (1968) is the basic text on Wolfe's problems dealing with race and nationality in America; C. Hugh Holman, whose many essays and books on Wolfe, rethought and rewritten in his 1975 opus *The Loneliness at the Core*, first assured Wolfe a prominent position in the American literary canon; Aldo P. Magi and John S. Phillipson, who, as editors of *The Thomas Wolfe Review* (originally *The Thomas Wolfe Newsletter*), have indefatigably published the lion's share of Wolfe scholarship and criticism since 1977; Suzanne Stutman, whose *My Other Loneliness* (1983), an edition of the correspondence of Thomas Wolfe and his mistress, Aline Bernstein, first opened discussion on the issue of Wolfe's treatment of women in his fiction; John Lane Idol, Jr., whose 1987 *A Thomas Wolfe Companion* serves as the most-readable general introduction to Wolfe; Leslie Field, whose humane textual study, *Thomas Wolfe and His Editors* (1987), provides the final word on the Halberstadt – Kennedy controversy of the early 1980s, an academic brouhaha and public debate over the collaborative nature of Wolfe's posthumously published novels; Francis Skipp, whose 1987 edition of *The Complete Short Stories of Thomas Wolfe* single-handedly resurrected interest in Wolfe as a short-story writer; and Margaret Mills Harper, whose elegant 1990 study, *The Aristocracy of Art*, explores the nature of autobiographical fiction in the novels of Wolfe and James Joyce.

In addition, the dimensions of Wolfe scholarship have been defined and redefined by his three major biographers, Elizabeth Nowell (the savvy Bryn Mawr graduate who served as Wolfe's literary agent from 1933 until his death and in 1956 published the standard edition of his letters) whose 1960 biography, *Thomas Wolfe*, first describes Wolfe's relationships with his editors and the literary marketplace; Andrew Turnbull, whose less successful 1967 biography based largely on Wolfe's published correspondence focuses on Wolfe the man and Wolfe the legend; and David Donald, whose Pulitzer Prize-winning biography, *Look Homeward: A Life of Thomas Wolfe*, remains the standard, an unexpurgated study of Thomas Wolfe, writer and genius, as he was – not as many perhaps would have wanted him to be – written by one of the foremost historians of the late twentieth century.

Of these eighteen defining figures, one is a retired auto worker, and fourteen function(ed) in academia as college and university professors. Rubin, Kennedy, Reeves, Stutman, Idol, Skipp, and Harper are Wolfeans whose published work on this author began as dissertations. Kennedy completed his dissertation, "A Critical Biography of Thomas Wolfe to His Thirty-Fourth Year," at Harvard under the direction of Howard Mumford Jones in 1953, one year before Rubin completed his dissertation, "Thomas Wolfe: The Weather of His Youth," at Johns Hopkins.

Professors Reeves and Skipp both completed their dissertations at Duke University under the direction of Arlin Turner. Professor Idol prepared his dissertation, "Thomas Wolfe's Satire," at the University of Arkansas under the direction of H. B. Rouse. Professors Stutman and Harper belong to yet a third generation of Wolfe scholars: Stutman's dissertation, an edition of the Bernstein-Wolfe correspondence, was produced at Temple University under the direction of Richard S. Kennedy; Harper's was completed at Chapel Hill under the direction of Louis Rubin, Jr. Two of these studies were produced in the forties, three in the fifties; four were the product of the sixties; two were produced (or, in the case of *The Thomas Wolfe Review*, first published) in the seventies; five were published in the eighties; and one in the nineties.

The socially conscious formalist and Marxist critics of the thirties and forties generally found Wolfe's writing unsatisfactory for their purposes (although Wolfe was courted by both the Agrarian and Marxist critics in the last years of his life). The work of Rubin, Watkins, and Holman first established the grounds on which Wolfe's reputation was built in the fifties, but many of their conclusions about the nature of Wolfe's literary career were to be redefined in the sixties when a turnover in leadership of the Estate of Thomas Wolfe provided scholars and critics with freer access to and permission for publication of previously unpublished documents and manuscript materials. Much of the manuscript material that Wolfe left at the time of his death (and which William B. Wisdom bought for three thousand dollars in the early forties, when that amount meant something) had been deposited by the late forties in the Wisdom Collection in the Houghton Library at Harvard. Here Kennedy, just returned from fulfilling his military commitment during World War II, first worked in the late forties and early fifties, completing in his dissertation by 1953 what would become the first section of his study, *The Window of Memory*.[1]

Critical Themes

The elements in Wolfe's writing addressed by his critics are as diverse as the critics themselves; still, there remain about a dozen major themes around which Wolfe studies seem to revolve: 1) Wolfe's discovery of America; 2) his concepts of time, loneliness, death, and the search for the

---

[1] The best study of Richard S. Kennedy's productive career is John Idol's entry, "Richard S. Kennedy," printed in volume 111 of *The Dictionary of Literary Biography: American Literary Biographers* (Second Series), ed. Steven Seraphin (Detroit: Gale Research, 1991), pp. 117–127.

father; 3) his depiction of the artist; 4) his verbosity and style; 5) his attitudes toward the North and the South, urban America and rural America;
6) his craftsmanship; 7) his formative years; 8) his social awareness; 9) his
use of autobiographical elements; 10) his collaboration with his editors;
11) his depiction of race and gender issues; and 12) his influences on
other writers and their influences on him.

The most authoritative critical treatments of all these themes appear in
Kennedy's *The Window of Memory* and Donald's *Look Homeward*, the premier Wolfe studies. Much of the information in these two books overlaps,
but never unnecessarily so. Kennedy's study is no biography; it is a
highly sophisticated analysis of Wolfe's intellectual and literary growth,
aimed at an audience of academics and scholars. Donald's biography,
though equally well documented, is written for a more general audience
interested in the historical Thomas Wolfe. In addition to these two books,
a number of important Wolfe studies have been written on each of these
themes.

Maxwell Perkins, Wolfe's first editor, in his 1938 article "Scribner's
and Thomas Wolfe," was among the first to suggest that Wolfe's primary
subject is the discovery and celebration of America. Others dealing with
this theme include John Peale Bishop, who argues that Wolfe's attempt to
present a myth of American greatness was stymied by the American Depression ("The Myth and Modern Literature"), and Herbert Muller, who
comments that, to the contrary, the American Depression was not the
cause of Wolfe's failure, but the means to his faith (*Thomas Wolfe* 8–14).
Kennedy's description of Wolfe's notebooks as focusing on the American
experience ("Thomas Wolfe and the American Experience") and Holman's *Three Modes of Modern Southern Fiction* also include important arguments suggesting that the American self was Wolfe's one true subject.

Clustered, the concepts of time, loneliness, death, and the search for
the father also produced significant critical response. The best study of
Wolfe's use of time is Karin Pfister's *Zeit und Wirklichkeit bei Thomas Wolfe*
(1954), a full-length study in German which deals with Wolfe's indebtedness to the thought of Proust and Bergson. Pfister's writing, however,
is uneven, and the value of her work is undermined by her focus on the
reflections of the philosophies of these two figures in Wolfe's writing
rather than on the writings themselves. Two of the best American studies
are W. P. Albrecht's "Time as Unity in the Novels of Thomas Wolfe"
and Margaret Church's "Dark Time." Albrecht's article defines two concepts of time in Wolfe's novels, linear (the river) and cyclical (the recurring seasons), while Church's article contrasts Wolfe's concepts of time to
those of Bergson and Proust. In his "Thomas Wolfe: Time and the
South," Louis Rubin argues that *Look Homeward, Angel* is dominated by

themes of mutability; and, several years later, Morris Beja would conclude that Wolfe uses memory to recapture and fix the past in his first two novels, but not in the last two ("Why You Can't Go Home Again").

The most comprehensive study of the theme of loneliness in Wolfe's writing is Holman's intellectually astute full-length study, *The Loneliness at the Core*. Wolfe, Holman writes, is bent on discovering America, but the major theme in his writing is that of loneliness and the isolation of the incommunicable self. It was a theme with which Wolfe obviously had some first hand experience. As Perkins's biographer A. Scott Berg notes, Perkins expressed concerns on several occasions about Wolfe's isolation as a writer; Wolfe was quite capable, Perkins explained, of going without seeing or talking to another human being for weeks at a time. Perkins rather casually introduced the idea of a young man's search for a father he has never known as a possible plotline for Wolfe's second novel during one of his brainstorming sessions with Wolfe. To Perkins's surprise, Wolfe restructured that suggestion into a profound philosophy and theme. The symbol of the search for the father in Wolfe's writing came to represent the universal search for certainty and authority. Joseph Warren Beach, one of the first American critics to study the technique of the novel, focuses on this theme in "Thomas Wolfe: The Search for a Father." Holman, however, suggests that the search for the father in Wolfe's fiction is, at best, an afterthought, a topic developing out of the more general theme of loneliness in Wolfe's writing. J. Russell Reaver and Robert I. Strozier add an interesting twist to their discussion of the theme of *loneliness and isolation* in Wolfe's writing. They argue that "Wolfe thought of isolation as a kind of death," a redemptive rather than a destructive process. They perceive Wolfe's use of the death of his brother, Ben, in *Look Homeward, Angel* as the means by which Wolfe provides Eugene with new creative energies ("Thomas Wolfe and Death").

Louis Rubin first suggested a link between Wolfe's depiction of the artist and the poverty of Wolfe's cultural and social background in 1963 in *The Faraway Country* and in 1973 in his article "The Sense of Being Young." Several decades later, Margaret Mills Harper's *The Aristocracy of Art*, the first full-length study of this theme, developed this concept more fully. Wolfe's depiction of the artist, Harper concludes, "rests primarily upon a working assumption that the artist is superior to and detached from his environment." Wolfe and Joyce, she suggests, redefine the criteria by which society evaluates individuals to create a sense of an artistic aristocracy which surpasses class and economic status structures (13). This may be one of the reasons that Wolfe fell into such disfavor with the Marxist critics; his early novels deny the existence of those very class structures that the Marxists perceived to be in revolt. Richard Walser's

"The Angel and the Ghost" treats Wolfe's concept of the artist in *Look Homeward, Angel* as a primary theme of that novel. The ghost/angel of Ben, he argues, returns in the last pages of that novel as a means of arousing Eugene Gant's dormant artistry. It is for Eugene alone that the marble statues and the memories of his past, both representing the creative powers of the imagination, come alive. When Ben's ghost/angel tells Eugene "*You* are your own world" (*Look Homeward, Angel* 624), he is providing the impetus for the kind of autobiographical fiction that Eugene, like Wolfe, ultimately writes. Other treatments of this theme appear in Maxwell Geismar's *Writers in Crisis* (1942) and Pamela Hansford Johnson's *Hungry Gulliver* (1948).[2]

If the critics disagree most violently on any single issue in Wolfe studies, it is in the ongoing debate on the quality of Wolfe's prose style. Howard Mumford Jones[3] in his 1935 review of *Of Time and the River*, "Social Notes on the South," was among the first to attack the structural and verbal failings of Wolfe's writings: "Just now," he writes, "Mr. Wolfe is riding on top of the wave, but whether the public will be willing to follow him through the two and a half million words which this gigantic scheme implies is a debatable question" (455). Just over a half decade later, Alfred Kazin, in his *On Native Ground*, attacked Wolfe's prose style more forcefully (though the fact that he included Wolfe in the study at all was a notable departure from his Marxist value systems). Wolfe, he suggests, is "the Tarzan of rhetoric." His prose style, Kazin continues, "pilfered recklessly from the Jacobeans and Sir Thomas Browne, James Joyce and Swinburne, Gilbert Murray and the worst traditions of Southern oratory, was a gluttonous English instructor's accumulation" (480). Robert Penn Warren, one of the younger Agrarians, argues that Wolfe's rhetoric was astonishingly loose, "sometimes grand . . . more often tedious and tinged with hysteria" ("A Note on the Hamlet of Thomas Wolfe" 205–206).

Equally as many talented critics find Wolfe's prose style to be sublime. The same Edwin Berry Burgum pilloried by Wolfe in *You Can't Go Home Again* for his mean-spirited comments on *Of Time and the River*, in retrospect maintained that the periodic sentences and the consolation of abstract statement in his later writings made Wolfe one of the great stylists in the English language ("Thomas Wolfe's Discovery of America"). One of the more detailed discussions of Wolfe's rhetoric, Maurice Natanson's "The Privileged Moment" suggests that Wolfe's style presents a

---

[2] The text of Johnson's study used in this book is that of the first American edition, *Hungry Gulliver*, which was published in 1948.

[3] Howard Mumford Jones taught both at Chapel Hill and Harvard, but not at the same time that Wolfe was enrolled at either institution.

"profound dimension of language . . . the power of language to epiphanize transcendent meanings through its own instrumentality" (144). Floyd Watkins in "Rhetoric in Southern Writing: Wolfe" (1958) cast his vote with Burgum and Natanson, concluding that Wolfe's prose style is nothing less than poetic, attracting "the large audience to which many modern poets claim they cannot appeal" (79).

It is not surprising that the fifties and sixties with their concern for urban sprawl, suburban values, and regional biases were the environment for a number of works defining Wolfe's attitudes toward the North and the South and toward urban and rural America. Wilbur Cash in his 1941 study, *The Mind of the South*, was the first critic to deal successfully with Wolfe's ambivalence toward the region of his birth. Rubin in "The Historical Image of Modern Southern Writing" (1956) and Holman in "The Dark Ruined Helen of His Blood" (1961) both suggest that for Wolfe, as for many other young Southern writers of the period, the North is the foe and New York City is the bastion waiting to be assailed. Holman's study, the more ambitious of the two, attempts to explain the ambivalence in Wolfe's writings about the South (an ambivalence that drew a good deal of criticism from the Agrarians in the thirties with their focus on the rejuvenation of the Southern rural tradition). Although several of Wolfe's critics argue to the contrary, Holman maintains that Wolfe was a *true* Southerner. He writes that Wolfe shares "the Southerner's willingness to accept and find delight in paradox" for "at the heart of the riddle of the South is a union of opposites, a condition of instability, a paradox: a love of individualism combined with a defense of slavery and segregation, a delight in polished manners and at the same time a ready recourse to violence, the liberalism of Thomas Jefferson coexisting with the conservatism of John C. Calhoun" (189). The earliest dissertation dealing with Wolfe, Blanche Gelfant's "Urbanization as an Influence on Dreiser, Dos Passos, and Wolfe," prepared under the direction of Frederick Hoffman at the University of Wisconsin in 1948 and later published as *The American City Novel* in 1954, focuses on the motif of urbanization in all three novelists. Gelfant perceives Wolfe's unique distinction as a "city novelist" to reside in his "personalization" of the city. "Wolfe," she explains, "found in its various and changing scenes the objective correlative to his own volatile emotions as well as to what he held to be timeless and impersonal truths" (119).

These decades ushered in a period of social protest and reform in America, producing a large number of studies on Wolfe's social awareness or on what many perceived to be his lack of social awareness. No fewer than a dozen articles written between 1950 and 1970 deal with this issue (see, for example, Edward Wagenknecht's "Gargantua as Novelist" [1952], William F. Kennedy's "Economic Ideas in Contemporary Literature" [1953], Walter Fuller Taylor's "Thomas Wolfe and the Middle Class Tradition" [1953]; H. M. Ledig-Rowohlt's "Thomas Wolfe in Berlin" [1953]; Irving Halperin's "Man Alive" [1958]; Holman's "Thomas Wolfe's Berlin" [1967]; and Richard H. Cracroft's "A Pebble in the Pool" [1971]). Many of these studies are concerned with Wolfe's Brooklyn experiences during the Great Depression, others with his introduction to the evils of Nazi Germany during his 1936 visit; all, however, suggest that toward the end of his writing *Of Time and the River*, Wolfe's attitudes toward his responsibilities as a critic of society changed significantly. The most remarkable example of this change occurs in Wolfe's "The Party at Jack's." The vital elements of this story are its social criticism, which spans capitalism and class structure, urbanization, and material pride. In "The Party at Jack's" even the members of the working class are corrupted by the Jack's affluence. Yet, as Richard S. Kennedy so incisively notes in *The Window of Memory*, despite the symbolic suggestions of revolution in the work, it remains quite unlike the average proletarian novel of its day: there is no clear-cut distinction between corrupt property owners and stout-hearted workers (348). Wolfe as deftly sidestepped the fads of politics as he did the passing fancies of the literary community.

Wolfe raised the issue of the autobiographical element in his writing in the prefatory note to *Look Homeward, Angel*; and it came back to haunt him. Robert Penn Warren entered the fray in May 1935 with his "A Note on the Hamlet of Thomas Wolfe," reminding his readers that Shakespeare had written *Hamlet*, but not been Hamlet. But it did not become a hotly debated critical issue until Bernard DeVoto in a scathing 1936 review of Wolfe's *The Story of a Novel*, "Genius Is Not Enough," noted that among several indications of Wolfe's "shoddy craftsmanship" in *Of Time and the River* were a number of instances in which Wolfe had failed to translate the first person "I" of his narrative to the third person "he," thereby confusing the author with the protagonist of his novel. Wolfe had lost his objectivity as a novelist. To emphasize the point, DeVoto's article featured a photograph of the critic with a cheshire-cat grin, gun in hand, ostensibly aimed off of the page at Thomas Wolfe. Thomas Lyle Collins a half decade later refuted the arguments of both critics in his *Sewanee Review* article, "Thomas Wolfe." Warren and DeVoto, he continues, in making their arguments against the autobiographical elements in Wolfe's writing, demonstrated the loss of their own objectivity by focusing on the author of the work rather than on the literary work itself. Assuredly, however, the final word in this discussion belongs to Margaret Mills Harper, who argues eloquently in her study *The Aristocracy of Art* that DeVoto and Warren confuse the genre of autobiographical fiction with autobiography. The autobiographical elements in the writings of Wolfe and Joyce, she argues, are integral to those texts, in which the burden of the reader's acceptance of the aesthetic of the protagonists lies to a considerable extent in the reader's recognition that the protagonists will become the artists who write the books. Without the autobiographical element, the works become meaningless.

Wolfe raised yet another controversial critical issue in his *The Story of a Novel* when he detailed the assistance he had received from his editor, Maxwell Perkins, at Scribners, opening up the issue of collaboration. DeVoto raised this issue as well in "Genius Is Not Enough," using the kind of technical metaphor common in the age of industrialization, suggesting that although Wolfe had manufactured the parts of the "carburetor," it was the assembly line at Scribners and Maxwell Perkins who put the carburetor together. This issue was a particularly sensitive one since it denied Wolfe his identity as a professional writer. The result of this debate was to force Wolfe to leave Scribners to prove that he could write successfully without Perkins's help. Wolfe's move to Harpers, however, ultimately raised yet another collaborative controversy. Reviewing Wolfe's posthumously published novel *You Can't Go Home Again* in the pages of *The New Republic* in 1940, Hamilton Basso, one of Wolfe's correspondents as well as a good friend of Maxwell Perkins, expressed significant concern over Edward C. Aswell's claim that Wolfe had completed his posthumous novels and turned them over to his publisher prior to his death in 1938. Basso, referring to a letter he received in July 1937 from Wolfe in which Wolfe indicated that these novels had not yet taken shape, suggested that Aswell and Harpers had not been entirely accurate in their presentation of these works.

By 1980, this issue had developed into a teapot tempest, referred to by Wolfeans, in an age which had begun to question the corruption of authority figures, as "Wolfegate." The heated debate between the young Yale graduate John Halberstadt, who insisted that Aswell had *written* Wolfe's posthumous novels, and the well-established Wolfean Richard S. Kennedy, who insisted that Aswell had simply functioned in a fashion necessary for protecting the Wolfe Estate at the time of Wolfe's death, found its way into the pages of *The New York Times Book Review, The New York Review of Books, The Chronicle of Higher Education, The Boston Globe, The San Francisco Chronicle*, and several other publications. Ultimately, the web of innuendo which brought Halberstadt such notoriety was unwoven by a third party, Leslie Field of Purdue, whose early studies of Wolfe had required him to become familiar with Wolfe manuscript material. Reviewing once again the manuscript materials at Chapel Hill and Harvard in his full-length study *Thomas Wolfe and His Editors* (1987), Field details how

Aswell handled Wolfe's manuscripts. This study, which prints many and describes many more of Wolfe's manuscripts in these collections, successfully reestablished the authority of Wolfe's posthumous novels while acknowledging both the pitfalls of producing a *true text* from manuscripts left unfinished at the time of an author's death and the responsibility of the editor to face those *pitfalls* if in fact the works were ever to be published.

Wolfe's mountain-bred biases against a variety of American ethnic groups – Jews, American Indians, African Americans, and Asian Americans – is the subject of Paschal Reeves's 1968 study *Thomas Wolfe's Albatross: Race and Nationality in America*. Reeves argues that Wolfe's early uncritical acceptance of the prejudices of his countrymen changed toward the end of Wolfe's life at which time it was too late to alter the satirical fictional portraits of these groups which had been published in his earlier works. Ruel Foster in his 1973 *American Literature* article "Thomas Wolfe's Mountain Gloom and Glory" explores the impact that the bowl like rim of the Blue Ridge Mountains had on the imagery and language of Wolfe's four novels.

Nearly fifteen years later, riding a wave of feminist criticism, Suzanne Stutman's edition of the correspondence of Wolfe and his mistress, Aline Bernstein, *My Other Loneliness*, opened up critical discussion to the treatment of women in Wolfe's fiction. The Wolfe/Bernstein correspondence is a particularly valuable companion to the edition of Wolfe's letters published by Elizabeth Nowell and the notebooks published by Kennedy and Reeves. Wolfe, Stutman concludes, suffered from the same virgin-whore syndrome that afflicted Joyce and Lawrence. Bernstein played Wolfe's modern-day Scheherazade, enticing him to entertain her with the stories of his youth night after night, many of which became scenes in Wolfe's first novel. Carole Klein, the author of the standard Bernstein biography, *Aline*, comments in a 1988 article that "Wolfe believed that any behavior of his, no matter how outrageous, should be acceptable to Aline Bernstein." When Bernstein complained about this Jekyll and Hyde behavior to her psychiatrist, Dr. Beatrice Hinkle, Hinkle responded that the absorption of self in the creative process, in terms of conventional maturity, can produce a man who remains a child forever (Carole Klein "Thomas Wolfe: The Aggrieved and Greedy Lover" 83). Be that as it may, the power of Bernstein's influence on Wolfe was enormous and the correspondence of these two fine writers is a particularly passionate one.

Gathering the abundant studies focusing on Wolfe's indebtedness to other authors and their indebtedness to him, the reader can only conclude that Wolfe influenced everyone and was, in turn, influenced by everyone. The comparisons are endless: Wolfe to Coleridge, Wordsworth, Carlyle, Nietszche, Whitman, and Shaw; Wolfe to Shakespeare,

In addition, he charges Wolfe with having a fire phobia, refers several times to the "feminine" element in Wolfe and Perkins in a way that implies a homoerotic aspect in their relationship, charges that if Wolfe had not died in 1938 he would have gone insane, and suggests that Wolfe's break with Scribners and Perkins had taken place because of Wolfe's Communist leanings.[6]

There was, of course, no evidence for any of these charges aside from Fisher's own overwrought "psychological insight." Nowell, passionately loyal to Wolfe and Perkins, was appalled. In letters to Aswell written during that same period, she attributes Fisher's articles to both his envy of Wolfe's success as a writer and his bitterness toward Perkins for rejecting his first novel. She wrote Fisher immediately, labeling his articles "psychological crap." "I think this psychological over-simplification with no horse sense [is] the real basic objection I have to your article, and to psychiatry and psychiatrists in general," she wrote Fisher. "They build themselves up a lovely fabric and in their own vision and conviction that psychiatry is right and everything else is wrong, they stray far far away from truth, and seem ludicrous to an ordinary dumb laymen like yours truly" (Nowell to Fisher, 29 August 1950, UNC-CH).

Nowell insisted that Fisher remove her name and Aswell's from the articles. Fisher, responding to Nowell's request, labeled her attitudes toward psychology "unworthy of a high school freshman with an IQ of 90," but swore that he would never compromise her by referring to her in either of the articles (Fisher to Nowell, 4 September 1950, UNC-CH). Although Fisher did replace references to Nowell and Aswell in his *Tomorrow* articles and in the reprinting of "My Experiences with Thomas Wolfe" in the Cargill memorial volume, *Thomas Wolfe at Washington Square* (substituting the more vague phrase "a friend of Wolfe" for their names), he chose to insert their names back into those essays when they were reprinted in his collection, *Thomas Wolfe as I Knew Him*, which was published in 1963, several years after the deaths of Nowell and Aswell.

It is clear from their correspondence with each other and with Fisher that much of what he wrote was a distortion of their attitudes and that

---

[6]Numerous entries in Wolfe's notebooks deal with his rejection of Communist ideals and values. See *Notebooks*, p. 705, for instance, in which Wolfe writes: "I have heard Communists I know in New York talk gloatingly about our people sodden with despair, muttering with revolution, long in a miserable degraded state of utter hopelessness – but by such foolishness they betray their ignorance, their feeble grasp, their failure to know anything about the country they are going to revolutionize – The American hope is fantastic, staggering, mad – ."

neither Nowell or Aswell, had they been alive, would have approved of Fisher's use of their names in this context.

Fisher's monomania extends even to his notes. On page 50 of *Thomas Wolfe As I Knew Him*, he writes, "Miss Nowell's letters to me reveal that she thought that in these two essays I had written too frankly about Wolfe and the Wolfe-Perkins relationship." None of Nowell's letters printed in *In the Shadow of the Giant* or filed in the University of North Carolina collection at Chapel Hill suggests that Nowell is the least bit concerned about Fisher's "frankness"; she is concerned, however, about the fact that, in maligning Wolfe and Perkins, Fisher portrayed both of them inaccurately.

Aswell managed to be philosophical about the Fisher essays, reminding Nowell that "People are free to write whatever they like, which means among other things that they are free to be as foolish as they like" (*In the Shadow of the Giant* 50). He felt that in the long run Fisher's articles would neither help nor harm Wolfe's reputation. His response to Struthers Burt's defense of his "Catalyst for Genius," which had been published in the Letters to the Editor section of the 11 August 1951 *Saturday Review of Literature* was, however, not nearly so even-tempered.

Struthers Burt's "Catalyst for Genius," filled with lavish praise for Max Perkins – but vilifying Wolfe, appeared in the 9 June 1951 issue of *The Saturday Review of Literature*. Although the article focused ostensibly on Perkins, Burt made several unsubstantiated charges against Wolfe in the periphery of his discussion. In the first paragraph of his essay Burt introduces Perkins, referring to him not only as Wolfe's "collaborator," but also as a "greater genius" than Wolfe. In the second paragraph, Burt drops a bombshell by announcing that there "is not the slightest question in the minds of the few who knew Maxwell Perkins intimately that the Tom Wolfe episode killed him." Wolfe's betrayal of Perkins (defined by Burt as Wolfe's decision to leave Scribners after the publication of *The Story of a Novel* and to sign with Harpers) had been, Burt indicates, the point at which Perkins began to die (6). In addition, he charges that Perkins was deeply offended by Wolfe's caricature of him as Foxhall Edwards in *You Can't Go Home Again*.

The article generated a series of letters to the editor, two of which appeared in the 11 August issue of that magazine, with responses written by Burt. In the first letter, Ridgely Cummings of Hollywood, California, questions Burt's failure to substantiate his charges against Wolfe, noting that whatever betrayal Wolfe had been guilty of must have certainly taken a long while to kill Perkins, who died nearly a decade after Wolfe did. Burt's acerbic response states that the facts of Wolfe's betrayal of Perkins were so widely known that they needed no documentation. Referring to the length of time between Wolfe's death in 1938 and Perkins's death in 1947, Burt's defense lay in circumnavigating the facts. He writes:

> Frequently it takes a man – or a woman – a long time to die, especially if the wound is spiritual. People do not die directly of such things . . . . What is meant is that when the time comes they do not put up the proper kind of fight. Maxwell Perkins died of pneumonia, a disease where the will to live is a paramount factor in recovery. Tom Wolfe had pneumonia in Portland when he wrote his famous letter to Maxwell Perkins. But he recovered. Ten weeks later he died of a brain infection. (23)

Burt's argument that people die not of pneumonia but of "disappointment" is about as astute as Vardis Fisher's attempts to psychoanalyze the dead. In addition, Burt had his facts all wrong. Wolfe never did recover from pneumonia – the stress of the illness is believed to have opened up a tubercular lesion which spread to the brain and resulted in Wolfe's death. Also, Wolfe developed pneumonia not in Portland, but in Seattle.

The second letter challenging Burt's assertions was written by Wolfe's brother, Fred, who lived in Spartanburg, South Carolina. Fred Wolfe refers to an article written by Perkins appearing in the Autumn 1947 issue of the *Harvard Library Bulletin* ("Thomas Wolfe") in which Perkins describes his break with Wolfe as the result of the critical charges (made by Bernard DeVoto and others) that suggested that Wolfe could not write without Perkins's guidance. "No writer," Perkins wrote, "could possibly tolerate the assumption, which perhaps Tom almost himself did, that he was dependent as a writer upon anyone else. He had to prove to himself and the world that this was not so. And that was the fundamental reason that he turned to another publisher" (273). In addition, Fred Wolfe referred indirectly to a libel suit which Scribners had decided to settle out of court in a manner that not only financially damaged Wolfe but provided precedence for individuals who believed themselves to be the originals of his characters to sue him. These, he wrote, were the real reasons leading to Wolfe's decision to end his association with the publishing firm that had printed his first two novels.

Fred Wolfe argued emotionally in defense of his brother: "Tom Wolfe never for one second betrayed Maxwell Perkins, nor did Max ever betray Tom. I, however, say here unhesitatingly that Burt by his statements in this article . . . has betrayed both Tom and his friend Maxwell Perkins, who in his wonderful, gentle, fine way would be the first to call Burt a fantastic liar" (Letters to the Editor 24).

Burt's response printed directly beneath Fred Wolfe's letter (which Burt had been allowed to edit before it appeared in print) was condescending. "Mr. Wolfe," he writes, "mixes his straws with his camels . . . . He seems to be equally ignorant of the inner workings of publishing houses." Scribners, Burt insists, would never have let Wolfe starve.

Aswell was incensed that Harrison Smith, the editor of *The Saturday Review of Literature*, had published Burt's article without checking the facts behind Burt's sensationalist charges (later he found that the *Review* had substituted Burt's article for another piece at the last moment – failing in the ensuing rush to publication to verify Burt's charges before the issue appeared). Although he initially felt that Burt's charges were too fantastic to be believed and concluded that he could only exacerbate the problem by responding to them, he decided after the appearance of the Cummings and Wolfe letters and Burt's response to them in the 11 August issue to set the record straight. In charging that Wolfe had "killed" Maxwell Perkins by moving to another publisher, Burt had not only libeled Wolfe, he had come close to libeling Aswell, who had enabled Wolfe to make that move, and Harpers, which had provided Wolfe with a contract and an alternative literary home.

As a means of apologizing for the mistake that had resulted in Burt's article going unchecked to press, *The Saturday Review of Literature* printed Aswell's lengthy response to Burt, "Thomas Wolfe Did Not Kill Maxwell Perkins," in its 6 October 1951 issue. In this article Aswell not only defended Wolfe against the charges that Burt had leveled against him, but also detailed the sequence of events that resulted in Wolfe's moving from Scribners to Harpers. Aswell's argument was two fold: 1) that the professional break between Perkins and Wolfe had not destroyed their friendship, as was attested to by Wolfe's decision to name Perkins the executor of his estate after Wolfe had moved to Harpers and by Perkins's willingness to serve in that capacity; and 2) that as the executor of the estate of Thomas Wolfe, Perkins had personally approved the "Foxhall Edwards" caricature in *You Can't Go Home Again*. "If Mr. Burt will examine the book," Aswell wrote, "he will discover that it is copyrighted in the name of Maxwell Perkins" (17).

Depicting Wolfe's frustrating attempt to locate a publisher after his break with Scribners, a frustration bred of the fact that most of the publishers to whom he offered his work in phone calls from Asheville believed those calls to be pranks and by the fact that his initial contact with a potentially new publisher, Houghton-Mifflin (Aswell's "publisher X"), failed to secure him a contract, Aswell detailed the events that led to his securing a contract and cash advance for Wolfe at Harpers. By the time Aswell appeared on the scene ready to offer Wolfe a ten thousand-dollar advance on his next book, Wolfe had come to the desolate conclusion that nobody wanted him. Wolfe's anxiety-ridden state during their initial meeting at Wolfe's apartment at the Chelsea, mirrored his fears that in breaking from Scribners he would have to start his literary career anew. Aswell writes:

> I think I have never been so profoundly moved as I was by this spectacle of a great man momentarily as alone and frightened as a lost child. He said he was running out of money, and felt he was also out of friends to whom he could turn. There was always Max, of course, but Tom couldn't go back . . . . That night he needed desperately some immediate and tangible evidence that someone else believed in him, too. (46)

Perkins, he added, understood the full details of what had happened. He knew that Wolfe could no longer work with Scribners because of the entanglements that threatened his financial and artistic autonomy. Perkins was also aware that Wolfe had not been lured away by Harpers. Citing his own friendship with Perkins, which developed after Wolfe's death, as further refutation of Burt's argument, Aswell concluded his article by referring to Perkins as "not only the greatest editor of our time, but a great man"(46).

R. T. Clay, the reviewer for the *Durham Morning Herald* pegged the problem with the two-volume *Correspondence of Thomas Wolfe and Homer Andrew Watt* and *Thomas Wolfe at Washington Square* when he reviewed that set in the 14 February 1954 issue of that newspaper. "As Cargill and Pollock see it," he wrote facetiously, "the focal point of Wolfe's brief life was not Asheville or Chapel Hill or Cambridge or London or Munich, but 'those experience drenched hours' he spent in New York City between 1924 and 1930 on the faculty of the Washington Square College of NYU." Originally intended to be a memorial to Wolfe providing the university with a means of raising funds for a scholarship in his name, the volumes were instead filled with the remnants of bitterness and hostility that Wolfe's personality and success had evoked in his colleagues while he taught at New York University just prior to the publication of his first novel. Cargill's introduction to the memoirs Wolfe's university colleagues prepared for him, originally intended to be laudatory, turned out to be defamatory, describing Wolfe as a poor teacher, insensitive to the needs of his Washington Square students, an anti-Semite, and a writer who held all pedagogues in contempt.

Both Aswell and Nowell agreed that in all likelihood Wolfe had been far too concerned with his own writing during the years that he taught at Washington Square to have courted the approval of his students or fellow teachers, but Aswell felt that a *memorial* volume was not the place to vent ancient hostilities. Originally drafting a *white-hot* letter to Cargill denying him permission to publish the Wolfe manuscript material in the volume,

Aswell later yielded to Nowell's advice and decided to talk the problem over with the volume's editors, Pollock and Cargill.

Taking Melville Cane, the Scribners attorney, along "for moral and legal support," he proposed that Pollock and Cargill make two separate books; one containing the Wolfe-Watt letters, which would be published with Aswell's permission as executor of the Wolfe estate, the other including Cargill's highly revised introduction and the memoirs of Wolfe prepared by the faculty of the Washington Square English department who had worked with him, which would not require Aswell's approval. Aswell wrote to Nowell, this "device will relieve me of my twin embarrassments of being a party to what seems to me a biased and rather hostile interpretation of Tom and of being put in the position of having to censor Cargill's views. In other words, I shall be associated with one volume but not with the other" (*In the Shadow of the Giant* 123).

Despite the ineptitude which produced these distorted portraits of Wolfe and his work, the fifties also produced a number of important and responsible studies on Thomas Wolfe. In 1953, the noted Wolfean Richard Walser published the first of his books on Thomas Wolfe, a collection of essays exploring the range of critical responses to the writing of Wolfe since 1929. *The Enigma of Thomas Wolfe*, published by the Harvard University Press, is divided into three sections, each of which contains reprints of what Walser perceives to be the most important (and occasionally least accessible) of the critical studies of Wolfe's writings. Part I, "The Writer," deals with a series of articles written by people who knew Wolfe: Don Bishop, Henry T. Volkening, John Skally Terry, Maxwell Perkins, William Braswell, and Jonathan Daniels. Part II includes reviews and comments on Wolfe's books by Edward C. Aswell, Maxwell Geismar, Robert Penn Warren, Henry Seidel Canby, Bernard DeVoto, Clifton Fadiman, and Stephen Vincent Benét. Part III deals with commentary on Wolfe's writings by Thomas Lyle Collins, Edwin Berry Burgum, Monroe M. Stearns, E. K. Brown, W. M. Frohock, W. P. Albrecht, Margaret Church, Nathan L. Rothman, Franz Schoenberner, and Betty Thompson.

"The book," Walser wrote, "is rather like a contest with the reader acting as the entire committee of judges" (x). An attack on Wolfe's rhetoric or formlessness on one page, he continues, is generally followed by a counterattack some pages further. In the process of selecting and arranging these articles, Walser successfully provided Wolfe scholars with a valid method of exploring the nature of Wolfe's writing within the context of the critical community, a method that welcomed rather than suppressed divergent opinions on the nature and quality of Wolfe's writing. Walser was among the first to attempt to define the critical debate on the Wolfe canon that at the time of the appearance of *The Enigma* had enlivened Wolfe studies for some two and a half decades.

"It must be remembered, too," Walser writes to those "admirers" of Wolfe who he feels may question the inclusion in the book of essays unflattering to Wolfe, "that the most perceptive critics reserve their most stringent examination for the greatest artists" (x). Walser recognized the truth of the old saying that "no publicity is bad publicity" and rephrased it for the present purpose to read that "no review is a bad review." The initial decision made by any reviewer or critic is not whether he or she will applaud or attack the writing in any document, but whether that document is in itself important enough to be reviewed at all. It is the quantity of critical analysis devoted to Wolfe, as well as the quality and nature of that analysis, that together define the value of his literary estate and the impact made by his writings.

Louis Rubin's fascinating study of Wolfe and mutability, *Thomas Wolfe: The Weather of His Youth*, was also a product of the fifties. Like Muller's study, Rubin's broadly defines Wolfe's technique, but Rubin's is the first full-length study of Wolfe's writing focusing not on a single work or group of works, but on a single theme. Refusing to accept the charges that Wolfe's writings are formless, Rubin analyzes all four novels as a single work constituting "a progression, sometimes steady, sometimes wavering, toward responsibility" (24). The form of the novels, he explains, "is the principle of development that carries the autobiographical protagonist from immaturity toward maturity, from rebellion toward acceptance, from romanticism toward realism .... It is a progression from an anguished, first-person art toward the kind of artistry represented in *The Hills Beyond*: third person, objective, representational fiction" (25).

While working at the Houghton, Elizabeth Nowell encountered Richard S. Kennedy, whom she encouraged to continue working on Wolfe. Their relationship was a congenial one, even though Aswell's denial of Kennedy's request to publish Wolfe manuscript material in his dissertation (a denial that cost Kennedy his job at the University of Rochester) was, as Aswell explains in a December 1953 letter to Nowell, based on his decision to provide her with the opportunity of being Wolfe's biographer after John Skally Terry's death. Although he considered several other possible candidates for this position, including Kennedy, Aswell felt strongly that whoever wrote the official Wolfe biography should have firsthand knowledge of Wolfe. His letters to Nowell also suggest that he was personally loyal to her and recognized her need to work on income-producing projects. Nowell, who had worked closely with Wolfe as his literary agent, became Aswell's first choice as Wolfe's biographer. "The decision is mine and mine alone," he wrote to her discussing his decision to deny Kennedy permission to publish Wolfe manuscript material, "and I am prepared to take the blame for it. There would be no sense in encouraging the writing of two biographies at the same time. You have the green light, and this means that until your book is out the light will have to be red for all others" (*In the Shadow of the Giant* 163).

Two years later, Nowell was diagnosed with breast cancer, but despite the agonies of chemotherapy and the pain of several surgical procedures, she continued to work devotedly on *The Letters of Thomas Wolfe* (published in 1956) and her *Thomas Wolfe: A Biography* (published in 1960, two years after her death). Richard S. Kennedy, an innocent bystander to this drama, published his brilliant critical study of the development of Wolfe's prose works as *The Window of Memory* in 1962, cutting from the text much of the original biographical material that it contained and reworking and renaming the work to emphasize its focus on Wolfe's literary career instead of on his life, so as not to conflict with the Wolfe estate's commitment to Nowell. Several factors together – the publication of the Nowell *Letters* in 1956, the biography in 1960, and Kennedy's *The Window of Memory* in 1962, with their heavy reliance on the manuscript material; less rigid criteria for publication by the estate; and the meticulous editing of Wolfe's notebooks by Kennedy and Reeves in 1970 – spurred and made possible the textual studies of Wolfe that have proven to be so prolific over the past three decades, providing numerous opportunities for responsible editors to publish previously unpublished Wolfe material three, four, and five decades after his death.

2: "The Stuff of Human Experience"

"**I** AM," WROTE Thomas Wolfe in *Look Homeward, Angel*, " . . . a part of all that I have touched and that has touched me" (192). These words capsulize Wolfe's life and art, which are often inseparable. By many objective standards he ranks among the most significant writers of the twentieth century, along with William Faulkner, F. Scott Fitzgerald, Ernest Hemingway, and Sinclair Lewis. In their Nobel Prize speeches, both Faulkner and Lewis praised him effusively, and the reading public soon echoed their praise. Critics, however, have always been ambivalent about Wolfe's writing, but even they have never been indifferent to it.

Born on 3 October 1900, at the beginning of the new century, in Asheville, North Carolina, a small town nestled among the Blue Ridge Mountains in the southwestern portion of that state, Wolfe was the youngest of the eight children born to his mother, Julia Westall Wolfe, and her husband, the Pennsylvania tombstone cutter William Oliver Wolfe. Of those children all but three reached maturity, and of those three, Grover, who died in St. Louis in 1904 of typhoid in the guest house his mother had set up to cater to visitors to the Louisiana Purchase Expedition, and Ben, who died of pneumonia in 1918, would be immortalized by their youngest brother in his first novel. In addition to them, Wolfe would take all of the major figures of his first novel *Look Homeward, Angel* from his family.

Had Wolfe been born in the 1990s, he would have recognized that his family was dysfunctional. W. O. Wolfe was an alcoholic, and the members of his family in adapting to his alcoholism became like Sherwood Anderson's characters, *grotesques* of what they might otherwise have been. Wolfe's mother was possessed by the idea of making a fortune in real estate; dealing with her passion and learning from it enabled Wolfe to write with some understanding about the emotional impact of the Great Depression in his later fiction. Writers describing the impact of alcoholism on the family often note that as the result of coping with the alcoholic, family members end up role-playing.[1] Julia's role as real-estate tycoon and

---

[1]For an extended discussion of the impact of alcoholism on the Wolfe family, see Elaine P. Jenkins, "The Gants in a Bottle," in H. G. Jones, ed., *Thomas Wolfe at Eighty-seven* (Chapel Hill: North Caroliniana Society and the North Carolina Collection, 1988), pp. 71–78.

her need to establish her family financially in Asheville may well have been a reaction to what she perceived to be her husband's fiscal irresponsibility. Wolfe's sense of drama and the narrative voice of the young artist in his novels was quite likely born in the verbal and emotional violence than he witnessed in his youth and in his need to assume a role other than that of silent observer.[2] If, as Maurice Natanson suggests in his essay "The Privileged Moment: A Study in the Rhetoric of Thomas Wolfe," the power of Wolfe's rhetoric is the result of his cumulative epiphanies, it needs to be remembered that the need for the transcendence produced by epiphanies is strongest in those who try to make sense of the fragmented and painful realities that either they or those they love experience. Unfortunately, this kind of role-playing leads to a basic dishonesty that often fragments the family. As Wolfe and his brothers and sisters grew up in the shadow of their parents' realities, they were caught hopelessly in the crosscurrents of their parents' decisions.

By the time Wolfe was eight, the family had split into two separate units, each dominated by one of the parents. W. O., the failed artist, whose dreams of carving the soft-stone face of an angel were never achieved, lodged behind his stone-cutting shop on Pack Square. Julia lived a few blocks away at her boarding house, referred to by the family as *My Old Kentucky Home*, a humorous reference to the Stephen Foster song. The children moved randomly from one parent's abode to the other's. Wolfe settled in with his mother and nursed his resentment toward both parents. His idyllic depiction of "Monk" Webber's daydreams of his father, whom the family calls a bad man, but whom Monk perceives as living in an "enchanted" world, in the opening pages of *The Web and the Rock* (9–10), comes as close as anything Wolfe ever wrote to reconstructing what he saw to be an unsatisfactory relationship with his father.

---

[2] One of the American authors to whom Wolfe has been most frequently compared is Walt Whitman. Both Wolfe and Whitman wrote powerful prose-poetry which culminates in epiphanies, both attempted to describe the breadth of the American experience, both wrote works that were highly autobiographical, both used the self as a microcosm for mankind, both depicted their autobiographical protagonists as heroes. Whitman (allegedly), like Wolfe, was the product of a family in which a parent was an alcoholic. In both instances these writers were strongly compelled to rewrite the less-than-perfect reality of their youths and make it "right." I am not suggesting that "alcoholism" is necessary for the production of great literature, only that some talented individuals confronted by the pressures of the alcoholic family think of themselves as rising above the circumstances of their life to correct the wrongs of the world in which they and their loved ones have suffered. The alternative to becoming a "God" figure who can change the course of history is to become the "artist" figure who can re-create it as it should have been.

Several critics – Stutman, Maxwell Geismar, and Alfred Kazin, for example – find much of Wolfe's aberrant behavior rooted in his relationship to his mother. Although it is clear that she encouraged and financially supported him as he worked toward becoming a writer, standing behind him when all of her friends and neighbors turned on him, it is equally clear that he blamed her for the deaths of his brothers, Grover and Ben, and for the fragmentation of the family. As Stutman has so successfully shown in her edition of the Wolfe/Bernstein correspondence, *My Other Loneliness*, Wolfe's "madness," the term he used to describe his ambivalence toward the woman he loved, and at the same time seemed unable to love, may well have originated in the powerful relationship he shared with Julia Wolfe. Narrative, the psychiatrists suggest, inevitably lies, while imagery is always truthful – and the imagery of Wolfe's correspondence with his mistress reveals an ambivalence toward women that is at times haunting. He writes to her in August 1928:

> The terrible mystery of living has laid its hands upon my heart and I can find no answer. All about me I see the jungle rut and ramp – the little furtive eyes all wet with lust, and the brutes heavy of jowl and gut, and ropy with their sperm.
>
> I see the flower face, the compassionate eyes of love and beauty, the pure untainted loveliness – I see it under the overwhelming shade of darkness: the hairy stench, the thick blunt fingers fumbling at the heart, the foul wet belly . . . .
>
> My heart is smothering in its love for you . . . . but you are imprisoned in a jungle of thorns, and I cannot come near you without bleeding. (*My Other Loneliness* 189–190)

But the family history alone does not explain the extraordinary tenderness and love, the gentle and innocent humor, with which Wolfe treats his family as it is translated into the Gant family of Altamont in *Look Homeward, Angel*. And aside from the obvious surface of the narrative, it is difficult to tell just when and where Eugene Gant's family is interchangeable with Wolfe's. Clearly the fictional family and the real family are similar, but it would be an enormous error on the part of any critic to fail to distinguish between *similarity* and *identity*. His mother, Julia – as Eliza Gant – grasps at wealth and controls her family with an almost Orestean energy, at the same time impressive and frenetic, but she manages nevertheless to hold an unwieldy family together. W. O., the Pennsylvania outsider, vents his spleen against the entire Southern tradition of his wife's family, the Pentlands, and the middle-class society of Asheville, to which he refuses to belong. Still, when he comes home from the West, the children run to him, shrieking "Papa's home!" (*Look Homeward, Angel* 80).

The Gant family pulses with an energy that abates only in moments of stillness, as at the end of chapter 19, when Eugene focuses his attention with photographic intensity on his father in the town square and even the water fountains stop flowing, suspended in time. All that Wolfe as a boy must have perceived as dull and tedious or perhaps even as painful and unjust in his own family and in Asheville is miraculously transformed in *Look Homeward, Angel.* The distance of time (memory) and the distance of space provide him with a double vision that enables him to perceive even the commonplaces of life with wonder. An epiphany occurs for Eugene (and for Wolfe) when he comes to realize the loss he feels for the people and places of his childhood, at that very juncture in time when the past and the future meet, just beyond the other side of an *unfound door.*

At the age of twelve, precocious and already a heavy reader, Wolfe was enrolled in the North State Fitting School, where he found additional material for his novel in the persons of Mr. and Mrs. J. M. Roberts (the Leonards of *Look Homeward, Angel*). They instructed him for four years until, at the not-so-ripe age of almost sixteen, the young boy, little more than an adolescent, entered the undergraduate program at the University of North Carolina in Chapel Hill – beginning those long, inevitable train rides which produced the powerful rhythm of some of his most memorable prose passages.

Home from the university for the summer of 1917, he had an innocent love affair with a young boarder, Clara Paul (Laura James of *Look Homeward, Angel*), and on his return to Chapel Hill, he published his first work, a short poem titled "A Field in Flanders," which was printed in the university magazine. In the fall of 1918, he enrolled in Professor Frederick Koch's playwriting class at Chapel Hill, returning in October of that year to Asheville for the funeral of his brother Ben.

Wolfe's stereotyped mountain melodrama, *The Return of Buck Gavin,* was presented by the Carolina Playmakers in 1919. That same year he became editor of the *Tar Heel,* the student newspaper, and won the Worth Prize for his essay in philosophy, *The Crisis in Industry.* He graduated from Chapel Hill in 1920 and entered the Harvard Graduate School, where he studied playwriting under George Pierce Baker while taking courses from John Livingston Lowes and Irving Babbitt. While Wolfe was at Harvard, his plays, *The Mountains* and *Welcome to Our City,* were produced by Baker's famous 47 Workshop, although neither would be accepted for production outside of the academic community at Harvard.

Realizing that he needed a source of income in addition to the money he received from his mother, Wolfe signed on as an English instructor at the Washington Square College of New York University in 1924, where he taught intermittently for several years. In the fall of 1924 he sailed for

Europe returning to New York in the fall of 1925. That trip is particularly memorable for providing Wolfe with an introduction to Aline Bernstein, who later became his mistress. Upon meeting this woman on his return trip, Wolfe was astonished to find that she was carrying in her suitcase a manuscript of his play *Welcome to Our City*. Their turbulent love affair would be romanticized by the young novelist in *The Web and the Rock*. Bernstein, a wealthy New York set designer, encouraged Wolfe to write about his childhood, funding another trip to Europe for the two of them in 1926.

At no time in his life, however, does it seem that Wolfe had any other goal than that of being a writer. As he noted in his Purdue speech, delivered in 1938 less than six months before his death, he "had to write to live." "If I go on writing," he adds, "I must supply the sheer physical necessities of life out of the writing that I do. In one way or another, I have got to be paid for it; because I have no other money on which to live – and if writing as a means of support fails me, then I shall have to turn to other means that do not. And yet, even if that happened, I believe that, in some way, I would contrive to get my writing done. Because, from what I have told you, you will see that it has been in my life not only a physical and economic necessity; it has been, much more than that, a spiritual one" (31).

The novel that would become *Look Homeward, Angel* was completed in 1927, and in the spring of 1928 Wolfe made yet another trip to Europe. There he received word that Maxwell Perkins, representing Scribners, was interested in his novel. Twenty-eight years old, Wolfe had written three full-length plays, a complete novel, a semifictional travel journal, and numerous short stories. But aside from student work and a short newspaper article printed in *The Asheville Citizen* describing the Tower of London, he had yet to publish a line.

Wolfe's first meeting with Maxwell Perkins took place in the Scribners office on 2 January 1929. Penniless, he walked the distance from his apartment. He had come to discuss the publication of his manuscript, "O Lost," a loosely-structured novel that had been rejected by several publishers. It was with some surprise, then, that Wolfe found the conversation focusing not on that novel, but on a single chapter – the section in which W. O. Gant sells the marble angel to "Queen" Elizabeth, a local madam, to be erected over the grave of a twenty-two-year-old prostitute, Lily Reed. Wolfe, sensitive to the coarse suggestiveness of the section and aware that Scribners was one of the great voices of the Genteel Tradition, began to backpedal: "I know you can't print that!" he broke in. "I'll take it out at once." Perkins responded that to the contrary, it was one of the greatest short stories he had ever read. By the end of the session, the order of printing was decided. Wolfe was to revise the "Queen" Elizabeth section for *Scribner's Magazine* and Wolfe was to start reworking sections of the novel for publication (*Letters* 168–169; Turnbull *Thomas Wolfe* 138–139; and *Max Perkins* 131–132). Five days later, following a second meeting with Perkins, Wolfe emerged from that same office a professional writer; he had a contract for the publication of his first novel and an advance of five hundred dollars (*Letters* 164).

As he prepared his short story for *Scribner's Magazine*, he played with several titles. Because the story centered on the purchase of the angel, he decided to call it "Look Homeward, Angel," an allusion to Milton's "Lycidas." Later, he reconsidered and changed the title of the story to "An Angel on the Porch," but after some months as his first novel went to press and the Scribners editors urged him to find a new title for it, he recalled the earlier title, and chose to use it.

The circumstances surrounding the publication of "An Angel on the Porch" are intriguing. First, there is genuine disparity in critical response to it: Floyd Watkins describes the scene as "relatively minor" (*Thomas Wolfe's Characters* 18); yet Perkins thought it a great story and, prior to his first meeting with Wolfe, read the piece to Ernest Hemingway who agreed with him (*Letters* 168). Neither Perkins nor Hemingway could have known, as Charmian Green has only recently shown in her "Wolfe's Stonecutter Once Again: An Unpublished Episode," that the seed of that scene had existed in Wolfe's imagination as early as 1920. Nor, in choosing the story as a means of introducing Wolfe to the American public in *Scribner's Magazine*, could Perkins have foreseen the circumstances that would result in the renaming of the novel after the central symbol in the short story.

Perkins chose to publish the story for the same reason Wolfe had been willing to sacrifice it: the coarseness and unconventionality of the subject matter. In the late 1920s, the introduction of the owner of a house of ill repute and the description of a young prostitute's death from what appears to have been an abortion would have been considered sensitive. Scribners, with its long background of religious and academic publications was particularly conservative, but by 1928 the firm had reached a turning point. Perkins and some of the younger staff members at Scribners had come to feel that *Scribner's Magazine* and the publishing house it represented were in a rut. To rectify this, Perkins had, in early 1928, approached the author of *The Sun Also Rises*, Ernest Hemingway, about serializing his next novel in the magazine. Hemingway inititially hesitated, certain that the staff of *Scribner's* would try to censor his book. His hesitancy gave way to agreement only when Perkins offered sixteen thousand dollars for the serial rights (*Max Perkins* 110–111; 140–143). Just at the

moment when Wolfe's monumental manuscript was brought to his attention, Perkins was courting unconventional literature for the firm as a
means of undercutting the company's traditional conservatism.

"An Angel on the Porch" appeared in the August 1929 issue of *Scribner's Magazine*, an issue which featured the fourth installment of *A Farewell
to Arms*. The first installment of the Hemingway novel, published in the
May issue, had resulted in the banning of the June issue in Boston and in
a run on the remaining issues in other cities. Wolfe's story of an old
man's movement toward death and the purchase of a "soft faced angel" to
memorialize the grave of a young prostitute is lodged between the beginning of the fourth installment of Hemingway's novel, which begins on
page 169 and runs to page 181 of the August issue, and the conclusion of
the Hemingway episode, which begins on page 229. "An Angel on the
Porch," which was printed on pages 205 to 210, was thus securely teth-
ered at a point in the issue through which Hemingway's readers would
have to pass as they read the installment. This point occurs between what
many consider to be the coarsest scenes in Hemingway's novel, the scene
in which Frederic Henry returns to his unit prior to the attack on Capor-
etto, his discussion of syphilis with his friend Rinaldi, their concern that
the unit priest is also a victim of that disease, and the scene, several pages
later, depicting the implied seduction of two Italian schoolgirls.

Perkins, by choosing to publish "The Angel on the Porch" juxtaposed
with the fourth installment of Hemingway's novel, made his critical commentary on Wolfe implicit: here was another maverick writer, another
one of Perkins's unconventional generals, ready to storm the bastion of
conventional middle-class morality; here was another writer to be banned
in Boston, another writer ready and willing to offend the defenders of the
outmoded Genteel Tradition. Wolfe, in a letter to George Wallace, a former member of Baker's 47 Workshop who Wolfe believed had connec-
tions with Boston newspapers, demonstrated what he had learned from
his first publication in a letter dated October 1929. "Scribners," he wrote,
"do not want to have my book 'Banned in Boston' – they are a very fine
and dignified firm, and did not like the Hemingway ban, although it
helped the sale of the book. But – this is between *us* – if it does get
banned, I hope it makes a loud noise – for God's sake try to get some
publicity out of it for me" (*Letters* 206).

In a 9 August 1929 letter to Henry T. Volkening, Wolfe describes his
response to the publication of his first story: "I was more madly in love
with myself than ever when I read it. I had expected convulsions of the
earth, falling meteors, suspension of traffic, and a general strike when the
story appeared – but nothing happened" (*Letters* 195). Wolfe's *nothing* was
about as accurate as Edmund's at the beginning of Shakespeare's *King*

Lear. Something *had* happened, something that would provide Wolfe with the emotional strife he believed had bypassed him. Although he does not mention it to Volkening, he had received a response to the publication of "An Angel on the Porch" from Margaret Roberts, his teacher at the North State Fitting School, expressing some concern about what Wolfe had written and about how it might affect his family. For the first time Wolfe admits that his writing might result in some pain to the citizens of Asheville whose lives he had translated into his novel. "I tremble," he continues in his letter to Volkening, "now that the thing's done – I loathe the idea of giving pain; it never occurred to me as I wrote; it is a complete piece of fiction but made, as all fiction must be, from the stuff of human experience" (*Letters* 196). To Margaret Roberts he was more specific: "I hope you may be wrong in thinking what I have written may distress members of my family, or anyone else. Certainly, I would do anything to avoid causing anyone pain – except to destroy the fundamental substance of my book. I am afraid, however, that if anyone is distressed by what seemed to me a very simple and unoffending story, their feeling when the book comes out will be much stronger" (*Letters* 197). Toward the end of August 1929, as Wolfe and Perkins finished deciding on the cuts to be made in *Look Homeward, Angel,* Perkins began to realize "with horror" that Wolfe's characters were based on his family and on real people who lived in the town of Asheville. In September, Wolfe returned home to tell his family what the book was about (*Max Perkins* 135; *Letters* 201).

With the final proofing of the manuscript completed, Wolfe left New York and traveled south to Asheville. During his train ride, he ran into an old friend and Chapel Hill classmate, Jonathan Daniels, who was also on the verge of publishing a novel (*A Clash of Angels*) with a far less prestigious publisher. Daniels listened, resentfully, as Wolfe enthusiastically outlined the hoopla that Scribners had planned for launching *Look Homeward, Angel.* Later Daniels admitted, in his *October Recollections,* that out of envy he chose to write a negative review of *Look Homeward, Angel,* "Wolfe's First Is Novel of Revolt," in the *Raleigh News and Observer.*

Wolfe arrived in Asheville on the morning of 7 September. His mother and his sister Mabel met him at the station. After breakfasting with his mother, he went to Mabel's for lunch and dinner. Later that week, Wolfe and his brother Fred traveled first to Anderson, South Carolina (which Wolfe describes as "that hot dismal town – ever the same – the pretty drawling girls with bribing word of rape, red clay, cotton, bigotry and murder" [*Notebooks* 365]), to visit their sister Effie Gambrell, and they caused commotion as in a drunken state both he and Fred meandered home through Greenville, South Carolina, and Hendersonville, North Carolina. By the end of the trip, both Fred and his brother were in tears: Fred because he believed that he had been insulted in Henderson-ville; Wolfe because he suddenly realized that he was one of the family "and couldn't get along without them." "Yet tonight," he continued in his pocket notebook "seems strange and terribly sad and unreal – still feel all the country around, the vast rolling depressing Piedmont, South Carolina, corn-licker depression, the incident at Hendersonville – the tears, the neurosis, and O God the sadness, the sadness, the sadness and the loneliness of my life – to *what* did I belong, to *what* do I belong – *who* wants me? Mama's old weak eyes and face puckered fumily with sleep as she looked at us – No more do I belong!" (*Notebooks* 367).

Several days later he sent a postcard to Perkins, assuring him that the town was "full of kindness and good will and rooting and boosting for the book. My family," he adds "knows what it's all about, and I think is pleased about it" (*Letters* 203). He had told them hardly anything.

Wolfe returned to New York for the opening of classes at the Washington Square campus on 24 September (*Notebooks* 362), and, on 18 October, *Look Homeward, Angel* was officially published – launched by Scribners with a massive publicity campaign that included a display of the novel in the store-front window of the company's main office in Manhattan. Wolfe walked back and forth in front of the window so regularly that he drew the attention of the police and came close to being arrested. Within the week, the Asheville and North Carolina reviews began to pour in.

The American Reviews

Two of the earliest of the North Carolina reviews were written by Jonathan Daniels and appeared in the *Raleigh News and Observer*. Neither was very kind. In his column "Looking Both Ways" printed on 18 October, Daniels indulges in the identification game of matching characters with their Asheville originals. The book, he concludes, is no novel, but "the prize puzzle book of the year." Two days later in an article entitled "Wolfe's First Is Novel of Revolt: Former Asheville Writer Turns in Fury upon N.C. and the South," Daniels extends his observations to a full-length review. Describing the novel as a "curse" on the South and attacking the sanity of the Gants, Daniels writes: "Seeing any section through the Gant family would be like looking upon that section through the barred windows of a madhouse." *Look Homeward, Angel*, he adds, picturesquely, "is a book written in a poetic realism, the poetry of dissolution and decay, of life rotting from the womb, of death full of lush fecundity. The book is sensuous rather than cerebral. It pictures a life without dignity – cruel and ugly and touched only by a half-mad beauty. It moves slowly but at almost hysterical tension through twenty years of the life of the lower middle class Gant family, a life stirred only by the raw lusts for food and drink and sex and property"; all of this, he comments, is the product of Wolfe's bitterness toward the region of his birth. The author, he charges, has "turned with all his fury" on the South and has written a work in which he "spat" on that region.

On the same day (20 October) that Daniels's second review appeared in Raleigh, Lola M. Love, the fiancée of Wolfe's friend George McCoy, wrote glowingly of Wolfe's novel in *The Asheville Citizen*: *Look Homeward, Angel*, she concludes, is a work of "genius" and the Gants are "intensely alive." "It was this vigor," she notes, "– translated to the dreamer and the visionary of the family – which made the pattern of life, in all its tragic and meaningful beauty, a thing of wonder." As comforting as this review must have been for Wolfe, it was assuredly written with blinders on; the only reference to autobiography or to the similarity of Wolfe's characters to Asheville citizens is a brief side note to the effect that "each man is his own story in real life, and other people exist only as they seem to him." The review concludes with an eight-paragraph biography of Wolfe focusing on his life in Asheville ("Stirring First Novel by Local Man Making Big Hit in Literary World").

The competing Asheville newspaper, *The Asheville Times*, was not nearly as enthusiastic in its reviews. The first of these two articles was signed by Walter S. Adams, the managing editor of that newspaper, and the unsigned second review was probably written by him as well. The title of the first review, which appeared on the front page of the newspaper on the same day that the Love review appeared in the *Citizen*, pretty much defines the concerns that the citizens of Asheville had about the novel: "Amazing New Novel Is Realistic Story of Asheville People." Throughout his review, Adams focuses on the fact that Wolfe paints himself, his home, his neighbors, his friends, and his acquaintances in the book, "sparing nothing and shielding nothing." "Most of the Asheville people who appear in the novel," he concludes, "wear their most unpleasant guises. If there attaches to them any scandal which has enjoyed only a subterranean circulation, it is dragged forth into the light. If they have any weaknesses which more tolerant friends are considerate enough to overlook, these defects are faithfully described." Asheville citizens, he adds, would read the work despite its lack of literary merit, "because it is the story, told with bitterness and without compassion, of many Asheville people."

The second review appearing in *The Asheville Times* on 27 October, "Wolfe Novel Causes 'Stir' in This Section: Lauded in New York," is actually the more interesting of the two, describing as it does the reactions of the people of Asheville who had read the novel. The reaction to the book in the Asheville community, the article reads, has been sensational and tremendous. The bookstores and libraries are experiencing strong demands for it from patrons, largely out of curiosity. Arcade Bookstore owner Leon McNeinery is quoted as advising the public that he is selling the book as "literature" not "smut." Much of the article is given over to reprinting a review by New York critic Margaret Wallace which had appeared that same day in *The New York Times Book Review*, praising the novel. The attention given the novel in Asheville, *The Asheville Times* article notes, comes from the fact that word has gotten out that the book is not a novel at all, but a "biography" of Thomas Wolfe.

By 21 October, Wolfe had received copies of the 20 October reviews written by Daniels, Love, and Adams. Apparently recognizing his complicity in the writing of some of the more-negative reviews, Wolfe wrote in his pocket notebook, "Live and learn" (*Notebooks* 377). Several days later, Wolfe wrote his friend George Wallace that although fine reviews will be published in *The New York Times* that coming Sunday (Margaret Wallace's review) and in *Scribner's Magazine* in December (Robert Raynolds's review), he has yet to receive reviews from any place other than North Carolina. "And, Boy!" he notes, "they are blowing off steam" (*Letters* 205). By 28 October, however, he could write with obvious relief to his sister, Mabel Wolfe Wheaton, who of all the family was probably the most hurt by the novel, which damaged in-roads she had made into Asheville society. "Read *New York Times* review for last Sunday," he tells her, "also *Herald Tribune* for next Sunday or the week after. No matter what Asheville thinks now, they will understand in time that I tried to write moving, honest book about great people. That is the way the world outside Asheville is taking it" (*Letters* 207–208).

Elsewhere in North Carolina, reviews of the book followed the pattern of the Asheville reviews, but without the personal animosity displayed in Asheville. Like Daniels, Richard L. Young, whose 15 December 1929 review appeared in the Charlotte *News*, had also been a classmate of Wolfe at Chapel Hill, but his review of his classmate's novel is far more enthusiastic than Daniels's. Wolfe, he predicts, will become "one of our greatest contemporary writers." An undated, unidentified review in the Caroliniana Collection at Chapel Hill, titled "Thomas Wolfe Tells Startling Story of North Carolina Life," is far less complimentary, suggesting that the novel is true to life in Asheville but that reading it "one will want to cast the book aside and go bathe." At Chapel Hill, John Mebane launched into effusive praise of the novel in his 2 February 1930 *Carolina Magazine* article, calling it "brilliant"; while down the road at Duke, Thomas J. Shaw wrote in the March 1930 issue of the *Archive* that the novel would provide professional teachers of English, everywhere, a chance to make good use of their blue pencils.

In a letter to his mother dated 6 November 1929, Wolfe best sums up his attitude to the responses his book had found in Asheville and in other regions of North Carolina. As in earlier letters to his sister Mabel and George McCoy, Wolfe stresses the fine reviews that his book had received outside of Asheville and reiterates his oft-stated claim that the work is fictional. "The characters and scenes in my book," he writes, "are of my own imagining and my own making – they have their roots in human experience, but what life and being they have, I gave to them. There is no scene in my book that is supposed to be literal, and I will not talk to damned fools who ask me if so-and-so in the book is meant to be such and such a person living in Asheville" (*The Letters of Thomas Wolfe to His Mother* 155). Whatever Wolfe's family thought of the book in private, in public they supported his novel. Julia proclaimed, as she later revealed to Haydn Norwood, who printed her comment in *The Marble Man's Wife*, that whenever asked about the novel that her son had written, she responded that he was the only Asheville author ever to sell ten thousand copies.

Despite Perkins's fears to the contrary, no Asheville citizen ever sued Wolfe or Scribners for libel. It may be that as time went by they were secretly pleased to be included in a work that had received so much national attention; it may be that none of them really wanted to own up to being the original for the character that they believed represented them.

In chapter 22 of *You Can't Go Home Again*, Wolfe's alter ego and protagonist George Webber, whose novel *Home to Our Mountains* has just been published, writes of the critical response from the hometown friends and neighbors in a way that echoes Wolfe's comments on his own initial experience with publication in his notebooks and correspondence:

> What did such people think he had been trying to write – nothing but an encyclopædia of pornography, a kind of prurient excavation of every buried skeleton in town? He saw that his book had unreefed whole shoals of unsuspected bitterness and malice in the town and set evil tongues to wagging. The people he had drawn upon to make the characters in his book writhed like hooked fish on a line, and the others licked their lips to see them squirm.
>
> Those who were the victims of all this unleashed malice now struck back, almost to a man, at the hapless author – at him whom they considered to be the sole cause of their woe. Day after day their letters came, and with a perverse satisfaction in his own suffering, a desire to take upon himself now all the searing shame that he had so naïvely and so unwittingly brought to others, he read and reread every bitter word of every bitter letter, and his senses and his heart were numb.

They said at first that he was a monster against life, that he had fouled his own nest. Then they said he had turned against the South, his mother, and spat upon her and defiled her. Then they leveled against him the most withering charge they could think of, and said he was "not Southern." Some of them even began to say that he was "not American." This was really rather hard on him, George thought with a wry, grim humor, for if he was not American he was not anything at all. (337)

Outside of Asheville and North Carolina, however, Thomas Wolfe's *Look Homeward, Angel*, like George Webber's *Home to Our Mountains*, received a much better reception.

There is, of course, no accurate means of gauging the impact of any promotional campaign on an author's career, either in terms of sale or reputation; the elements contributing to each are simply too complex and ill defined to be dealt with in terms of one-to-one relationships. However, an examination of Scribners' promotion of Wolfe suggests how that firm regarded him as a marketable commodity and the nature of the public image it felt would make him salable. The whole question of advertising, Roger Burlingame notes in his study of Scribners, *Of Making Many Books*,[3] is seen in proportion to sales. If the sale of a book does not justify what the publisher spends promoting it, then the publisher loses money. Since much of a promotional campaign is planned before publication, much of the advertising strategy is a matter of guesswork, an expression of the publisher's confidence in the ultimate success of a work. Before the publication of *Look Homeward, Angel* in 1929, few at Scribners could have anticipated its success. The earliest *New York Times Book Review* advertisement is an unframed 2 square-inch[4] blurb quoting Thomas Beer. "Mr. Wolfe," it reads, "seems to me to be the most interesting writer of fiction to appear in America since Glenway Westcott" (3 November 1929, 19). This note appears near the bottom of a full-page, 117 square-inch collective advertisement, dwarfed by framed advertisements for Hemingway's *A Farewell to Arms*, Galsworthy's *A Modern Comedy*, Edwin Franden Dakin's *Mrs. Eddy*, Theodore and Kermit Roosevelt's *Trailing the Giant Panda*, and Will James's *Smoky*, each of which was at least five times the size of the Wolfe note.

On 18 October 1929, Scribners invested in a first printing of 5,540 copies of *Look Homeward Angel*, some 3,000 more copies than they had invested in the first novel of another young author, F. Scott Fitzgerald, only

---

[3] (New York: Scribners, 1946). Burlingame took the title of his book from an early discarded title for Wolfe's *The Story of a Novel.*

[4] Dimensions of advertisements have been rounded off to the nearest inch.

nine years earlier, but some 15,000 fewer copies than they printed of that by-then-established author's third novel, *The Great Gatsby*, in 1925. By 6 November, *Look Homeward, Angel* had entered a second printing of 3,000 copies. Scribners had increased its investment by over 50-percent and, subsequently, stepped up its promotional campaign, tripling the size of the advertisement for the book in the 24 November issue of *The New York Times Book Review*, framing it, and positioning it at the top center of the page, next to the advertisement announcing the fifth printing of *A Farewell to Arms*. By 1 December *Look Homeward, Angel* had entered its third printing. Advertisements appearing in the 1 and 8 December issues of *The New York Times Book Review* measured 9 square inches and 25 square inches, respectively (27; 16). The latter of these, for the first time, focused attention on Wolfe as well as on the book, featuring a drawing of the author in profile.

The change in size and prominence of these advertisements reflects the change in the publicity department's perception of the salability of *Look Homeward, Angel* over a two-month period, but there was also a change in the nature of these advertisements. These changes suggest the nature of the public image that Scribners felt would make Wolfe most marketable. By the time *Look Homeward, Angel* reached its second printing, the bland assertion of interest evident in the Thomas Beer blurb had been replaced by quotes from reviewers focusing on the vitality, raw energy, and unconventionality of the book. According to these blurbs, the book breathed the spirit of youth and was "vigorous and striking" with the "buoyant health of the roaring Elizabethan tales of Nashe and Greene." The writer, the advertisement continues, had dodged "neither life's vulgarity, bestiality, profanity, and horror nor its fine strivings, its hopes and its invincible optimism" (8 October 1929).

Although according to legend Wolfe's *Look Homeward, Angel* burst like "lightning" onto the American literary scene, the national reviews of Wolfe's first novel were in general ambivalent. While praising Wolfe's vitality and prose style, the critics inevitably alluded to the autobiographical nature of the work. This, they assumed, was the result of the fact that the novel was Wolfe's first. Most suggested that it would not be until Wolfe wrote a second novel (implicitly, one that did not rely so on autobiographical material) that his success as a novelist could be evaluated. Several of the reviews were condescending, and a few, such as Harry Hansen's "Ah, Life! Life!" that appeared in the 26 October 1929 issue of *The New York World* successfully poked fun at the novel. Wolfe's intrusive prose style, like George Meredith's, Hansen writes, was thirty years out of date. "In the days of James Lane Allen it became a bit cloying . . . . to-day," he notes, "it is something of a surprise." Hansen concludes his review by questioning whether Wolfe will be more than a "one-book" man. The same sentiment was echoed by John Chamberlain in an untitled review in *The Bookman*, Frances Lamont Robbins in the *Outlook and Independent*, Carl Van Doren in the Literary Guild publication *Wings*, and Franklin P. Adams in *The New York World*.

In his column "The Conning Tower" in *The New York World*, Franklin Adams rehashes the reception that the book had received in Asheville and quotes from a letter he had received from that town depicting the widespread response to the book: ministers denounced it from the pulpits, and a Mother Superior at a big Catholic Hospital promised to confiscate and burn every copy of it. "It is not allowed," this writer continues, "on the shelves of the local library." That month, Donald Davidson, who that same year would contribute his "A Mirror for Artists" to the Agrarian symposium *I'll Take My Stand*, reviewed the novel in the *Nashville Tennessean*. Like Jonathan Daniels, Davidson saw in the book a "hatred and loathing" for the South and pegged Wolfe as a "defeatist." Focusing on the lack of "purpose" and "conviction" in the novel, Davidson concludes that "brilliant and powerful as it is," it "has a sickness in its marrow."

Writing to Hamilton Basso on 14 October 1936, after the publication of *Of Time and the River*, Wolfe alludes to the Hansen review and the critics who had reserved judgment until the publication of a second novel:

> Knowing what I did about the career of the book, how the entire population of my home town wanted to draw and quarter me, how eminent reviewers, such as Mr. Harry Hansen, headed their reviews with such master strokes of sarcasm as "Ah, Life, Life," etc., how everybody asked if I could ever write another book and how quickly they began to say I never would – I say I was able to smile a trifle grimly a year ago after the publication of "Of Time and the River," when I read that my career had been a bed of roses from the beginning, that "Look Homeward, Angel" had been greeted with a hurricane of applause, that my path from that time on had been as smooth as velvet. I know what happened then. I think I know what is likely to happen to me now until I get another book done. It's not going to be easy to take. But it's not going to be quite the bitter and disillusioning experience that it was five or six years ago. You know, as well as I do, how quickly they can turn, how desperately hard it is to prevail, when they make up their minds about you. (*Letters* 549)

By 1937 Wolfe would include Hansen's column in his pocket notebook on a list of "Potential Fascist Literary Groups and Individuals" (*Notebooks* 887).

One of the few completely negative reviews appeared in the Unitarian *Christian Register* on 9 January 1930. Written by Edwin Fairley, the note reads:

> We gather from the jacket that the publishers kept this book three years before they published it. In our judgment, they ought to have burned it. It is the small-town life of a small-town family of futilitarians. But why write of them? They could swear, and visit brothels, and quarrel no end; but what of it? Even the similes in this foul book are vile . . . . One disgusting situation follows another until we are nauseated. Why did a reputable house put out such a book? (31)

Two decades later, the editorial staff of this same Boston-based newspaper would admit to being "amused" by the vehemence of this reaction to "an undoubted masterpiece" (Nanette Senior to Myra Champion, 10 August 1953, Pack Memorial Library, Asheville, North Carolina).

Much as with Antony's Caesar, *the evil* that Wolfe's critics did *lived after them* and the *good* was *oft interred with their bones*; Wolfe's correspondence and pocket notebooks seem to fixate on the negative elements in the reviews of *Look Homeward, Angel*, forgetting some of the most positive responses that the book received. Margaret Wallace, the reviewer for *The New York Times Book Review*, was effusive in her praise. "Mr. Wolfe," she writes, "has a very great gift – the ability to find in simple events and in humble, unpromising lives the whole meaning and poetry of human existence." She goes on to describe Wolfe's prose style as "enormously sensuous" and "shrinkingly sensitive," "sprawling," "fecund," "subtly rhythmic" and "amazingly vital." She calls his ability to twist language to his own needs "masterful" and concludes with the statement that the book is to be "savored slowly and reread" ("A Novel of Provincial American Life"). Similarly, Margery Latimer in a review titled "The American Family" in *The New York Herald Tribune Books* praises Wolfe's descriptive talents. "He isn't content to describe a meal in a sentence, but he uses a page," she writes, "bringing the food before you until it is so tangible it is intolerable, until it is so rich and abundant that it pierces you with the awe of life." Scribners hand-picked the young poet and novelist, Robert Raynolds, to review the novel in the December issue of *Scribner's Magazine*, in which he likened Wolfe's novel to Melville's *Moby-Dick* and Whitman's *Leaves of Grass*. Wallace received a brief thank-you note from Wolfe (*Letters* 207), and Latimer found a place on Wolfe's 1929 Christmas List (*Notebooks* 386). Robert Raynolds became a good friend of Wolfe on the basis of his review and later accepted Wolfe's assistance in getting his own work published (*Letters* 336).

When Wolfe's critics chose to quote from the novel, they inevitably chose the prose poem at the beginning of the novel as representing

Wolfe's style at its best: "Naked and alone," Wolfe writes, "we came into exile. In her dark womb we did not know our mother's face; from the prison of her flesh have we come into the unspeakable and incommunicable prison of this earth. Which of us has known his brother? Which of us has looked into his father's heart? Which of us has not remained forever prison-pent? Which of us is not forever a stranger and alone?" (see, for instance, Margaret Wallace, "A Novel of Provincial American Life" and Kenneth Fearing, "A First Novel of Vast Scope"). Or they chose to quote from the scene in which Ben returns at the end of the novel, half ghost, half angel, to tell Eugene that he is his own world (see Harry Hansen, "Ah, Life! Life!"). Only Burton Rascoe, writing in *Arts and Decorations*, found the novel's conclusion unsettling, a sudden "switch" from realism to fantasy. He did not recognize that what appeared to be an inconsistency was in fact the climactic moment of the text, an epiphany in which Eugene's creative imagination is set loose, free to re-create the world as it *should be*, free to bring a beloved brother back to life. In making his brother, Ben, return at the end of the novel, Wolfe (like Eugene who watches the inanimate objects of the square come to life and speaks to the ghost of his brother) uses his art to conquer death.

Apparently, the only literary journal reviewing Wolfe's first novel was *The Virginia Quarterly Review* (Stringfellow Barr, "The Dandridges and the Gants"). In that review Barr, a professor of Modern History at the University of Virginia and an editor of *The Virginia Quarterly Review*, compared Wolfe's novel to Stark Young's *River House*. In contrast to Daniels and Davidson, Barr praised Wolfe's attitude toward the South. "The life of the white Southerner has been for political and traditional reasons so compact of legal fictions and dying social shibboleths that it has been difficult to do anything with it unless one sentimentalized . . . " he wrote. "Thomas Wolfe, on the other hand, has constructed a really tremendous novel out of the mean and sordid life of a North Carolina town." Although, Wolfe is not concerned with the survival of Southern culture, Barr continues, he has enabled the South to contribute "to the literature of the world a novel, strongly provincial in its flavor, universal in its terrible tragedy."

There was, however, yet one more American voice to be heard on Thomas Wolfe's *Look Homeward, Angel*, and that voice belonged to the American novelist Sinclair Lewis. Lewis had never met Wolfe but had been impressed by the young author's first novel. Receiving the news that he had won the Nobel Prize for Literature in early November 1930, Lewis took time to mention several American authors who had not won the award: Cabell, Dreiser, Hemingway, Cather, and Wolfe. Focusing on Wolfe, Lewis commented in his 5 November press conference that Wolfe, of all of them, "may have the chance to be the greatest American writer" (*The New York Times*, 6 November 1930). One month later when he received the award in Sweden, he repeated his praise for Wolfe. "There is," he noted, "Thomas Wolfe, a child of, I believe, thirty or younger, whose one and only novel, *Look Homeward, Angel*, is worthy to be compared with the best in our literary production, a Gargantuan creature with great gusto of life." [5]

Not normally self-effacing, Wolfe found the praise so unexpected that he was a bit disconcerted by it. "The Great American Writer business," he wrote Perkins from Paris in the last days of 1930, "is pretty tough stuff for a man who is on his second book, and I hope they won't be gunning for me. Also I have begun to come to a way of life — I meant what I said about *obscurity*: . . . I want to write famous books, but I want to live quietly and modestly" (*Letters* 288). Scribners did not seem to hear him, however, and within days of Lewis's press conference, the advertising department slapped a wrap-around band on the remaining copies of the first edition of the novel quoting Lewis: "SINCLAIR LEWIS *says of* THOMAS WOLFE 'I don't see why he should not be one of the greatest world writers. His first book is so deep and spacious that it deals with the whole of life.'"

Wolfe, in turn, wrote an extended discussion of Lewis's (Lloyd McHarg's) championing of the young writer George Webber into the opening pages of chapter 33 of *You Can't Go Home Again*.

The English and German Reviews

The English edition of *Look Homeward, Angel* is an example of the kind of liberties publishers seemed to be willing to take with Wolfe's work. It is clearly thirteen pages shorter than the American edition; however, a sight collation of these two editions suggests the true dimensions of the liberties taken (possibly on both sides of the Atlantic) with Wolfe's text. The English edition of *Look Homeward, Angel*, published by Heinemann nine months after the Scribners edition, differs from its predecessor in 975 point: 911 of which are accidentals and sixty-four of which are substantive.

Several of the substantive changes in the English edition are fairly lengthy. The largest of these is a cut of twenty-five consecutive pages at the end of chapter 24 — which in combination with a four-page cut appearing earlier in that chapter — reduces the length of that chapter from thirty-one to two pages. The most complicated of these changes is the

---

[5] *The Man from Main Street: Selected Essays and Other Writings, 1904–1950*, edited by Harry E. Maule and Melville H. Cane. New York, 1953, p. 17.

movement of three pages of material from the end of chapter 23 to the end of chapter 21. The most maladroitly handled of these changes is a cut of some nine pages from the end of chapter 28 and some two pages from the beginning of chapter 29 – which resulted in dropping the chapter break and heading for chapter 29 in the English edition. The material from the twenty-ninth chapter retained in that edition is appended to the end of chapter 28 – which is then immediately followed by chapter 30. There are, in addition, two lengthy passages added to the English edition which are not present in the American edition – twenty lines on page 341 focusing on the pretentiousness of nationalism and the folly of war and two pages – following almost immediately thereafter – burlesquing English war books. Altogether, the English edition differs substantively from the American edition in about sixty pages – or 10 percent of its text.

The sixty-four substantive variants seem to fall into three categories: 1) expurgations, deletions of references to British historical or literary figures that would have proven distasteful to English readers and deletions of or clarifications of distinctly American references, 2) variants representing attempts to correct logical inconsistencies in the text, and 3) variants that coincide with material that was subject to contention in the American edition.

The most complicated variant reading involves moving three pages of material describing Eliza's trip to Florida during Eugene's fourteenth year from the end of the twenty-third chapter in the American edition to the end of the twenty-first chapter in the English edition. Although the authority for this change is undocumented, its motivation, the correction of a logical inconsistency, is self-evident.

Eugene begins study at the private school set up in Altamont by John Dorsey Leonard and his wife, Margaret, in August 1912, about a month before Eugene's twelfth birthday. Chapter 22 in the American edition begins "Toward the beginning of Eugene's fourteenth year, when he had been a student at Leonard's for two years, Ben got work for him as a paper carrier." The rest of the chapter, in typical Wolfean fashion, describes Eugene's "Niggertown" route, which requires him to rise at 3:30 every morning – tracing it through all four seasons, at least one year, possibly more. Chapter 23, however, begins with Eugene's decision not to tell the Leonards about his paper route, knowing that they will oppose it as potentially dangerous to his health and damaging to his studies. Chapter 23 concludes with the three pages of variant material in question. These three pages describe Eliza Gant's extended trip to Florida (a trip which enables her to make stops in Miami, Palm Beach, and Orlando) – explicitly stating that this trip took place during Eugene's fourteenth year and that Eugene boarded with the Leonards while his mother was in Florida.

It would have been highly unlikely, then, that Eugene, who began his paper route at the beginning of his fourteenth year and arose at 3:30 every morning to work his route, could have kept it a secret from the Leonards during that indeterminate period in his fourteenth year when he was boarding with them.

The English edition corrects this logical inconsistency by moving the material relating to Eliza's trip to Florida from the end of the twenty-third chapter to the end of the twenty-first chapter and deleting from the first sentence in chapter 22 the clause specifying that Eugene began his paper route at the *beginning* of his fourteenth year. In the English edition, Eliza's trip to Florida now physically precedes the passage describing Eugene's employment as a paperboy, the time frame for which is given less specifically, not "at the beginning of his fourteenth year," but "when he had been a student at Leonard's for two years." Given the fact that Eugene would be at least fourteen after two years with the Leonards, it is plausible that Eliza could leave Altamont for an extended Florida visit – leaving Eugene to board with the Leonards – and return, sometime in Eugene's fourteenth year, *prior* to his decision to take on a paper route, enabling Eugene to keep that route a secret from the Leonards.

The remaining changes – involving what adds up to over forty pages of material – are clustered in chapters 24, 25, and 33. The documentation for these changes, surprisingly, exists not in Wolfe's correspondence with his English editor, A. S. Frere-Reeves, but in his correspondence with Scribners editor John Hall Wheelock concerning the galleys of the first edition of *Look Homeward, Angel.* On 19, 22, and 23 July 1929, while in Ocean Point, Maine, where he was reading the galleys for the novel, Wolfe posted three successive letters to Wheelock (*Letters* 182–191). The context of the discussion is that Wolfe has received galleys 1 to 100 for the novel. Galleys 1 to 70 have been proofed by Wolfe, returned to Wheelock, and already set in page proof. Galleys 79 to 100 remain in Wolfe's hands. On 19 July, Wolfe comments on the disturbing news that the seventy-five pages of edited typescript used as setting copy for those galleys has disappeared. He is concerned, but not overly concerned, because a second complete copy of the unedited typescript is being held in the Scribners office. "Of course," he adds, "what revisions were made in those 75 pages I don't know" (186–187).

By 22 July, as he returns galleys 79 to 90 to Wheelock, Wolfe is more agitated about the missing typescript pages. "Will you please urge the printer again to try to recover it?" he asks. "There are several places here that cause me difficulty. Naturally, without the manuscript I cannot remember word for word the original, but it seems to me that there are omissions in several places that are not covered by the cuts Mr. Perkins and I made" (187).

The references in Wolfe's letters to Wheelock are to galley numbers, but the context of his discussion and specific references to identifiable material on galley 85 (a reference to a German book, Der Zerbrochene Krug, that appears on page 319 of the American edition) and galley 94 (on which Wolfe adds a sentence beginning "Having arranged to meet her" that appears on page 352 of the American edition) make it possible to locate the points of Wolfe's concern. These points occur in chapters 24 and 25 of the novel, coinciding with those points at which the American edition differs from the English edition. These points are, respectively: 1) "the boys-going-from-school scene," pages 324 to 348 in the American edition, a twenty-four page segment in which Wolfe scans the characters and scenes of Altamont, which is all but eliminated from the English edition; and 2) a burlesque of English war books, a passage some five pages in length appearing in the English edition which does not appear in the American edition.

Wolfe mentions the boys-going-from-school scene in his letter to Wheelock of 22 July. It is, he feels, the passage most damaged by cuts made in the galleys, cuts that he does not remember authorizing. "Mr. Perkins and I," he writes, "took out a big chunk, but there is now a confusing jump that nullifies the meaning of several speeches" (Letters 187–188). In this segment of chapter 24, Eugene, after asking the Leonards' permission, runs off to town and meets George Graves on the way, and the two encounter and comment on dozens of Altamont characters and sights before stopping at Wood's Pharmacy to order two chocolate milks from the soda jerk. Among the characters introduced are Mrs. Van Zeck, the wife of a lung specialist; William Jennings Bryan; Old Man Avery; and Colonel Pettigrew. In short order, Wolfe traces the pattern of the town – race, culture, and background. He juxtaposes German and English quotes, German and English phrases, and German and English descendants – only to conclude in a description of Colonel James Buchanan Pettigrew, head of the Pettigrew Military Academy, adorned in a Confederate cape and discussing war with two pimply cadets. It is a section in which English and German are carefully balanced – and unauthorized cuts could easily throw them out of balance. Wolfe writes to Wheelock, "I do hope people will not look on this section as a mere stunt . . . it is not a stunt" (Letters 188). The cuts, he adds, have caused problems – gaps – he seems unable to solve without the help of the missing pages of edited typescript – and he is having difficulty filling the holes. The entire segment – and an additional five pages of material at the beginning of chapter 24 in which the school boys at the Leonards' play with glib false readings of German texts – are deleted from the English edition.

It is possible to imagine a number of scenarios accounting for the deletion of thirty pages of material from the English edition coincident with material that Wolfe, although pressured to cut from the American edition, struggled to retain: 1) Wolfe, involved in making cuts in the text for his British publisher, found it easiest to choose passages that Wheelock and Perkins had suggested could be cut; 2) the setting copy for the English edition was galleys or page proofs for the American edition – with Wheelock's suggested cuts marked; 3) Wheelock made suggestions to Heinemann about cuts that he wished had been made in the American edition; or 4) Wolfe gave up trying to reconstruct passages that seemed to have been mangled in editing and for which the edited typescript had been lost, and he decided to cut them. It is fairly clear that in July 1929, at least, Wolfe felt strongly enough about this section to buck Wheelock and Perkins and insist on its retention. This argues strongly for the authority of the American rather than the English edition at this point.

However, Wolfe's correspondence with Wheelock, these same three letters, suggests the authority of the English text over the American at another point. An additional eighty lines of material which do not appear in the American edition, two closely related passages, the largest of which is more than two pages long, appear on pages 342 to 344 of the English edition. In this segment, Eugene (who has been studying the literature of romanticized war enchantment under the direction of the pro-British Leonards) after reading Rupert Brooke imagines himself composing an excessively literary letter at the front: "'It's no use, mater,' he wrote six hours before the attack in which he fell, 'I simply can't bring myself to hate these Huns. I dare say they are mostly chaps like me with their own Pollys and Paters, and dear little flaxen-headed Tommies somewhere back home.'" This "last letter" is followed by the eulogy of his close friend, George Graves, transformed in Eugene's imagination into Captain George Albert Fortescue Graves, D.S.O. Eugene's fantasy precedes by seven lines the sentence that Wolfe writes Wheelock he has inserted on galley 94 ("Having arranged to meet her . . . "). Had the war fantasy segment been included in the American edition, then, it too should have appeared on, or in the vicinity of, galley 94.

Wolfe's letter to Wheelock of 23 July indicates that this was, in fact, where he expected to find it. "There was originally a burlesque of the English war books on galley 94 – was this omitted in the cuts?" (*Letters* 189). This variant may or may not have been coupled with the shorter twenty-line passage inserted one page earlier in the English edition, in which an omniscient narrator breaks into John and Margaret Leonard's maudlin pro-British war sentiments to comment in two paragraphs on the folly of nationalism and war: "They were lifted up on the wings of their enormous folly . . . . They were drunken, inspired, by that great false vision of Arcadia unvisited."

Several other variants, all in chapter 33 and all deleting reference to Eugene's employment as an American armaments worker (about eight pages altogether) may also hinge on the addition of these two passages to the English edition. Because Wolfe broadly mocked British war efforts and nationalism in chapter 25, Wolfe or his editors may have been unwilling to focus on Eugene's employment *behind the lines* in the English edition. It is possible that they feared that Eugene's employment in the armaments factory might cause British reviewers to draw unsympathetic comparisons between Eugene's service at home and the real hardships faced by those British soldiers (the subject of his humor) who had served at the front.

In these ways, the English edition of *Look Homeward, Angel* differed significantly from the novel read by the American critics. All of the English reviewers, except for Richard Aldington, who based his review on the American edition of the novel, read the Heinemann edition published on 14 July 1930.

Although much has been written about the negative responses to Wolfe's first novel by his family and friends in Asheville, little has focused on Wolfe's response to two particularly critical reviews of his work published in England in the summer of 1930 and written by Frank Swinnerton and Gerald Gould. Reading through Wolfe's letters, it is evident that what Richard S. Kennedy describes in his *The Window of Memory* as "frenzied antics" following the English publication of *Look Homeward, Angel*, even given Wolfe's admitted oversensitivity to criticism, was unprecedented. These reviews came at a time when Wolfe was particularly vulnerable: young enough to care what the reviewers said (he had used the positive reviews of the New York critics to shield himself from the adverse reactions to the book in Asheville – quoting them at length in his letters home to suggest the proper response of sophisticated readers to the novel) – but too young to have yet formalized his own literary theory, as he would five years later in *The Story of a Novel*. In 1930 he had essentially no way, other than brief interviews, of responding to his critics: no way, that is, except to include that response in his second novel. It is important then to demonstrate how hard Wolfe took the English reviews of *Look Homeward, Angel* – and why he found these reviews so devastating.

On Wolfe's fifth visit to Europe in 1930, his English publisher, Frere-Reeves, met him in Paris and introduced him to Richard Aldington, the English poet and critic, and Aldington's wife, the Imagist poet, Hilda Doolittle (*Notebooks* 429). Aldington's highly favorable review of *Look*

Homeward, Angel was among the first of the English reviews that Wolfe read. Writing in the 6 July 1930 *Sunday Referee*, Aldington praised the book for the "gusto" and "exuberance" with which it was written. "I rejoice over Mr. Wolfe," he adds, "I think this mighty David has slain once for all the tedious Goliath of 'objective' fiction down to the bottommost dog of them all . . . . There is no *chichi* about this young man, no sterile tootling on the super-highbrow flute acquired at second hand and by petty larceny from last season's Paris modes in literature; he has something to say, knows what is is, and, by the Nine Gods, he says it." "For me," Aldington continues, "this young American goes at one jump straight to the top-notch novelists." Concluding his essay with a review of Faulkner's *Soldiers' Pay*, recently published by Chatto and Windus, he suggests that he considers it also a good novel, but he can not be as enthusiastic about it as he might otherwise have been because it comes "pat on top of Mr. Wolfe's book." Later that month another English review, "*Look Homeward, Angel,*" filled with praise for the novel appeared in the *Times Literary Supplement.* Unsigned, the article notes that the native force of Wolfe's writing is largely unknown in England. "It is impossible," the writer adds, "to regard this unstinting output of magnificent, raw vigour without a thrill and a hope that it will be channeled to great art."

Lulled into an unrealistic sense of security by these early English reviews sent to him by Frere-Reeves, Wolfe forgot the promise he had made to himself not to read any of the English reviews. The depression that he experienced following his reading of two of these reviews, Frank Swinnerton's review, appearing in the 8 August 1930 issue of *The London Evening News,* and Gerald Gould's, appearing in the *London Observer* on 17 August 1930, is dealt with at length in his notebooks and letters.

Like many of his American predecessors, Frank Swinnerton attacks the autobiographical element in the novel and the exuberant prose style, depicting Wolfe as the representative of a "new generation" of less-than-artistic writers. Unlike the American reviewers who balanced their negative criticisms of Wolfe's novel with almost unilateral praise for his prose and predictions of literary success, however, Swinnerton's review is completely negative. The autobiographical element, Swinnerton writes in a final paragraph capitalizing on a particularly crude simile, "is the difference between copying and creating, that the artist tells what he imagines, and gives his tale the air of truth; while the less-than-artist, having all his experience no farther down, as it were, than his crop, brings it all up again like an owl's undigested remnants."

Swinnerton's attack was followed nine days later by Gerald Gould's review of the novel in the *London Observer* — a review that was truly a writer's nightmare. Attacked by Swinnerton for his lack of artistry, Wolfe was to find his prose viciously ridiculed by Gould. The review begins, "A voice, sleep-strange and loud, forever far-near spoke. Eugene! Spoke, ceased, continued without speaking, to speak. In him spoke. Where darkness, son, is light. Try, boy, the word you know remember. In the beginning was the logos. Over the border the borderless green-forested land. Yesterday, remember." Gould continues, "That is the way in which Mr. Thomas Wolfe writes at his most ecstatic! – I can see no reason why anybody should abstain from writing like that: I can see no reason why anybody should read the result." After weeks of "gnawing" away at the book, Gould confesses that he cannot form the remotest conception of what it is about. He describes the Gants as "an untidy American family" and Eugene as "perhaps by a shade more violently silly than the others."

On 18 August, the day following the publication of the Gould review, Wolfe wrote at least three letters. One, to his English publisher, Frere-Reeves, states simply, "I'm pretty badly hit by these reviews." A second, to Scribners editor John Hall Wheelock, begins "Dear Jack: Thanks very much for your good letter. There is very little that I can say to you now except that . . . I have stopped writing and do not ever want to write again." The third, to Maxwell Perkins, requests that Scribners prepare a statement of money due him: "I shall not write any more books, and since I must begin to make other plans for the future, I should like to know how much money I will have." Wolfe's letter to Wheelock continues to suggest that Wolfe's creative vitality has been extinguished by his literary critics: "What reward in the world can compensate the man who tries to create something? My book caused hate and rancor at home, venom and malice among literary tricksters in New York, and mockery and abuse over here. I hoped that that book, with all its imperfections, would mark a beginning: instead it has marked an ending" (*Letters* 252–258).

A letter written by Wolfe to Maxwell Perkins only days after the Gould review and clearly in the midst of Wolfe's depression, offering Scribners the opportunity to sever relations with him, outlines the "enemy" – the "person who will always appear to cheat you of what you most desire." In a paragraph that clearly foreshadows the Starwick confrontation in *Of Time and the River*, he continues, "He has no talent . . . he is nothing; he has no life save that you gave him, but he is there to take all you want away from you. Thus, if you love a woman, and your Opponent is millions of people, thousands of miles away, he will come to trick her from you" (*Letters* 258–259).

Eugene's rejection of the overly-mannered Starwick in the eighty-eighth chapter of *Of Time and the River*, the rejection of the aesthetic poseur, is clearly important to Eugene's development as an artist; it is just as clearly a means by which Wolfe chose to respond to the Swinnertons and Goulds who had attacked and parodied his first novel. The tension in the relationship between Eugene and Starwick throughout the novel develops not out of the barest hint of an undercurrent of homosexuality remaining in the novel after its many cuts, but out of the genuine adulation Eugene and the general public feel for an inferior talent dressed up as an artist. As his friend contemplates a still-life at the Boston Museum, in one episode cut from the novel, Eugene mumbles "foolishly" before Starwick. He is only one of a group of bystanders who stand in hushed silence before the young dandy. Even though Eugene prefers the larger canvasses of the Dutch and Flemish schools, he is incapable of articulating his preference because he lacks the knowledge of the critical jargon used by Starwick (*The Starwick Episodes* 18–20).[6] In a way that ties in to Wolfe's response to the critics of *Look Homeward, Angel*, Starwick represents the darling of the literary establishment (he is after all Hatcher's protégé). He personifies the *urbane* and *restrained* writer that the critics have chastised Wolfe for not being. "The great man," Eugene jeers, "is closeted in his sanctum composing . . . . Not *writing*, mind you, but *composing* with a gold-tipped quill plucked from the wing of a Brazilian condor" (*Of Time and the River* 317). Starwick's threat to Eugene exists in the very refinement and elegance of his imposture – which enables Starwick to impress Ann, although as an artist and as a man he is essentially impotent. Eugene's choice is either to emulate Starwick, winning the approval of Ann and the literary community, or to absolutely reject him as his enemy. To Eugene's credit, he chooses the latter.

The thirty-eighth chapter of the novel, in which Starwick unmasks himself to admit that he and Ed Horton share the same midwestern background (and, by implication, the same quality of talent), contains an extended discussion of art and the artist. Starwick's language in describing evil (and, ironically, himself) focuses at length on "the eunuchs of the arts," "men who have the lust, without the power for creation, and whose life goes dead and rotten with its hatred of the living artist and the living man." The implication, since Starwick describes himself as not having "the great well and power" in him necessary to produce art, is that as Ed Horton's talents will cause him to gravitate toward advertising, Starwick's will cause him to gravitate toward the critical. For Eugene, choosing to follow Starwick (just as choosing to listen to those critics who have charged him with only "3,264 fundamental faults, which are absolutely, profoundly and utterly incurable and uncorrectable" would be for Wolfe [*Letters* 450]) – would be to place himself in the hands of his "mortal"

---

[6]In his 1989 edition, *The Starwick Episodes*, Richard S. Kennedy prints a number of scenes cut prior to publication from the original manuscript of *Of Time and the River*.

enemies. "The *fault*, the *fault* always, as *you* should know," Wolfe writes to Perkins a month after the publication of *Of Time and the River*, "is not that we exceed the vital energy of life but that we fall short of it – and that a horrible misbegotten race of anaemic critics whose lives have grown underneath a barrel call out 'monster' and 'exaggeration' at you the moment you begin to approach the energy of life" (*Letters* 447).

The phrase "horrible misbegotten race of anaemic critics" echoes the phrasing used by Starwick in the thirty-eighth chapter of *Of Time and the River* to describe himself, phrasing filled with references to misbirth and deformity. In the middle of their discussion of art, Starwick quotes Shakespeare twice to describe himself – he is "puny, feeble, ugly, and diseased – as King Richard said about himself, brought into the world 'scarce half made up'" and was "still born from his mother's womb" (321). Earlier in the chapter, Eugene chastises Starwick for his "grand airs and mysterious manners": "Is it that like Cæsar you were from your mother's womb untimely ripped?" (318).

Eugene and Starwick's language poignantly foreshadows the references Wolfe makes to himself and *Of Time and the River* in a 7 April 1935 letter to Max Perkins discussing his critical enemies. They are, Wolfe writes, "so much more numerous than you expect – they include, in addition to the Henry Harts, Wassons, and others of that sort, the Benéts, the I.M.P.'s, the F.P.A.'s, the Morelys, the Nathans, the Mark Van Dorens, the Mike Golds, and others of that sort . . . . [who] make a rubber stamp under the name of 'criticism.'"[7] Fearing the critical response to his second novel, Wolfe makes a reference that Perkins cannot fail to recognize, a reference that parallels his own situation to Starwick's: "Max, Max, I cannot go on, but I am sick at heart – we should have waited six months longer – the book, like Caesar, was from its mother's womb untimely ripped – like King Richard brought into the world 'scarce half made up'" (*Letters* 446). Attacked by the critics, Wolfe begins to believe that he will

---

[7]Ben Wasson, William Rose Benét, Isabel Paterson, Franklin Adams, Christopher Morley, and Robert Nathan. A Henry Hart worked in the publicity department at Scribners, but Wolfe is probably referring to the critic, Henry Hart, who published in *The New Masses*; Ben Wasson was a friend of Aline Bernstein and a literary agent; Isabel Paterson was the book reviewer for *The New York Herald Tribune;* Franklin Adams was at various times a reviewer for the *New York Evening Post* and *The Saturday Review;* Robert Nathan was a poet and novelist and a friend of Aline Bernstein; Mark Van Doren never reviewed Wolfe's work but commented in the 25 April 1934 issue of *The Nation* on Wolfe being a one-book novelist; and Mike Gold wrote for *The Liberator* and *The New Masses*. For a description of an early confrontation between Wolfe and William Rose Benét, see David Donald, *Look Homeward: A Life of Thomas Wolfe* (Boston and Toronto: Little Brown, 1987), p. 164.

necessarily have to face his greatest fear, the public humiliation of reduction to the mediocrity of a Francis Starwick – the fear that he would at last fall into the hand of his mortal enemies, the defeatists and literary snobs who critique art rather than create it.

German readers were introduced to Thomas Wolfe in the early thirties when Sinclair Lewis's Nobel Prize Acceptance Speech was printed in *Das Tagebuch* and *Die Literatur*.[8] In the late twenties, American Literature, primarily the novel, emerged in the minds of literate Europeans as a positive cultural force, consciously national in its character. A group of American writers, Theodore Dreiser, Upton Sinclair, Jack London, Ernest Hemingway, and Sinclair Lewis, captured the German imagination during this period. Their work, often underrated in America, was lionized in Germany. By 1932–33, Charlotte Demming, writing in the German Catholic journal *Gral*, called for an American literature which in metaphysical reality would correspond with the gigantic territorial size of the New World. Thomas Wolfe's *Look Homeward, Angel* was waiting in the wings, ready to fulfill German needs for a patriotic national literature that described the length and breadth of America in ways that complemented German values while not challenging the values of Hitler's Third Reich.

Although Wolfe's publisher, Rowohlt Verlag, announced the publication of *Schau heimwärts, Engel!* in 1932, the book was first run in serial form in Berlin's *Vossische Zeitung*, edited by Monty Jacobs, before it finally appeared in book form in 1933. By World War II, the sensitive Rowohlt Verlag German-language edition of the novel, translated by the remarkable Hans Schiebelhuth, had sold close to nine thousand copies.

---

[8]My discussion of the reception of Wolfe's writing in Germany in this text is based on five important studies: Bella Kussy [Milmed]'s "The Vitalist Trend and Thomas Wolfe," *The Sewanee Review*, 50 (July-September 1942), 306–324; William Pusey's "The German Vogue of Thomas Wolfe," *The Germanic Review*, 23 (April 1948), 131–148; H. M. Ledig-Rowohlt's "Thomas Wolfe in Berlin," *The American Scholar*, 22 (Spring 1953), 185–201; C. Hugh Holman's *The Loneliness at the Core* (Baton Rouge: Louisiana S U P, 1975), pp. 141–154; and Leslie Field's "You Can't Go Home Again: Wolfe's Germany and Social Consciousness," in John S. Phillipson, ed., *Critical Essays on Thomas Wolfe* (Boston: G. K. Hall, 1985), pp. 99–112. In addition, I have made use of a three-page document of translated excerpts of the German reviews of *Look Homeward, Angel* provided me courtesy of the Wisdom Collection in the Houghton Library, Harvard University (AC9.W8327.LZ999g. Box 1). Although unidentified by the Houghton, this document is mentioned in a 1933 letter sent to Maxwell Perkins by Wolfe in 1933 (*Letters* 380). It is a series of German "excerpts" sent to Wolfe by Rowohlt Verlag and either translated by them or by Scribners before being sent on to him. I have also made use of a selection of new translations of German reviews prepared for me by Pascale Jarlman and Sharon Beckett.

As William Pusey notes, the importance of Schiebelhuth's translation to the German reception of Wolfe's novel cannot be overestimated. Schiebelhuth, a noted translator of Chinese, French, and English texts, was also a lyric poet whose work had achieved some critical success. He was born in 1895, lived in Darmstadt, and died in the United States in the mid-forties. Schiebelhuth excelled in rendering Wolfe's evocative and ecstatic prose style, as critics from Sigismund Radecki, to Wolfgang von Einseidel, to Otto Karsten noted. Reviewing the novel in the October 1933 issue of *Der Querschnitt*, Radecki referred to Schiebelhuth's translations as careful, painstakingly accurate, and poetically distinguished. Von Einseidel, in a review of *Von Zeit und Strom* written in 1936, praised Schiebelhuth for conveying the power of Wolfe's language: "the rush of the ocean that is called music." Karsten, writing in the February/March 1936 issue of *Die Literatur*, argued that Schiebelhuth's unbeatable, subtle, and congenial translation enabled Germans to read the novel without questioning the superlatives used to describe it.

Indeed, in the German critical responses to this novel, which appeared in a variety of right-wing, middle-of-the-road, and liberal journals, there were superlatives aplenty. The winner of the 1946 Nobel Prize in Literature, Hermann Hesse wrote glowingly of *Schau Heimwärts, Engel!* in *Die Neue Rundschau*: "We do not wait impatiently for the next book of this superb writer merely because we are eager to drink up another hundred pages of his overwhelming and wonderful hymns in celebration of nature, of eating and drinking, of sensuality, of intoxication, of the perfume of flowers, of animals, of foods, of women – but because his next book must bring this young Siegfried to the place where the beauty and the desolation of the world may no longer be represented side by side, where, amid gigantic throes, some reconciliation must be found"(Translations 2). By 27 April 1933, he would conclude, in an article printed in Switzerland in the *Neue Züricher Zeitung*, that *Schau Heimwärts, Engel!* "is the most powerful piece of work from contemporary America with which I am familiar." By December 1935, while awaiting the publication of the German-language edition of Wolfe's second novel, *Von Zeit und Strom*, he wrote even more about Wolfe, comparing his novel to Faulkner's *Light in August*. Hesse writes in the December 1935 issue of *Die Neue Rundschau*:

> Two years ago, I read the first book of the American author Wolfe with joy and surprise: *Schau Heimwärts, Engel!* – for years the most notable impression of American literature . . . . At the same time I learned about the German translation (by Rowohlt) of a new American storyteller: William Faulkner and his novel "Light in August." Similar to Wolfe's book (I consider Wolfe to be the greatest storyteller), this novel works its way through the strength and vivid images, through the immense

closeness to reality to the sensuality of youth in which you can actually hear Southern voices. (670)

In the *Berliner Börsen-Courier*, Erich Franzen described his response to the novel: "The brilliance of its presentation, the superb sweep of its spiritual outlook, and the almost fanatical verisimilitude of the whole thing, make the book one of the most significant of our time. It must be looked upon as the voice of the entire younger American generation . . . ." (Translations 1). Ullrich Sonnemann in the *Berliner Tageblatt* called the novel "superb." "Here," he wrote, "is greatness." Hermann Linden writing in the *Frankfurter Nachrichten* compared Wolfe's talent to a fiery comet, and Ludwig Winder in the *Deutsche Zeitung* writes of the novel, "In this book you will find magic, passion, rebellion, youth: all the things that you miss in the carefully groomed older American novelists. Thomas Wolfe is a great hope." In the *Neue Freie Presse* Kurt Münzer added his words of praise for the novel, writing that "Wolfe did not write this book, he sang it . . . . He is shamelessly creative before our very eyes, he is shamelessly truthful down to the very nakedness of the soul itself, he is shamelessly intoxicated with the wonders of man and of the earth" (Translations 1–3).

The party-line critic, A. E. Günther, writing in his *Deutsches Volkstum*, was one of the few critics to make even the most cursory of negative comments about the novel. Comparing Wolfe's novel to Sinclair Lewis's *Ann Vickers*, he writes: "Wolfe, who has been influenced less by Europe than Sinclair Lewis, does not have even the rudimentary traces of structure which are to be found in 'Ann Vickers.' Episodes follow each other according to the calendar, not according to any plan on the part of the author. Nevertheless Wolfe is more genuinely creative than Lewis. Out of the bitter and brutal descriptions of a primitive but in no sense innocent civilization, there breaks forth in Wolfe an elemental love for America, the germs of a true national spirit" (Translations 3).

The very qualities that displeased Wolfe's American critics – his individualism, egocentrism, and his mysticism, even his formlessness – pleased the German critics. Much like DeCrèvecoeur in his *Letters from an American Farmer* and Thomas Jefferson in his *Notes on the State of Virginia*, Wolfe was perceived to have written a work that issued a declaration of independence to the American spirit, a novel that opened up a kaleidoscopic view of the true America to European observers.

Wolfe wrote to Maxwell Perkins in August 1933 about the favorable German reviews:

> I think some sort of publicity also should be given to the fact that the book got fine reviews in Germany. Jack Wheelock read me the advertisements the German publishers sent me and the excerpts which they used from some of the leading papers of Germany, Austria and Switzer-

land, which are as good or better than anything I ever got in this country. Why should we conceal this fact? I notice that publishers of other writers use foreign reviews which cannot touch these notices and make full use of any favorable foreign publicity they get. The publicity I kicked about was that which seemed to me to be personal and gossipy and irrelevant and not substantiated by fact, but I see no reason at all to be ashamed of the fact that my book got fine reviews in Germany and Austria, and I do not see why that is not publicity which could be honorably and creditably used. (*Letters* 380)

3: A Matter of Form

WHAT IS IT that empowers *Look Homeward, Angel?* Critics write about Faulkner and Fitzgerald, Hemingway and Dos Passos; they write about *Of Time and the River, The Web and the Rock*, and *You Can't Go Home Again*, but when they turn to Wolfe's *Look Homeward, Angel*, they turn inward – choosing to describe their early responses to the novel – before they go on to evaluate or analyze it. The novel, they admit, more often than not, changed their lives, or altered their perception of reality, or encouraged them to achieve goals that they believed beyond them. C. Hugh Holman writes in *The Loneliness at the Core*,

> The structure of *Look Homeward, Angel* and the maturing of the protagonist are consonant; between the outer view of society and the inner seeking of the soul there is a shared and constant dream, the aspiring dream of every middle-class provincial American boy who has turned his back upon home to seek triumphs in the citadels of culture and power. *Look Homeward, Angel* is structurally the most satisfying of Wolfe's novels not only because the *Bildungsroman* has a built-in pattern and wholeness but also because the American boy's dream is at its center – a dream not yet torn by fundamental doubts: its realization is not only possible, it seems almost within the outstretched grasping fingers. (91)

Holman almost never becomes autobiographical, but his understanding of those "outstretched grasping fingers" is so energized an image that the reader comes to suspect that there may be something autobiographical behind this assessment. The parallels between Wolfe's life and Holman's are unusual. Both were the product of small provincial Southern towns (Holman was brought up in the small towns of Goldville and Clinton in South Carolina); both had mothers who ran boarding houses to support the family; both longed for fathers (Holman's had died when he was young); both were voracious readers; both wrote novels (Holman wrote detective fiction); and both received degrees from Chapel Hill. One went on to establish a national reputation as a teacher and a scholar; the other went on to write great fiction. If anything, Holman's passion for achievement was even more powerful than Wolfe's. Wolfe's parents provided for his education at the North State Fitting School, Chapel Hill, and Harvard. Holman's father died during the early years of the Depression, and his mother died only a few years later. Neither left any financial provisions for their son. Enrolled at Presbyterian College, Holman worked at whatever jobs he could find. He showed films at night in a Goldville movie theater, drove a school bus, and in addition to being a full-time student, worked a full eight-hour shift in the textile mills, a physical strain that took a significant toll on his health. Wolfe, writing as many as eighteen hours a day, drowned himself in coffee to stay awake, limited himself to a single meal a day, and went weeks without talking to a soul. Both men were impassioned by their need to succeed, by their need to rise above the cards that life had dealt them (James Skinner, "Hugh Holman: From Goldville to Clinton").

Another major Wolfe critic, Holman's colleague at the University of North Carolina at Chapel Hill Louis Rubin, had a similar experience with Wolfe, as he writes in his 1973 essay, "The Sense of Being Young," which first appeared as the Introduction to his *Thomas Wolfe: A Collection of Critical Essays*:

> My own encounter with the Wolfe novels – if I may become confessional for a moment in order to make what I hope is an important point – has been a lifelong affair. I first came upon Thomas Wolfe in 1943, when I was 19 years old and a Private First Class in the Army of the United States . . . . To say that I was enthralled with Thomas Wolfe scarcely describes what happened. I read *Look Homeward, Angel*, and straightaway I was transported into a realm of literary experience that I had not known could exist. No writer, as Thoreau once remarked of Whitman, can communicate a new experience to us; but what he can do is to make us recognize the importance of our own experience, so that we become aware, for the first time, of what it is that we feel and think and what it can mean for us. This is what Thomas Wolfe did for me . . . . For a young reader such as myself there could be an instantaneous and quite exhilarating identification, not only with the youthful protagonist, Eugene Gant, but with the autobiographical author who was describing Eugene's experience with so much approval and pride. (3)

In his 1968 review of the Turnbull biography, "The Shade of Thomas Wolfe," William Styron also writes about his initial response to this novel:

> It would be hard to exaggerate the overwhelming effect that reading Wolfe had upon so many of us who were coming of age during or just after the second world war. I think his influence may have been especially powerful upon those who, like myself, had been reared as Wolfe had in a small Southern town or city, and who in addition had suffered a rather mediocre secondary education, with scant reading of any kind. To a boy who had read only a bad translation of *Les Misérables* and *The Call of the Wild* and *Men Against the Sea* and *The Grapes of Wrath* . . . , the sudden exposure to a book like *Look Homeward, Angel*, with its lyrical torrent and raw, ingenuous feeling, its precise and often exquisite rendition

of place and mood, its buoyant humor and the vitality of its characters and, above all, the sense of youthful ache and promise and hunger and ecstasy which so corresponded to that of its eighteen-year-old reader – to experience such a book as this, at exactly the right moment in time and space, was for many young people like being born again into a world as fresh and wondrous as that seen through the eyes of Adam. (96)

Styron's *Sophie's Choice*, with its focus on a young Wolfe clone, Stingo, and its constant references to Wolfe and his writing, suggests that several decades later, Styron was still being influenced by the writer he had read as a young man.

Moving on from the world-war generations, it is also important to note the influence that Wolfe's first novel has had on the generations of the eighties and nineties. Three young scholars, David Wyatt, David Strange, and Phillip Horne, compiled a keepsake detailing their initial responses to Wolfe in 1990 (*How I Got Hooked on Thomas Wolfe*). Wyatt writes, "I first read *Look Homeward, Angel* when I graduated from college. I was saturated then with the scientific method – a system of analysis that seemed to drain the 'enormous beating color' from life, leaving a world of black and white. Thus when I read this wonderful book, my unprepared senses were in desperate need of such stimulation. I was overwhelmed with Wolfe's collage of imagery and his sensational command of language" (2). David Strange describes his young wife's concern when he chose to take *Look Homeward, Angel* along on their honeymoon (10–11). And Phillip Horne recalls that while in college at Chapel Hill, each night "as his roommate read his Bible . . . I took down my *Look Homeward, Angel*" (18).

For many of these writers and critics *Look Homeward, Angel* is more than text, it is a reflection of their own condition – and, perhaps, even a guidebook to escaping that condition. The work of Faulkner and Hemingway is truly remarkable and worth writing about, but their writings do not seem to affect people's lives as Wolfe's *Look Homeward, Angel* does. It is remarkable, then, as we look at the critical evaluations of this novel made in the forties and fifties and in the sixties and after – in light of our own understanding of what this work has meant to so many readers and authors – to come across critics for whom the quality of Wolfe's work was still a subject of debate.

The 1940s and 1950s

Two of the earliest assessments of *Look Homeward, Angel* appeared in 1942. Maxwell Geismar and Alfred Kazin included evaluations of Wolfe's first novel in their book-length studies of American fiction, *Writers in Crisis: The American Novel Between Two Wars* and *On Native Grounds: An Interpretation of Modern American Prose Literature*, respectively.

Geismar, who four years later would edit *The Portable Thomas Wolfe*, a confusing series of excerpts from the writings of that author, examines *Look Homeward, Angel* in the broad context of the American novel and concludes that Wolfe's first novel takes as its subject the idea of "the lost paradise." That "lost paradise," however, passes through several incarnations in the course of his discussion. It begins, innocuously enough as the "lost paradise" of Genesis and Wordsworth, is transmuted into the primal American landscape (similar to that described by Fitzgerald in the concluding pages of *The Great Gatsby*) and then somehow mutates into the lost garden of the pre-Civil War South (194). W. O. Gant, functioning in the novel, according to Geismar, as a Northern consciousness, can compare the tawdry town of Altamont, disparagingly, to the "rich meadows, corn, plum trees, and ripe grain" of his Northern home. "It is Gant . . . ," Geismar writes, "who recalls the 'great, forgotten language, the lost lane-end into Heaven' . . . . Lost indeed the Gantian South with its gray and withered Altamonts, its squalid Toytown cities, the 'pasteboard pebbledash' hotels. The muddy clay roads. The slattern people. The rows of yokels strung like apes along the fences." From this, Geismar leaps to the same conclusion voiced by Daniels and Donald Davidson, that in order to write *Look Homeward, Angel*, Wolfe had to become disloyal to his origins, lose faith in his neighbors, and literally lose whatever affection he might have for his home. "Wolfe," he concludes, echoing the charges made by these earlier reviewers, "was born in the South, but he shared with it little except the accident of birth"(196).

Wolfe's lack of loyalty to his family and native region, Geismar attributes, in a period far more tolerant of chauvinism than our own, to emotional deficiencies, the burdens of a young man coping with an overambitious mother willing to offer up any human sacrifice to achieve her "insensate freedom" (199). Failing to recognize that the voice of the narrator in *Look Homeward, Angel* is at points ironic, that it is the reflections of an older-wiser consciousness that has come to value the characters and situations of his youth looking back on his early misunderstanding of those characters and situations from a distance, and completely missing the tenderness of Wolfe's tone and the gentle humor with which he explores the various characters in Altamont, Geismar concludes that Eugene comes to hate Eliza, and then Gant as he is affected by Eliza, and then himself. Wolfe's "preposterous rhetoric," he suggests, "provides a richness of words for the vanished richness of fact" and his long elaborate depictions of hunger and food arise from the poverty of the material and spiritual life in Altamont that he condemns.

Alfred Kazin is equally unsympathetic to the character of Eliza Gant, whom he describes as the "enemy" in the novel. "Her greed, and lovelessness and talk, the burning acquisitiveness which found its symbol in the boardinghouse that supplanted their home, the family's slow disintegration, his newspaper route in the early winter mornings," he concludes, were the causes of both Eugene's and Gant's torment. Examining Wolfe's deficiencies, his failure to mature beyond the egotism of childhood, in the light of Kazin's own Marxist views, he concludes that Wolfe proved himself the most "self-centered" novelist of his day. "His imagination," he writes, "was a perpetual tension between his devotion to himself and his devotions to his self interests." Unlike Whitman, who recognized that the generic "I" contained multitudes, at bottom Wolfe's sense of tragedy was "always a personal complaint, an imperial maladjustment."

But Kazin's assessment of Wolfe's writing, though apparently more bitingly critical, is ultimately far less negative than Geismar's. Kazin recognizes that in the final analysis Wolfe's focus on the truth of his own experience, rendered symbolic in the novel, explains how he was able to incorporate and even surpass the best methods of American realism. Before going on to evaluate Wolfe's later novels, Kazin concludes in a manner that seems to surprise him as much as it surprises his readers, that though Wolfe "often seemed determined to prove himself the sickliest of romantic egotists, he was, ironically enough, the most alert and brilliant novelist of depression America" (477–478).

Wolfe's satire, humor, and rhetoric in *Look Homeward, Angel* also provided material for analysis for critics of the forties and fifties. The evaluations of Wolfe's use of humor in his writing are especially important in understanding why young people are so attracted to the novel and why there is such a range in the critical response to it. Those critics who perceive the humor in Wolfe's depiction of the follies of young-manhood tend to be more positive in their discussions of Wolfe's rhetoric; on the other hand, those critics who turn a deaf ear to Wolfe's humor frequently focus on the unevenness and "mawkishness" of his prose style. Many of Wolfe's early reviewers picked up on what they called the "exuberance" of Wolfe's fiction, but none of the reviewers focused significantly on the response of the readers to what are clearly humorous exaggerations in the text.

One of the earliest discussions of humor in Wolfe's first novel appears in Edgar Johnson's *A Treasury of Satire*, published nearly two decades after the appearance of *Look Homeward, Angel*. Johnson describes Wolfe as a clumsy ironist, "a young giant who has no idea of his strength and who

imagines he is being delicate and restrained when he is flattening something beyond recognition" ("Thomas Wolfe and the American Dream"
742). In *Look Homeward, Angel*, Johnson continues, the satire is almost entirely personal, centered upon the members of Eugene Gant's family.
The examples he provides include old Gant's roaring and bombast;
Eliza's miserliness; Steve's bullying swagger; Helen's wild laughter;
Luke's stammering; Ben's bitterness; and Eugene's emotional outbursts
(743). Whereas many of the earlier critics analyzed Wolfe's depictions
of his family as criticism of a dysfunctional family, Johnson, more sensitive to Wolfe's tone, picks up on the innocent humor and love in his attitude toward the family. This humor is invariably located in Eugene's
consciousness, as he reflects on the exaggerated moments of trauma and
humiliation in his youth. This humorous oversensitive response of the
young protagonist of the novel to his family, typical as it is of so many
adolescents, is one of the most endearing elements in *Look Homeward, Angel.*

Although it is difficult to understand how any reader could fail to recognize the humorous sub-text to Eugene's world in Wolfe's first novel,
Edwin Berry Burgum (Wolfe's colleague at New York University in the
late twenties who, by the mid-thirties, had along with Harold Stearns and
others become an editor of the Marxist journal *Science and Society*) seems to
have done just that. In his "Thomas Wolfe's Discovery of America," published in *The Virginia Quarterly Review* only a year after Johnson's book on
satire was published, Burgum charged Wolfe's prose style in *Look Homeward, Angel* with almost every possible inadequacy. The style, he writes, is
uneven, the prose is lifeless, the rhetoric is adolescent, and the structure is
formless. "There is," he concludes, "no humor in *Look Homeward, Angel*,
only a hypnotic identification with the violence of despair." What "gusto"
there is in the novel, he continues, belongs to old Gant, rather than to
Eugene. It is only in the social criticism of his later novels, Burgum con-
cedes, that Wolfe's work rises above overly romanticized adolescent
reminiscence (422–423).

In a frequently overlooked but nevertheless impressive study of
Wolfe's prose style and humor first appearing in the spring 1955 issue of
the *Arizona Quarterly*, "The Durable Humor of *Look Homeward, Angel*," B. R.
McElderry, Jr., focuses on the extravagant joy in Wolfe's earliest novel,
the innocent exuberance of the twenties that McElderry feels was responsible for making the novel so popular in the traumatized Depression years
of the thirties. Where Burgum found "no humor" and Johnson found
only heavy-handed satire, McElderry found subtlety and the work of one
of the finest humorists in American letters. Wolfe's humor, he continues,
surpasses even that of Twain. "It is the tolerance, the lack of malice, that

gives distinction to Wolfe's humor in this novel," McElderry writes. "In this he is often superior to Twain, for much of Twain's humor is overshadowed by his obvious desire to score off somebody else as more stupid than himself, or sometimes to get even with himself for being stupid . . . . Wolfe is more natural, and more varied" (123–124).

Supporting his argument, McElderry reproduces more than a half dozen of what he perceives to be the novel's most humorous scenes: the first meeting between Eliza Pentland and her future husband, W. O. Gant, in which Eliza as a book agent sells him a book of poems, *Gems of Verse for Hearth and Fireside*, for his soul and *Larkin's Domestic Doctor and Book of Household Remedies* for his body (11); Gant's exaggeration of the world of his early schooling, "constantly three feet deep in snow, and frozen hard" (50); Eliza's shrewd puncturing of Gant's pretended death, a scene that ends delightfully in Eliza's inside joke "Some day . . . you'll cry wolf-wolf once too often" (281); Queen Elizabeth's self-aggrandizing remarks on her contributions to the world's oldest profession as she purchases a tombstone for Lilly Reed ("'And she was such a fine girl, Mr. Gant,' said Elizabeth, weeping softly. 'She had such a bright future before her. She had more opportunities that I ever had, and I suppose you know' – she spoke modestly – 'what I've done'" [266]); the unsuitable inscription she and Gant decide on for the tombstone (268); Eliza's absent-minded rambling about vanilla extract, soda, and coffee in the face of Gant's unexpected return from his travels in the West (78); the Shakespeare pageant ("The pageant had opened with the Voices of Past and Present – voices a trifle out of harmony with the tenor of event – but necessary to the commercial success of the enterprise. These voices now moved voicelessly past – four frightened sales-ladies from Schwartzberg's, clad decently in cheese-cloth and sandals, who came by bearing the banner of their concern" [374]); and the parodies of Eugene's youthful daydreaming, written "years before Walter Mitty," in which Eugene Gant sees himself as Mainwaring, the young minister, Bruce Glendenning, and "The Dixie Ghost" (104–108; 273–274).

Within months of the appearance of McElderry's article, C. Hugh Holman would also focus on the humor in *Look Homeward, Angel* in an early version of his often-reprinted and as frequently revised "The Loneliness at the Core," published in the 10 October 1955 issue of *The New Republic*. Holman's claims for Wolfe's humor are, however, far less grand than McElderry's:

> I think the first thing that strikes the mature reader who goes back to
> *Look Homeward, Angel* is the realization that it is a book enriched by a
> wealth of humor and saved from mawkishness by a pervasive comic

spirit. This quality of the book is usually lost on its young readers, because the young very seldom see much amusing in themselves . . . .

The author looks back at youth with longing and love, but also with
a steady but tolerant amusement. This is nowhere more apparent than
in the hyperbolically presented day-dreams of "Bruce-Eugene" and in
the very youthful posturing of the college student so earnestly set upon
dramatizing himself. The humor is itself sometimes very poor and very
seldom of the highest order. It is satire directed with crude bluntness; it
is hyperbole lacking in finesse; it is *reductio ad absurdum* without philosophical seriousness. Wolfe is not a great comic writer, but his comic
sense gives distance and depth to his picture of his youthful self. (16)

Floyd Watkins, to the contrary, in his 1958 essay "Rhetoric in Southern Writing: Wolfe," in which he describes *Look Homeward, Angel* as
Wolfe's "best book" because of its subtle imagery and humor, suggests
that what critics perceived as exaggerations of rhetoric in Wolfe's style
was more frequently than not the result of his comic intent. Focusing in
on Eugene's visualization of himself in a motion-picture theater as the
"Dixie Ghost," Watkins suggests the complexity of a verbal stance overlooked by earlier critics.

In this scene, Wolfe uses an exalted rhetorical stance to portray the
comic melodrama of childhood, as Eugene Gant, better known as the
Dixie Ghost, rescues the "young dancing girl" from the lechery of Faro
Jim, whom the Ghost kills off with a "barking Colt" just one-sixth of a
second before the gambler could fire. As the astonished onlookers ask his
name, the Ghost responds:

> "In the fam'ly Bible back home, pardner," the Stranger drawled, "it's
> Eugene Gant, but folks out here generally calls me the Dixie Ghost."
> There was a slow gasp of wonder from the crowd.
> "Gawd!" some one whispered. "It's the Ghost!"
> As the Ghost turned coolly back to finish his interrupted drink, he
> found himself face to face with the little dancing girl. Two smoking
> globes of brine welled from the pellucid depths of her pure eyes and fell
> with a hot splash on his bronzed hand.
> "How can I ever thank you!" she cried. "You have saved me from a
> fate worse than death."
> But the Ghost, who had faced death many times without a flicker of
> a lash, was unable to face something he saw now in a pair of big brown
> eyes. He took off his sombrero and twisted it shyly in his big hands.
> "Why, that's all right, ma'am," he gulped awkwardly. "Glad to be of
> service to a lady any time." (273)

Wolfe, Watkins notes, is not only portraying the imagination of a
child ruminating on young love, "but also sympathetically laughing at the
child and the movie."

Look Homeward, Angel, Watkins concludes, is the best of Wolfe's books because of its rhetoric, which luminously captures the emotions and the imagination of a sensitive youth. The decline of Wolfe's rhetoric in *Of Time and the River* and *The Web and the Rock* is the result of Wolfe's descriptions of the emotions of an "older if not more mature hero." In these novels, the finely honed rhetoric that keeps wishful humor from collapsing into burlesque in Wolfe's first novel is missing. In them the rhetoric becomes "bombastic." Still, Watkins suggests, the decline evident in the rhetoric in these works is offset by Wolfe's use of Southern speech and oratory.

The discussion of rhetoric and humor in Wolfe's first novel by critics in the forties and fifties is intriguing. The debate seems to divide itself evenly between those critics who perceive *Look Homeward, Angel* to be humorless (most frequently the Marxists, like Burgum and Kazin) and those critics who recognize its humor (Johnson, McElderry, Holman, and Watkins, who because of their concern with language and focus on text in combination with biographical and historical interpretations can be describe as "contextual critics"). The ultimate conclusion is unavoidable that the Marxists responded negatively to Wolfe's first novel because their purpose, the creation of social change, was such an all-consuming passion that it left them essentially humorless. Without a sense of humor, they were tone-deaf to Wolfe's prose style and capable of analyzing only character and plot in a novel which concerns itself more with language, words, and the nature of youthful perception than with social change.

These same decades produced an abundance of scholarship comparing Wolfe's writing to that of other writers of his own and preceding generations. One of the earliest examples of this is also one of the most interesting, Monroe M. Stearns's 1945 *College English* essay on Wolfe and the Romantics, "The Metaphysics of Thomas Wolfe." Stearns, a psychological critic who at the time of the publication of his article was head of the English department at the Berkshire School in Sheffield, Massachusetts, suggests that *Look Homeward, Angel* is steeped in the ideas propounded by the English Romantics. Without referring to the fact (of which he was probably unaware) that Wolfe had studied with John Livingston Lowes while at Harvard, the critic whose masterful study of Samuel Coleridge, *The Road To Xanadu*, redefined Romantic scholarship, Stearns likens *Look Homeward, Angel* to *The Rime of the Ancient Mariner*. "What is *The Ancient Mariner*," Stearns asks, "but voyage – odyssey – literature – the journey of an outcast soul to find its salvation through torturous atonement?" (195). More specifically, he identifies the source of the opening phrase of the novel " . . . a stone, a leaf, an unfound door" which he finds has precedence in the third book of Wordsworth's *The Prelude*. In that poem, Wordsworth writes of his eye

> Which, from a tree, a stone, a withered leaf,
> To the broad ocean and the azure heavens
> Spangled with kindred multitudes of stars
> Could find no surface where its power might sleep . . . .
>
> (ll. 161–166)[1]

Wolfe, Stearns concludes, uses the same methods to rescue his generation from the futility of its existence that Wordsworth and Coleridge had used to rescue theirs. Like them, he preaches about a "return to the natural man, exalts the dignity and beauty of human nature, reaffirms man's divinity and purpose, and restores to his readers thereby a sense of their own value and importance" (199). Although Stearns's discussion bogs down in his Freudian attempt to analyze Wolfe's childhood as marred by a "spiritual wound," the result of his mother's rejection, his discussion of Wolfe's metaphysics is an excellent one. He does not, however, take it quite far enough.

There can be little doubt that the refrain that echoes so eloquently throughout Wolfe's first novel originates with Wordsworth. The prose poem to which so many of the critics of this novel repeatedly refer reads:

> . . . a stone, a leaf, an unfound door; of a stone, a leaf, a door. And of all the forgotten faces.
>
> Naked and alone we came into exile. In her dark womb we did not know our mother's face; from the prison of her flesh have we come into the unspeakable and incommunicable prison of this earth.
>
> Which of us has known his brother? Which of us has looked into his father's heart? Which of us has not remained forever prison-pent? Which of us is not forever a stranger and alone?
>
> O waste of loss, in the hot mazes, lost, among bright stars on this most weary unbright cinder, lost! Remembering speechlessly we seek the great forgotten language, the lost lane-end into heaven, a stone, a leaf, an unfound door. Where? When?
>
> O lost, and by the wind grieved, ghost, come back again. (2)

From its primary position in the book, aside from the power of its poetry, this epigram lays heavy claims on the novel. It sits, italicized, on the verso immediately preceding the first page of the first chapter – like a key left under a doormat, to provide entry to people by chance locked out of their

---

[1] References to Wordsworth's *The Prelude* are to the 1805 text reprinted and edited by Ernest De Selincourt and published in Oxford and New York by the Oxford University Press in 1970.

homes. And that is exactly what Wolfe meant it to be – a key to the meaning of the novel itself, an early injunction on how it should be read.

It was probably difficult for Wolfe, as gifted as he was with an enormously retentive memory (every bit as much a part of his inheritance from his mother as the "spiritual wound" to which Stearns so facilely alludes), that not all human beings shared his gift of absolute recall. Had he lived through the forties, he might have been surprised to find how long it took his readers and critics to recognize his reference to Wordsworth's *Prelude*, a reference that is even more important than Stearns suggests. There are significant similarities between Wolfe's first novel and the third book of Wordsworth's *Prelude* which extend beyond those of the refrain to which Stearns refers.

First, the title of the third book in Wordsworth's poem is "Residence at Cambridge." Even though this refers to the English university and not the city of Cambridge, Massachusetts, the site of Harvard University, Wordsworth's title must have immediately conjured up to Wolfe some sense of the ties that bound his experience to that of the renowned English poet. The verses of "Residence at Cambridge" refer to Wordsworth's education at King's College. Most modern readers are aware that Wolfe's novel will also deal with the education of a young man, but for those first readers of Wolfe, who opened the book in the last months of 1929 without having read the reviews, the subject of the novel was unknown. By referring back to Wordsworth's poem Wolfe suggests to this audience that his novel will also be concerned with the education of a young man similar to that of the *Prelude*.

Wordsworth writes in the fourth verse of that book:

> I was the Dreamer, they the Dream; I roam'd
> Delighted, through the motley spectacle;
> Gowns grave or gaudy, Doctors, Students, Streets,
> Lamps, Gateways, Flocks of Churches, Courts and
>   Towers:
> Strange transformation for a mountain Youth . . . .
>
> (ll. 28–34)

Had Stearns searched longer in Wordsworth's poem, he would have come across passages that reverberate throughout Wolfe's prose. For Wordsworth's *Prelude* is an undisguised autobiographical poem, a young man's remembrance of the past, just as *Look Homeward, Angel* is. Wordsworth continues:

> And here, O Friend! have I retrac'd my life
> Up to an eminence, and told a tale
> Of matters which, not falsely, I may call

The glory of my youth. Of Genius, Power,
Creation and Divinity itself
I have been speaking, for my theme has been
What pass'd within me. Not of outward things
Done visibly for other minds, words, signs,
Symbols or actions; but of my own heart
Have I been speaking, and my youthful mind . . . .
Points have we all of us within our souls,
Where all stand single; this I feel, and make
Breathings for incommunicable powers.
Yet each man is a memory to himself . . . .

(ll. 168–189)

It is to that "inner" life that Wordsworth describes in this poem that
Wolfe is referring in the subtitle of the novel, "A Story of the Buried
Life." His prose poem echoes Wordsworth's discussion of lost youth, of
inner worlds, and of incommunicable prisons.

Somewhat enlarging the focus on Wordsworth's poem, by referring
back not only to those specific lines that deal with "a stone, a tree, a
wither'd leaf," but also to the context within which those lines function in
the poem, yields yet additional understanding of the reasons for Wolfe's
decision to preface his novel with this prose poem. Wordsworth writes:

Unknown, unthought of, yet I was most rich,
I had a world about me; 'twas my own,
I made it; for it only liv'd to me,
And to the God who look'd into my mind.
Such sympathies would sometimes shew themselves
By outward gestures and by visible looks.
Some call'd it madness: such, indeed, it was,
If child-like fruitfulness in passing joy,
If steady moods of thoughtfulness, matur'd
To inspiration, sort with such a name . . . .
It was no madness: for I had an eye
Which in my strongest workings, evermore
Was looking for the shades of difference
As they lie hid in all exterior forms,
Near or remote, minute or vast, an eye
Which from a stone, a tree, a wither'd leaf,
To the broad ocean and the azure heavens
Spangled with kindred multitudes of stars,
Could find no surface where its power might sleep,
Which spake perpetual logic to my soul,

> And by an unrelenting agency
> Did bind my feelings, even as in a chain.
>
> (ll. 141–167)

Add to this the fact that Wordsworth lost his brother, John, early in his life, as Eugene lost his brothers Grover and Ben, that *The Prelude* was Wordsworth's attempt to write a history of the growth of his own mind, that both Wordsworth and Eugene Gant come out of the "mountains" to get an education, and the similarity between Wordsworth's age (seventeen) in that segment of the poem quoted to Eugene's age at the end of the novel, as he prepares to leave for college, and the parallels become even clearer. Wordsworth writes of the "chain" that bound his feelings and Wolfe speaks of an "incommunicable prison"; Wordsworth looks to the azure heavens "Spangled with kindred multitudes of stars" and Wolfe writes of loss "in the hot mazes, lost, among bright stars on this most weary unbright cinder, lost!"; Wordsworth searches for meaning in the exterior forms of nature, "a stone, a tree, a wither'd leaf" and Wolfe searches for the entrance to a lost knowledge under "a stone, a leaf, an unfound door."

Wolfe's allusion to Wordsworth is at once a vindication of the auto-biographical nature of his work, a citation of precedence for autobiographical literature, a reference to the dreams and perceptions of childhood "trailing clouds of glory" of which Wordsworth writes in his "Intimations of Immortality," a key to the tone of the narrative text, and a message to the reader to compare the story of the maturation of a young American writer to that of an already established English poet. The "forgotten language" is the language of childhood and nature, vibrant and alive in youth, but so frequently forgotten in middle age. The "lost" object is the sense of newness that youth brings to everything it envelopes. And, as a child, close to the ground, looks under every stone and leaf to find his reality, so the mature author returns to find that "door" which will lead him back to the original experiences of his youth. That "door," with its hinge already opened, is the book itself, the repository of memory, which brings with it a new existence, a new birth.

Aside from Wolfe's contemporary reviewers, several of whom noticed the similarity between the writing of Wolfe and James Joyce but did not develop their discussions of that relationship, Nathan Rothman was among the earliest of the critical analysts of Wolfe's writing to describe the similarity between Joyce's *Ulysses* and *Look Homeward, Angel* in any detail. Rothman, a teacher of English in the Richmond Hill High School in New York City, was completing a book on Joyce's influence on American writing when a segment of that book, "Thomas Wolfe and James Joyce: A Study in Literary Influence," was picked up by Alan Tate for his 1947 collection, *A Southern Vanguard.* Quoting the passage in *The Story of a Novel* in which Wolfe expresses his debt to Joyce's *Ulysses*, Rothman notes that Wolfe, unlike other writers, was never swallowed up by Joyce, although "he used all of Joyce that he could, and some elements of Joyce's that no one else had attempted or perhaps understood." However, Wolfe remains, Rothman argues, always free of purely derivative writing (53).

Rothman mentions several points of similarity between the two writers (similarities in their rhetoric and imagery; their use of stream of consciousness; their sense of time; their autobiographical focus on the artist as a young man) before focusing in on the fourteenth and twenty-fourth chapters of *Look Homeward, Angel,* which share, he notes, the Joycean technique of telescoping time. In addition, he likens Wolfe's prose poem at the beginning of *Look Homeward, Angel* to the fifty-eight fragmentary lines which Joyce places at the head of his Sirens episode. Wolfe's prose poem carries the "freight of themes" which will be scattered like seeds through Wolfe's first two novels: the grief for a dead brother, the phrase "a stone, a leaf, a door," which reappears in *From Death to Morning* in the story "No Door" (3) and on the second page of "Gulliver" (135) in that same volume and on page 604 of *Of Time and the River.* Throughout those first three books, Rothman continues, Wolfe also introduces other themes, weaving them into his original themes like the composition of a symphony.

Like Morris Beja, who writes about the deterioration of Wolfe's prose style in the posthumously published novel in his "Why You Can't Go Home Again," published two decades later, Rothman recognizes that this warp and woof pattern in Wolfe's writing does not continue after *From Death to Morning. The Web and the Rock* and *You Can't Go Home Again,* he argues, would have been good novels for other writers, but not for Wolfe. Unlike Beja, however, who merely speculates on the deterioration of Wolfe's posthumously published works, Rothman suggests that the problem was largely the result of Wolfe's caving-in to the criticism of the literary community. The critics, he notes, goaded Wolfe into writing for them when he should have continued writing in his own vein. *The Web and the Rock* and *You Can't Go Home Again,* he continues, are not weak works, but they are "built upon concessions to his critics, and they are deflected from the course Wolfe's work was taking at the end of *Of Time and the River*" (75).

One of the most frequently reprinted analyses of Wolfe's writing is Wilbur M. Frohock's rhetorical study, "Thomas Wolfe: Of Time and Neurosis," which first appeared in the Autumn 1948 issue of *The Southwest Review.* This article was reprinted in Frohock's 1950 study, *The Novel of Violence in America*; thereafter, it reappears at least once a decade in the major collections of Wolfe criticism until 1973. It was first collected in 1953 in Walser's *The Enigma of Thomas Wolfe*, later, in 1962 in Holman's *The World of Thomas Wolfe*, and finally, in 1973 in Rubin's *Thomas Wolfe: A Collection of Critical Essays*. The frequency of its reprintings alone argues for its importance in Wolfe studies.

In the process of describing Wolfe's *Look Homeward, Angel* as a "case history of the educated American" readjusting to two cultures, the urban and the rural cultures of the early 1900s, Frohock makes some interesting comparisons between the writings of Wolfe and the writings of his contemporary John Dos Passos. Whereas Wolfe's writing is largely autobiographical in the tradition of Jonathan Swift's *Gulliver's Travels* and the English Romantics, Dos Passos's detachment from his subject matter, in which fictional events are presented in the light of historical events, originates in a discipline that developed in France during the middle of the nineteenth century. Wolfe's writings, Frohock concludes, lack the discipline of technique in Dos Passos's but rise above Dos Passos's in their rhetoric. In an interesting aside (in an article full of such moments), Frohock likens the Gant family of *Look Homeward, Angel* to Aeschylus's Orestean family. Frohock writes of Wolfe,

> His ability to make incredible things seem credible is itself almost incredible. It is only when one goes back to *Look Homeward, Angel* that the Aeschylean family of the early book shows itself for what it is and the whole Pentland-Gant clan becomes implausible if not preposterous. W. O. Gant as Agamemnon home from the wars to die, Eliza as Clytemnestra (her refusal to admit that there is anything wrong with the old man being a kind of murder), Helen as Electra when she is not doubling as Cassandra, Eugene as the wretched Orestes . . . one feels that Wolfe cannot really have intended these things, and yet, vaguely, there they are! The people, if hardly the setting, of an *Oresteia*. The Family taint on which Eliza sometimes, and Helen always, dwells is the Curse upon the House. And on first reading . . . one accepts these things unthinkingly. (354)

After *Look Homeward, Angel*, however, Wolfe's continuous use of eccentric and abnormal personalities is far less impressive, and on rereading *Look Homeward, Angel* within the context of Wolfe's later writings, one finds that the Aeschylean family appears as only the first in a long succession of "crackpot figures."

In 1949, a member of the Duke University English department, Margaret Church, published an essay titled "Dark Time" in the September issue of *The Publications of the Modern Language Association*, contrasting Wolfe's use of time to Proust's and Bergson's. Developing an argument established by Herbert Muller in his 1947 study, *Thomas Wolfe*, Church refutes earlier arguments made by Mary M. Colum in her December 1936 discussion, "Literature of Today and Tomorrow," and Joseph Warren Beach in his 1941 study, *American Fiction*, in which they indiscriminately likened Wolfe's perception of time to Proust's and Bergson's.

In developing her argument, Church refers back to several important episodes in *Look Homeward, Angel*. Although at first the reader may find echoes of Bergson in Wolfe's urge to return to the past and the womb, it is only "Bergson modified by Wolfe's earthiness." Church continues, "Wolfe's emphasis is on the individual as a result of the generations that preceded and framed him. He says that if you could really examine your love affair ended yesterday in Texas, you could see elements it had in common with one begun in Crete four thousand years ago by a remote ancestor" (631). Bergson, on the other hand, would say that these two love affairs exist simultaneously. Referring to the scene at the end of *Look Homeward, Angel* in which Eugene meets the ghost of Ben in the square (*Look Homeward, Angel* 623), Church compares Wolfe's sense of duration to Proust's and Bergson's. Proust and Bergson would have argued, she suggests, that Gant lives in the present and the past at once, whereas for Wolfe, Gant lives in a temporarily arrested present that only seems to the observer of the scene to be like the past.

In 1959, Louis Budd in a study appearing in the Winter issue of *Modern Fiction Studies* compared Wolfe's writing to that of yet another author, Sherwood Anderson. Wolfe, Budd argues in a highly perceptive essay, stood closer to Anderson than he did to Joyce. In George Willard, Wolfe found much that he used in Eugene Gant, a hunger for emotional richness, the travail of an innocent spirit, and a common desire to "resolve the dilemmas of feeling by becoming writers" ("The Grotesques of Anderson and Wolfe" 307). *Winesburg, Ohio*, Budd notes, avoids ordered symmetry and *Look Homeward, Angel* is similarly shapeless. Both books deal with a series of loose sketches tied together by an autobiographical cycle. Anderson's penultimate sketch in *Winesburg*, in which George Willard takes leave of his home town, anticipates Eugene's midnight vision at the end of *Look Homeward, Angel*. Anderson writes,

> Suddenly something happens; he stops under a tree and waits as for a voice calling his name. Ghosts of old things creep into his consciousness . . . . If he be an imaginative boy a door is torn open and for the first time he looks out upon the world, seeing, as though they marched in procession before him, the countless figures of men who before his time have come out of nothingness into the world . . . . With a little gasp he sees himself as merely a leaf blown by the wind through the streets of his village . . . . Already he hears death calling. With all his heart he wants to come close to some other human, touch someone with his

hands, be touched by the hand of another. ("The Grotesques of Anderson and Wolfe" 308)

Budd believes that this passage provides at least a partial provenance to the famous phrase Wolfe used, "A stone, a leaf, a door." It is interesting in light of Monroe Stearns's earlier discussions of Wolfe's references to Wordsworth's *Prelude* with its references to a stone and a withered leaf, to note that Wordsworth's phrase includes a reference to a "tree," not to an unfound door. Although the leaf and the stone do not appear as insistently throughout *Winesburg* as they do in *Look Homeward, Angel*, the use of the "door" is Anderson's favorite metaphor for the escape from loneliness. It is quite possible that Wolfe's often-quoted cry was a hybrid of phrases and images he found in Wordsworth and Anderson, all of which pivot on that windblown leaf.

By the end of the fifth decade of this century, only a decade after Wolfe's death, both C. Hugh Holman and the English novelist Pamela Hansford Johnson could call for a reassessment of Wolfe's writing. Holman, in a bibliographical study of the Wolfe canon published in *Texas Studies in Literature and Language*, suggests that in many ways the writings of Thomas Wolfe had put American scholarship and criticism to the test – and that the scholars and critics had simply failed to come to grips with the major issues. "The great need today," he writes, "is for a thoroughgoing critical examination of Wolfe in the light of the aesthetic assumptions of the English Romantics" (445). Johnson, writing in 1959, seven months after the simultaneous publication of the fourth printing of the English edition of *Look Homeward, Angel* and the first printing of the English edition of Elizabeth Nowell's *Letters* (retitled *Selected Letters of Thomas Wolfe*) which took place on 15 September 1958, wrote in response to the largely negative criticism those works received. Cyril Connolly, she notes, reviewing the Heinemann books, refers to Wolfe as "an obsessional neurotic with a gift for words," while Edwin Muir concludes that most of Wolfe's writing had by the late fifties become unreadable. Only Doris Lessing, in an article printed in the *Manchester Guardian*, saw the negative responses as class oriented. "I have yet to meet a person born into any kind of Establishment," Lessing writes, "who understood Wolfe, I have yet to meet a provincial who has cracked open a big city who does not acknowledge that Wolfe expressed his own struggle for escape into a larger experience" (Johnson, "Thomas Wolfe and the Kicking Season" 77).

The trouble with Wolfe, Johnson concludes, is that he "runs counter to anything we have learned recently to respect. He is pre-eminently Bad Form – or would be if he had a form. He is politically reprehensible – or would be if he had any coherent difficulties." Johnson's conclusions about

Wolfe and his reception in the late fifties are equally relevant in the politically correct nineties. Judged by the political assessments of the day, Wolfe is both chauvinist and racist, resoundingly politically incorrect. The fact that he writes great literature seems only of peripheral interest. Most damaging to his reputation is the fact that in an age of "nonreaders" his works are simply too long to anthologize in those college texts which for so many are their first and last exposure to great American literature. When his short stories are anthologized now, it is not "The Angel on the Porch" with its humane characterizations, rich references to failed art, and humorous double entendres that is chosen for reprinting, but the more politically correct "Only the Dead Know Brooklyn" (as unWolfean a story as Wolfe ever wrote) or "Child by Tiger," generally reanalyzed and reinterpreted to provide a standard sociological reading of race issues in the South.

The 1960s and After

The last four decades of the twentieth century have been a particularly productive period in Wolfe scholarship. Three major biographies, Elizabeth Nowell's *Thomas Wolfe: A Biography* published by Doubleday in 1960, Andrew Turnbull's *Thomas Wolfe* published by Scribners in 1967, and David Donald's *Look Homeward* published by Little, Brown in 1987, were published during that period. Other important works published about Wolfe during this time include C. Hugh Holman's edition of *The Short Novels of Thomas Wolfe* and his critical study *The Loneliness at the Core*; Paschal Reeves's *Thomas Wolfe's Albatross*; the Kennedy and Reeves edition of Wolfe's *Notebooks*; John S. Phillipson's *Thomas Wolfe: A Reference Guide*; Suzanne Stutman's editions of the Wolfe/Bernstein correspondence, *My Other Loneliness,* and her edition of the previously unpublished *The Good Child's River;* Aldo Magi and Richard Walser's *Thomas Wolfe Interviewed;* Elizabeth Evans's *Thomas Wolfe*; John Idol and Louis Rubin's edition of *Mannerhouse*; Idol's edition of *The Hound of Darkness;* Francis Skipp's *The Complete Short Stories of Thomas Wolfe*; Leslie Field's *Thomas Wolfe and His Editors*; Carol Johnston's *Thomas Wolfe: A Descriptive Bibliography;* Mary Aswell Doll and Clara Stites's *In the Shadow of the Giant*; Margaret Mills Harper's *The Aristocracy of Art*; James Clark's edition of *The Lost Boy*; and Idol and Stutman's *The Party at Jack's*. In addition no fewer than eleven major collections of critical essays (a total of over 250 previously published and unpublished reviews and essays) appeared in print. These include C. Hugh Holman's *The World of Thomas Wolfe* published in 1962; Leslie Field's *Thomas Wolfe: Three Decades of Criticism* published in 1968; Paschal Reeves's *The Merrill Studies in* Look Homeward, Angel published in 1970 and his *Thomas Wolfe and the Glass of Time* published in 1971; Louis Rubin's *Thomas Wolfe: A Collection of Critical Essays* published in 1973; Reeves's *Thomas Wolfe: The Critical Reception* published in 1974; H. G. Jones's *Thomas Wolfe of North Carolina* published in 1982; Richard S. Kennedy's *Thomas Wolfe: A Harvard Perspective* published in 1983; John Phillipson's *Critical Essays on Thomas Wolfe* published in 1985; H. G. Jones's *Thomas Wolfe at Eighty-seven* published in 1988; and Harold Bloom's *Thomas Wolfe* published in 1987.

Despite this abundance of scholarly activity with its promise of a renaissance in Wolfe studies, one study is almost universally considered by Wolfeans to be the premier event of Wolfe scholarship in the decades following 1960: the publication of Richard S. Kennedy's *The Window of Memory: The Literary Career of Thomas Wolfe* in 1962. Without Kennedy's painstaking study of the manuscript materials at the Houghton, without his remarkable and sensitive multileveled readings of the Wolfe canon, without his detailed description of the complexities of Wolfe's themes and forms, without his careful analysis of the editing of Wolfe by Perkins and Aswell, scholarly study of the writings of Thomas Wolfe would not have come of age.

The Window of Memory deals with each of Wolfe's four novels, in eight segments, all of which revolve about a single recurring structure that deals first with the themes of the work, then with the process of its creation and form, and finally with discussions of the editing process. Unlike far too many critics who focus in on Wolfe the legend or Wolfe the man, Kennedy never forgets that readers study Wolfe not as an historical figure, but as the author of an incomparably fine succession of plays, novels, short stories, essays, and private documents. Without the literature that he produced, Wolfe vanishes into that very *manswarm* of activity that he describes in his later fiction. Where earlier critics questioned Wolfe's techniques, Kennedy documents those techniques; where earlier critics despaired of Wolfe's rhetoric, Kennedy explicates it on a variety of narrative levels; where other critics perceived formlessness, Kennedy finds a highly complex philosophical structure; where earlier critics hedged about the nature and quality of Wolfe's literary canon, Kennedy clearly recognizes the magnitude and complexity of the themes that pulse through Wolfe's writings.

Kennedy makes it clear from the beginning of his discussion of *Look Homeward, Angel* that it is the very abundance of that work that has troubled critics. "They are ready," he writes, "to see it as the animal a thousand miles long that Aristotle pictured when he warned about proper magnitude." Few of those novels which actually display the energy of life, he suggests, stay within the restricted forms described by the critics. *Look Homeward, Angel* transcends its imperfections because of "the intensity, vitality, and grandiose scope with which Wolfe rendered 'the vision of life which burned inside of him'"(143). If it appears formless, it is only because critics have not perceived the three planes of unified narrative which taken together in the text provide it with its full meaning. These narrative planes include the central story of the growth of Eugene Gant, the context of the family unit in which Eugene plays a small part, and the larger and more general biological interpretation of life, variously referred to as vitalism, emergent evolution, or creative evolution. By vitalism, Kennedy means the process by which an organism evolves from a "microscopic blob" to "man." Although it seems to move forward by blind chance, it has a certainty of purpose, a "Life Force" guiding it that is beyond mortal comprehension. That "Life Urge" eternally strives to fulfill its purpose over millennia. Within the chapters of the novel, Wolfe arranges an elaborate "overture" of themes and variations comprising "the rhythms of earth, the common activities of Altamont, the family business dealings, the growth of Eugene, and the problems of Time, Memory, Chance, and Illusion," linking in a series of brilliant episodes the personal, the familial, and the universal – displaying this life urge (137).[2]

The passage most representative of Wolfe's central concept of the eternally resurging Life Force is the prose lyric of the passing seasons which begins the second part of the novel:

> The plum-tree, black and brittle, rocks stiffly in winter wind. Her million little twigs are frozen in spears of ice. But in the Spring, lithe and heavy, she will bend under her great load of fruit and blossoms. She will grow young again. Red plums will ripen, will be shaken desperately upon the tiny stems. They will fall bursted on the loamy warm wet earth; when the wind blows in the orchard the air will be filled with dropping plums; the night will be filled with the sound of their dropping, and a great tree of birds will sing, burgeoning, blossoming richly, filling the air also with warm-throated plum-dropping bird-notes. (*Look Homeward, Angel* 165)

This passage precedes several scenes in which Eugene, wandering along his paper route, is inundated by life, milkmen, market vendors, and doctors. As the scene progresses it focuses on Eugene's questions about fixity and chance, passes into the world of his romantic fantasies, and then jumps back into the shabby reality of Dixieland. At its conclusion, Eugene's fantasies resurge, and he pictures an insane millionaire filling his hands with dimes. "Always be good to the birds, my boy," he cautions (*The Window of Memory* 136). Wolfe returns his reader to the developing

---

[2]For an interesting and sustained discussion of Vitalism, see Bella Kussy, "The Vitalist Trend and Thomas Wolfe." *The Sewanee Review*, 50 (July-September 1942), pp. 306–324.

child, the orchard, and the spring darkness – the point at which the entire panorama of the town began. The structure of this segment of the novel is certainly not chronological and not linear; its cyclical form is meant to suggest the continued renewal of the life force in each moment – outside of the specter of time – but it is nonetheless a structure, and it is a structure which is both thematically and philosophically appropriate to the work and to the questions of life and death and art posed in that work.

The precision of Kennedy's analysis and the quality of his discussion in *The Window of Memory* provide Wolfe's critics with a springboard to scholarly study of the complex rhetorical and structural elements in Wolfe's writing: after all that search for an "unfound door," it was Kennedy who first recognized it, unlocked it, moved in, and made himself at home.

In the wake of the publication of *The Window of Memory*, several other critics suggested additional unifying themes and symbols in the novel. Richard Walser, in his 1961 study, "Look Homeward, Angel," argues that the naming of the novel (an afterthought) biases the reader into identifying Eugene with an angel, obscuring the actual theme of the novel which focuses on the ghost of memory which was more apparent in its original title, "O Lost." In order to complete his transformation into the artist, Eugene must confront both his angel and his ghost. The ghost, Walser writes," is the source, the brightness, the inspiration of art," and the angel is the "permanence of art itself." In the final scene of the novel, both ghost and angel become manifest in Ben. Ben's appearance as ghost/angel prepares Eugene for the creative act by enabling him to recapture the past – which includes Ben – in the timeless form of art that becomes the novel, *Look Homeward, Angel.*

In 1962, J. Russell Reaver and Robert I. Strozier in a *Georgia Review* essay suggested that a major theme in the maturation process of Eugene Gant in the novel develops around his ability to face death. Reaver and Strozier perceive the novel to revolve around three major death scenes: Grover's death, the death of the young prostitute Lily Reed, and the revelation that W. O. Gant is dying of cancer. As he experiences these deaths, Eugene gains maturity and strength which he demonstrates in his reaction to a fourth death scene, Ben's death. No longer a child mourning the loss of life and shuddering at "the high horror of death and oblivion, the decomposition of life" ("Thomas Wolfe and Death" 101), he is ready to face life because he has learned how to face death. Wolfe's treatment of death, they conclude, places his fiction "outside the stream of contemporary naturalistic fiction" which cannot rise above the idea of death as the end of an irrational existence. "Wolfe," they write, "has faith even in death since his experience has taught him that it offers a release from an out-worn phase of life to a new height of spiritual promise" (350).

Louis Rubin, on the other hand, in "Thomas Wolfe: Time and the South," an essay first published in his *The Faraway Country* in 1963, sug-gests that the unifying theme in the novel is mutability. By writing *Look Homeward, Angel*, Wolfe fixes the transient world of his childhood into "changeless art" (104). Rubin focuses on the final scene of the novel in which Eugene speaks to the ghost of Ben: "The fountain in the square is suddenly motionless, frozen in time. The stone animals of the monu-ments get up and walk. All that he has seen and known parades before Eugene's unbelieving eyes. Then, in the climactic moment of the novel, he sees, coming along past the fountain carrying his load of newspapers, 'himself – his son, his body, his lost and virgin flesh.' His own childhood self passes by, the self lost in time, vanished down the years . . . . the boy had gone, leaving the memory of his bewitched and listening face turned to the world. O lost!' . . . Time, chronology, change; these are the only reality he knows."

By 1964, Kennedy was building on the arguments he had set forth in his *The Window of Memory* to suggest additional unifying elements in Wolfe's first novel: the use of the motif of the *Bildungsroman* and the use of style. In his *South Atlantic Quarterly* essay "Wolfe's *Look Homeward, Angel* as a Novel of Development," he likens Wolfe's novel to *The Red Badge of Courage, The Caine Mutiny, Great Expectations, Crime and Punishment*, and *An American Tragedy*. Like these novels, Wolfe's *Look Homeward Angel* is almost a classic example of the *Bildungsroman*. The story presents the struggle of a young man to break free from his environment and from a possessive mother; follows him through the standard childhood experiences of con-flicts with his siblings; opens up his imagination through books and sexual curiosity; follows him through intellectual and sexual initiations; and con-cludes with his reaching a new interpretation of life. Unlike other exam-ples of this format which demonstrate no literary value, like Alexander Laing's *The End of Roaming* or Betty Smith's *A Tree Grows in Brooklyn*,[3] however, Wolfe's *Look Homeward, Angel* has philosophic breadth, a func-tion of Wolfe's rich and varied style which makes good use of concrete detail, imagery, and stream of consciousness to enable him to create in full the complex universe inhabited by Eugene Gant.

---

[3] Alexander Kinnan Laing (1903-) is the author of *The Methods of Dr. Scarlett* (New York and Toronto: Farrar & Rinehart, 1937) and *Way for America* (New York: Duell, Sloan and Pearce, 1943). Betty Smith (1896–1972) is the author of *Joy in the Morning* (New York: Harper & Row, 1963) and *A Tree Grows in Brooklyn* (New York and London: Harper & Brothers, 1943).

Darlene H. Unrue, writing of Wolfe's use of the ghost in her study "The Gothic Matrix of *Look Homeward, Angel*" published in *Critical Essays on Thomas Wolfe* in 1985, describes it as an element of Wolfe's Gothic quest. The structure of the novel, with its focus on a dysfunctional family within a decaying mansion (Dixieland), is similar to that used by a number of Southern writers – Faulkner, McCullers, Williams, O'Connor, Capote, Warren, Welty, and Ellison. Similar elements in Wolfe's novel and the traditional Southern Gothic novels include his use of bells, darkness, wind, a decaying mansion, labyrinths, abysses, and eerie music. The journey of knowledge that forms the matrix of the Gothic novel includes confrontations with numerous dangers and evils against backdrops of thunder, lightning, howling winds, wailing ghosts, and screeching demons.

Applying her definition of Gothicism to a passage frequently criticized by Wolfe's early reviewers for its silliness, Unrue reaches some interesting conclusions. An adolescent Eugene recalls infant impressions of imprisonment within a crib:

> And left alone to sleep within a shuttered room, with the thick sunlight printed in bars upon the floor, unfathomable loneliness and sadness crept through him: he saw his life down the solemn vista of a forest aisle, and he knew he would always be the sad one: caged in that little round of skull, imprisoned in that beating and most secret heart, his life must always walk down lonely passages. Lost . . . .
>
> His brain went black with terror. He saw himself an inarticulate stranger, an amusing little clown, to be dandled and nursed by these enormous and remote figures. He had been sent from one mystery into another: somewhere within or without his consciousness he heard a great bell ringing faintly, as if it sounded undersea, and as he listened, the ghost of memory walked through his mind, and for a moment he felt that he had almost recovered what he had lost. (*Look Homeward, Angel* 37–38)

Eugene, she notes, contemplates his sad fate as an imprisoned Gothic hero, not within a gloomy castle, but within his crib. Permeated with feelings of isolation and terror, the passage evokes images of prison bars, dark passages, and ghosts. Like George Washington Cable, Faulkner, and other Southern Gothicists, Wolfe tethers his novel in a strong sense of time and place, pitted against the rampant industrial transformation of the South in the 1920s that threatened that *time* and *place*. "A part of the repugnance of Dixieland," Unrue writes, "a repugnance so strong that it evokes nightmare terrors, is that it represents the opposite of what Eugene wants. He wants aesthetic nourishment, and Dixieland is an ugly symbol of twentieth-century American capitalism and of his mother's total absorption in the profit motive" (54).

   Unrue's argument is convincing and thought-provoking. In addition to its romantic and lyric elements, *Look Homeward, Angel*, makes use of a distinctly Southern tradition, the archetypal Gothic images of the Southern experience. So, the critical reception of *Look Homeward, Angel* in America comes full circle, from the earliest of its reviewers (Jonathan Daniels) who charged that in his first novel Wolfe had "spat" upon the South, to the assimilation of the work into the very literary matrix of that region. There were elements in the South of the 1920s that made it ripe for Gothic fiction, and there were circumstances in Wolfe's experience, that made him turn naturally to the motifs and symbols of his own region as a means of describing the spiritual landscape of terrors and horrors within. The tradition of *Look Homeward, Angel* reaches not only backward to the Southern Gothicism of Poe, but forward to the black humor of Pynchon, Barth, and Vonnegut.

4: The Question of Genius

THE FIRST PRINTING of *Of Time and the River*, ten thousand copies, took place in February 1935, although Scribners did not officially publish it (that is, put the book on sale to the general public) until 8 March. Advertisements in *The New York Times Book Review* indicate that the book entered a "Fifth Large Printing on [the] Day of Publication." By the time the novel had entered its sixth printing in April, one month after its publication, two months after its first printing, and only three months after page proofs had been set, Scribners had printed thirty thousand copies. Advertisements in *The New York Times Book Review* heralded the advent of each new printing, much as they had in the campaign for Hemingway's *A Farewell to Arms* in 1929, creating a steamroller effect, the sense of a book so much in demand that new printings were required on a weekly basis.[1]

Considering the rapid succession of the first six printings of *Of Time and the River*, few corrections might be expected. In fact, nearly one hundred corrections were made in the first six printings. Many are substantives. Heinemann, Wolfe's English publisher, intending to set copy from galleys sent to them in January, was provided in February and April with corrections lists and caught most of the errors prior to setting type in August 1935. John Hall Wheelock chose to send Wolfe's German publisher, Rowohlt-Verlag, stitched gatherings of the sixth printing of *Of Time and the River* in March 1935, specifically because that printing incorporated all of the corrections made to that date. Wolfe first wrote about his awareness of the problems in the early printings of *Of Time and the River* on 31 March 1935 in a lengthy four-part letter to Maxwell Perkins (*Letters* 435–450). He sent a list of corrections, but 75 percent of the errors had already been corrected by the time his letter was received.

Wheelock explained the problem in a letter to Frere-Reeves at Heinemanns dated 19 April 1935. The manuscript of *Of Time and the River* had been given to a typist, in Wolfe's hand, to copy. The typist had difficulty decoding the handwriting, and as a result, the typescript which came into the printers' hands had a number of words which, although they made

[1]For an interesting article on the Scribners marketing campaign for Wolfe's contemporary Ernest Hemingway, see John J. Fenstermaker, "Marketing Ernest Hemingway: Scribners Advertising in *Publishers Weekly* and *The New York Times Book Review* 1929–1941," in Matthew J. Bruccoli and Richard Layman, ed. *Fitzgerald/Hemingway Annual* 1978 (Detroit, Michigan: Gale, 1979), pp. 183–195.

sense, were not the words that Wolfe had written. Where Wolfe wrote "transmuted," the typist read "transmitted"; where Wolfe wrote "loveliness," the typist read "loneliness"; where Wolfe wrote "clay," the typist read "day." Most of the corrections made by Scribners in the first six printings were of this nature; others, errors in pronoun usage, resulted from the failure of the Scribners staff to translate the first-person story published as "A Portrait of Bascom Hawke" in the April 1932 issue of *Scribner's Magazine* into the third person when that story was incorporated into the novel.

Wheelock's letter to Frere-Reeves admitted, in good, businesslike fashion, an embarrassing situation. Wolfe's letter to Maxwell Perkins, on the other hand, was frenzied and anxiety-ridden. Wolfe's fears were prophetic, though possibly not for the reasons he suspected. The nature of the advertising campaign for *Of Time and the River*, a campaign that finally focused on Wolfe as *The Great American Novelist*, made him vulnerable, if not to his "enemies," at least to those whose creative philosophies differed from his own. In addition, more by chance than by choice, the copy of *Of Time and the River* that fell into the hands of the critic writing for *The Saturday Review of Literature*, Bernard DeVoto, was a second printing, in which fewer than a third of the errors had been caught.

The Scribners campaign for *Of Time and the River* differs most significantly from the campaign for *Look Homeward, Angel* in its focus. Although its advertising blurbs continued to stress the vitality of Wolfe's novels, Scribners began to market the author as well as the product. On 10 March 1935, *The New York Times Book Review* contained a full-page advertisement promoting eleven Scribners books. Of the 130 square inches of space in that advertisement, nearly 75 square inches (more than half) were devoted to *Of Time and the River*. The section devoted to this book contained two illustrations, each measuring 9 square inches: a portrait of Wolfe and a facsimile of the dust jacket for the book. The 14-line blurb for the novel, printed in 18-point type, heralded a second printing and quoted from Sinclair Lewis's Nobel Prize speech describing Wolfe as, potentially, one of the world's greatest writers (17). Two weeks later, as the book entered its fifth printing, Scribners devoted over 80 square inches of a *New York Times Book Review* advertisement to *Of Time and the River*, dramatically reproducing the front pages of issues of *The New York Times Book Review*, *The New York Herald Tribune Books*, and *The Saturday Review of Literature*. All that is legible in these facsimiles are banners reading: "Mr. Wolfe's Pilgrim Progresses: 'Of Time and the River' Carries on 'Look Homeward, Angel'"; "The Ecstasy, Fury, Pain and Beauty of Life: Thomas Wolfe Sings and Shouts in His Gargantuan New Novel"; and "The River of Youth." Wolfe's portrait appears in all three facsimiles.

In addition, the advertisements quote from reviews by Peter Munro
Jack, Mary Colum, Herschell Brickell, Lewis Gannett, and Clifton
Fadiman. Of these five review blurbs, three refer to the book and two to
the author. Jack calls the novel a "triumphant demonstration that Thomas Wolfe has the stamina to produce a magnificent epic of American
life." Fadiman writes: "For decades we had not had eloquence like his in
American writing" (24 March 1935, 13).

On 7 April 1935, half of a 98 square-inch Scribners advertisement in
The New York Times Book Review was devoted to the new book, labeled "A
New National Best-Seller Enthusiastically Acclaimed by Leading Critics
from Coast to Coast." Wolfe's portrait, paraded in a single column along
the left-hand margin of the advertisement, appears five times. Of the nine
reviewers and reviews quoted, more than half focus on Wolfe and not on
the novel. Peter Munro Jack speaks of Wolfe's stamina; Mary Colum likens Wolfe to Joyce and Proust; James Gray calls Wolfe "a genius . . . a
terrific elemental force"; Sterling North comments that "never before in a
book by an American has there been such a raw and rich profusion of
life"; and Paul Jordan Smith remarks that "no man has ever told the story
of youth's tragi-comedy in such golden words" (13).

Two weeks later, in a 32 square-inch advertisement appearing in the
pages of *The New York Times Book Review*, Scribners quoted Harry Hansen,
who referred to *Of Time and the River* simply as "Thomas Wolfe's great
book," and John Chamberlain, who suggested that "Wolfe may supply
the motive to change our literature" (21 April 1935, 11). Later advertisements in *The New York Times Book Review* refer to *Of Time and the River* as
the "Greatest novel of the year" (28 April 1935, 15) and "the most remarkable American novel since 'Moby Dick'" (5 May 1935, 19) and liken
Wolfe to Dickens and Rabelais (12 May 1935, 13). Wolfe, one reads,
towers "head and shoulders above anyone now writing" (19 May 1935,
13).

The American Reviews

Before leaving for Europe on 2 March 1935 to escape the emotional furor
that he felt sure would surround the publication of *Of Time and the River*,
Wolfe dedicated his book to his editor, Max Perkins. The dedication
reads:

To
MAXWELL EVARTS PERKINS

A GREAT EDITOR AND A BRAVE AND HONEST MAN, WHO
STUCK TO THE WRITER OF THIS BOOK THROUGH TIMES

OF BITTER HOPELESSNESS AND DOUBT AND WOULD NOT LET HIM GIVE IN TO HIS OWN DESPAIR, A WORK TO BE KNOWN AS "OF TIME AND THE RIVER" IS DEDICATED WITH THE HOPE THAT ALL OF IT MAY BE IN SOME WAY WORTHY OF THE LOYAL DEVOTION AND THE PATIENT CARE WHICH A DAUNTLESS AND UNSHAKEN FRIEND HAS GIVEN TO EACH PART OF IT, AND WITHOUT WHICH NONE OF IT COULD HAVE BEEN WRITTEN.

Perkins had expressed his concern at the dedication which, with his usual foresight, he perceived could cause nothing but trouble. But Wolfe had persisted, and after countless rounds of editing sessions and concessions on Wolfe's part concerning the editing of the book, Perkins capitulated.

In addition, the "Publisher's Note" located on the page opposite the half title at the front of the book promised that *Of Time and the River* and *Look Homeward, Angel* were two of what would ultimately be a series of six books appearing under the title *Of Time and the River*, the first four books of which had already been written. This ruse was intended to ameliorate those critics who Wolfe and Perkins believed would attack the book as being incomplete or fragmentary.

Perkins and Scribners recognized that Wolfe could not continue to write under the burden of being a "one-book" author. Five years had passed since the publication of *Look Homeward, Angel*, and with each year questions of Wolfe's ability to write a second successful novel had become more burdensome. Taking matters into his own hands, Perkins sent the manuscript of *Of Time and the River* on to the typesetters while Wolfe was out of town on a brief vacation, without asking Wolfe's permission. By the time Wolfe returned, the book that he had expected to work on for another year was already being set. Aware of the book's flaws, Wolfe and Perkins decided that to ensure his emotional health Wolfe should be out of the country when the book appeared. Knowing how violently Wolfe reacted to the reviewers and critics, Perkins made Wolfe promise that he would not read any of the reviews while he was in Europe.

It required all the help of Wolfe's friends Belinda Jelliffe, Elizabeth Nowell, John Skally Terry, and Robert Raynolds and his wife to get Wolfe aboard the *Ile de France* in time to sail. At the last minute, he insisted on leaving boxes of his manuscripts with Perkins, buying fruit for the trip, and recovering some forgotten laundry. When he reached the ship, he found that the steward had replaced the bed in his room with an extra long one. Delighted, he waved good-bye to his friends.

Two days later, on 6 March 1935, Wolfe wrote Jelliffe from the middle of the Atlantic. The voyage had been uneventful, except for the heaving of the vessel, up and down, and side to side, that had evidently ruined some of the passenger's appetites, but not Wolfe's. The food, he commented, was excellent, the accommodations like a good hotel, and his only complaint was that the lurching of the boat from side to side made it difficult to sleep at night. He was, he noted, tossed from side to side in his bunk like a "delicate little 250 pound pea" in its pod. At sea, the sky was ash-grey, and the waves exploded "mountain-high" all around, tossing the poor little forty six-thousand ton boat about "like a rotten straw." His emotional state mirrored the physical state of the *Ile de France*. He writes,

> I have had little joy or peace or love yet – still tormented, still driven on by drink, goaded by useless requests, beset by wild and foolish apprehensions – wondering what the swine will have done to me or to my book by the time this reaches you, if there will still be heart and power in me to go on with my work if they damn me up and down and say that I'm no good . . . . (*Letters* 432–433)

Arriving in Paris on 8 March, the day that *Of Time and the River* was published, Wolfe received a glowing cable from Perkins: "Magnificent reviews, somewhat critical in ways expected, full of greatest praise" (*Letters* 434). Still, nothing could convince Wolfe that his book was a success. Wandering around Paris, drinking heavily, he felt dizzy and nauseated. He believed that he was going mad. In a lengthy letter to Perkins, dated 31 March, he described his lost weekend:

> I came home to my hotel one night – or rather at daybreak one morning – tried to get off to sleep – and had the horrible experience of seeming to disintegrate into at least six people – I was in bed and suddenly it seemed these other shapes of myself were moving *out* of me – all around me – one of them touched me by the arm – another was talking in my ear – others walking around the room – and suddenly I would come to with a terrific jerk and all of them would rush back into me again . . . . There were about three days of which I could give no clear accounting . . . . (*Letters* 438)

All this he felt had been the result of the pressure put on him by the critics who had questioned his ability to make a second book. He had, he wrote, been badly shaken by them, "driven" to the verge of despair and self-doubt by their questions about his ability to write another book and by their criticisms of his style, his rejection of Marxist politics, and his failure to take any political stance in his writing. "I allowed myself so seriously to be disturbed and shaken," he wrote, "that once or twice I may have been upon the very brink of total failure and submission" (*Letters* 439).

Even after Perkins wired him that the reviews were "magnificent" and "full of the greatest praise" and sent him excerpts, Wolfe wondered if Perkins had been honest with him and whether the excerpts had not been "*hand-picked.*" "God knows," he writes, "I could profit by a wise and penetrating criticism as much as any man alive, but as I grow older I am beginning

to see how rare – how much rarer even than *Lear*, *Hamlet*, the greatest productions of art – such criticism is" (*Letters* 444). He worried that the critics
would find the book episodic and chide him for taking five years to write a
book which he had really finished in one year.[2] In addition, as he reread the
text, he found countless errors in wording and proofreading, for which he
knew that he alone was to blame, but which stabbed him "to the heart."

Scribners had, he felt, been premature in publishing the novel, delivering
him into the hands of his enemies: "the Henry Harts, Wassons . . . , the
Benéts, the I.M.P.'s, the F.P.A.'s, the Morleys, the Nathans, the Mark Van
Dorens, the Mike Golds, and others of that sort"(*Letters* 447). Why is it, he
asks, that the American critical establishment seems so intent on destroying
its best writers, turning them into drunkards, dipsomaniacs, and creators of
"Pop-eye horrors" while in every country in Europe the artist is "honored,
revered, and cherished as the proudest possession that a nation has?" (*Letters*
449). Venting his confusion, he continues,

> The Paterson woman says my people are all seven feet tall and talk in bel-
> lowing voices – she says take away his adjectives, nouns, verbs, pronouns,
> words of violence, height, altitude, colour, size, immensity – and *where*
> would he be? The Mark Van Dorens say take away his own experience,
> the events of his own life, forbid him to write about what he has seen,
> known, felt, experienced – and where would he be? The Fadimans say
> take away his apostrophes, declamations, lyrics, dreams, incantations – and
> where would he be? The Rascoes say he has no sense of humour . . . . The
> Communists say he is a romantic sentimentalist, of the old worn-out ro-
> mantic school, with no Marxian code; and the Saturday Reviewers a de-
> picter of the sordid, grim, horribly unpleasant and surrealistic school – and
> so it goes – in Christ's name what do these people want? (*Letters* 449–450)[3]

Wolfe was oversensitive to the early critical response; the early reviews were, with few exceptions, remarkably good. It would not be until
the reviews appeared in the literary journals that Wolfe would come to
understand his full share of the burden of critical commentary.

---

[2]Wolfe spent much of the time between 1929 and 1936 working on several manuscripts:
"K-19," "The October Fair," and "The Vision of Spangler's Paul." Perkins discouraged
him from completing any of these.

[3]"The Paterson woman" was Isabel Paterson (I.M.P.), who reviewed *Of Time and the
River* in the 24 February 1935 issue of *The New York Herald Tribune Books*; Mark Van
Doren had referred to Wolfe as a one-book author in the 25 April 1934 issue of *The Na-
tion*; Clifton Fadiman reviewed *Of Time and the River* in the 9 March 1935 issue of *The
New Yorker;* Burton Rascoe reviewed the novel in the 10 March 1935 issue of *The New
York Herald Tribune Books*.

Few of the works published by Wolfe's contemporaries received reviews as enthusiastic as those devoted to *Of Time and the River*, and yet few works have ever been reviewed so ambiguously. The same critics who praised the book for its vitality, exuberance, and intensity, denounced it for being repetitious, overwritten, confused, and chaotic. The response of the reading public to the novel mirrored the response of the critics; in a straw poll appearing in *The Saturday Review of Literature*, *Of Time and the River* was voted both the *best* and the *worst* novel of 1935 ("The Results If Any").

In comparison to the enthusiastic reception awarded *Of Time and the River*, the critical response to *Look Homeward, Angel* appears relatively modest. Reviewers for the book sections of both *The New York Times* and *The New York Herald Tribune* responded to *Of Time and the River* with page-one reviews. Terms such as *genius* and *Great American Novel* were bandied about by the critics, as were comparisons of Wolfe's writings to Melville's, Whitman's, and Rabelais's.

In North Carolina the response to Wolfe's second novel was far more positive than the response to *Look Homeward, Angel* had been in 1929. Asheville critics, such as Elizabeth Wilson, whose review of *Of Time and the River* appeared in the Asheville *Bluets*, had been subjected to five years of national acclaim for their hometown-novelist-made-good in New York. By 1935 they seemed to be convinced of the quality of his writing and instead of resenting his intrusion into the privacy of their lives had come to feel honored by the national recognition he had brought to their community. Most of the local critics reviewing *Of Time and the River* confessed that the citizens of Asheville who had originally felt resentment toward Wolfe's using them in *Look Homeward, Angel* now voiced resentment at being omitted from the second novel. Joe Sugarman, in a review appearing in *The Carolina Magazine*, "Thomas Wolfe Hungers On," wrote that in his second novel Wolfe had risen from a regional to a national novelist. Sugarman takes pleasure in recounting Eugene's experiences in the North at Harvard and contrasting them to Eugene's experiences at Pulpit Hill. It was no longer Asheville, but Boston that writhed under Wolfe's satire. Journeying to Harvard, Sugarman writes, to perfect himself as a dramatist, Eugene's spirit "is badly bruised by the discovery of dilettantes, fakers, and hangers-on in the world of the creation of beauty. The superficiality of his instruction, the shallowness of his associates, and the generally patternless existence of the individuals in this academic-artistic realm revolt him and send him hurtling back to the Carolina hills where there is at least strength" (22).

Only the review in *The Asheville Citizen* written by Weimar Jones and published on 21 April 1935 echoed the negative local reviews received by

Wolfe in 1929. What does the book have, Jones asks, that has made it so popular with the public and the critics? It has, he concludes no plot, no action, only the most distorted characterizations, and no humor. The action of the novel, he continues, is spiritually immature; Wolfe depicts his alter ego as the only noble soul in a small town which is otherwise filled with caricatures. *Of Time and the River* he finally comments "is the work of a man who is warped." The book itself is "vividly unbeautiful; dully uninspiring; and obviously lop-sided, and therefore untrue." Wolfe's women, Jones writes, "are all 'breasts' and 'thighs'; they are in the world to be 'possessed.'" Wolfe, he adds, "paints sex as an ugly thing; yet the book is permeated with it" (123).

Jones's arguments about the absence of humor in *Of Time and the River* are reminiscent of the arguments about Wolfe's absence of humor in *Look Homeward, Angel* made by Edwin Berry Burgum and Alfred Kazin. Like them, Jones fails to recognize the way in which Wolfe exposes the absurdity of the familiar and the way in which he focuses the reader's attention on human idiosyncrasies, social conventions, and prejudices. There are, of course, numerous examples of humor in *Of Time and the River*.

However, there is a difference in the nature of the humor in Wolfe's first two novels. Wolfe's humor in *Look Homeward, Angel* develops more naturally out of the characters and the plot of that novel; it is often the result of the double vision of the young boy Eugene, who sees Asheville not only in terms of his youthful hopes and dreams, but in the light of his memory. In *Of Time and the River*, Wolfe's humor is less innocent and more heavy-handed. Instead of poking fun at his childhood fantasies and misapprehensions, he satirizes the various ethnic and intellectual groups he encounters in that novel. Among the best of these satiric moments in the novel are the scenes in which Eugene Gant, living with a family of Boston Irish in Cambridge, discusses his books with the family's youngest son, Eddy Murphy (a student at the Jesuit-run Boston College), who argues that the greatest writer of all times is "James Henry Cardinal Nooman" (164–165) and the scenes in which Professor Hatcher's students indicate their ludicrous misunderstandings of drama. Eugene describes these students of the *drama* as living men "writing, with amazing skill, dead plays for a theatre that was dead, and for a public that did not exist" (172). Two of the most interesting of these "Hatcher scenes" are the scenes in which Oswald Ten Eyck, leaving his eight thousand-dollar-a-year job with the Hearst Syndicate to enroll in Hatcher's famous course, finds that, dependent on a smaller budget, he can only write about food – and the expressionist drama read by another student, Miss Thrall, *You Shall Be Free When You Have Cut Your Father's Throat*, a strange mixture of

Eugene O'Neill, classic Greek drama, Yiddish burlesque, and Marxist sentiment which Wolfe quotes at length in the text:

THE CROWD: (with from their throats an even-stronger roar yet) E L E K T R A. It is Elektra!

ELEKTRA: (her voice even lower and more hoarse becoming, her eyes with the red blood-pains of all her heart-grief with still greater love-sorrow at the man-mass gleaming.) Listen, man. Slaves, workers, the of your fathers' sons not yet awakened — hear! Out of the night-dark of your not yet born souls to deliver you have I come! So, hear! (Her voice even lower with the low blood-pain heart-hate hoarse becoming.) Tonight must you your old with-crime-blackened and by-ignorance-blinded father's throat cut! I have spoken: so must it be.

A VOICE, HOMUNCULUS: (from the crowd, pleadingly, with protest.) Ach! Elektra! Spare us! Please! With the blood-lust malice-blinded your old father's throat to cut not nice is. (293)

The scene seems custom-made for the Borscht Circuit.

The appearance of a 912-page novel was, in itself, an event. In early March *The Saturday Review of Literature* printed a cartoon in which a group of angry New York reviewers picketed Scribners. They are shown carrying placards that read "Thomas Wolfe ignores 8-hour day; makes reviewers work twenty-four hours" and "Too much Wolfe at the door." But as John Chamberlain, the *New York Times* reviewer, noted in an 8 March 1935 article, "reviewers have no real complaint; it is not every day that they have a chance to read Thomas Wolfe." Four days later in a fuller *New York Times* review, Chamberlain referred to the novel as "a landmark in American literature." "Rich, sensuous, deliberately flying in the face of all recent tradition in the writing of novels," he continues, "containing satire, poetry, mysticism and even an occasional touch of balderdash," it is one of the most satisfying novels to have appeared in a long time. At *The New York World-Telegram*, Harry Hansen referred to *Of Time and the River* as "one of the most eloquent, most thoughtfully and verbally satisfying novels" of his day (8 March 1935). The next day Marion Starkey, in *The Boston Evening Transcript*, questioned whether Wolfe had become *The Great American Novelist*.

Clifton Fadiman reported in his 9 March 1935 review, "Thomas Wolfe," published in *The New Yorker*, that he had emerged from his reading of the novel feverish and groggy. Praising Wolfe's eloquence in passages such as his hymn to America, Fadiman at the same time argues that

Wolfe's writing needs more editing. Six months later he would print a heavy-handed parody of Wolfe's writing (much like Gerald Gould's review of *Look Homeward, Angel*) in the October 1935 issue of *The American Spectator*. His parody focuses on the scene in which Eugene Gant visits his Uncle Bascom in Cambridge (one of the scenes most frequently praised by Wolfe's critics and a scene which originated in one of Wolfe's most successful short stories, "A Portrait of Bascom Hawke"):

> At this very moment, so pregnant and prescient with the huge warp of fate and chance, the dark, terrific weaving of the threads of time and destiny, there was heard one of the loveliest and most haunting of all sounds, a sound to echo in the ears of Americans forever, surging in the adyts of their souls and drumming in the conduits of their blood. The doorbell tinkled.
>
> "A moment's – *beep!* – peace for all of us before we die," snarled, bellowed and croaked gaunt Uncle Habbakuk, prodding himself violently in the midriff with his hard bony fore-finger. "Give the goat-cry!"
>
> "Phuh-phuh! Ow-ooh! *Beep!*" came the goat-cry from without, and Aunt Liz opened the door. It was he, the youth of the tribe of the Gants, eleven feet, eight inches high, with slabsided cheeks, high, white, integrated forehead, long, savage, naked-looking ears, thirty-two teeth, one nose, and that strange, familiar, native alien expression to all the Gants, wandering forever and the earth again. ("Of Nothing and the Wolfe" 4)

Henry Seidel Canby, editor of *The Saturday Review of Literature*, printed his review of *Of Time and the River*, "The River of Youth," in the 9 March 1935 issue of that periodical. Canby begins his discussion of Wolfe's novel by referring to D. H. Lawrence's *Studies in Classical American Literature*. Lawrence, Canby notes, described an Old Indian Devil who was always plaguing the Americans with sudden flushes of paganism and sex. "It is not so funny now," Canby continues, "for some devil, Indian, Marxian, or psycho-analytic, has surely been torturing the best American writers of our era. They squirm, they lash, they spit out filth and imprecations, they whine, they defy. They are not at ease in this Zion of our ancestors."

Turning to Wolfe, he decides that the *Indian* curse on the writer of *Of Time and the River* is *impotence*. The rest of his review is predicated by the phrase "neither/nor." Wolfe's novel is neither autobiography nor fiction; poetry nor prose; fantasy nor fact. He likens Wolfe's artistic failure to that of Melville in *Pierre*. As good as *Of Time and the River* is at points, Canby concludes, it is "an artistic failure."

Had this been all that Canby had to do with the reviewing of Wolfe's second novel, Wolfe may well have left him alone. But as editor of *The Saturday Review of Literature*, Canby would make the final decision to publish Bernard DeVoto's scathing indictment of Wolfe's craftsmanship, "Genius Is Not Enough," in the April 1936 issue of that magazine. Several days after the appearance of DeVoto's review, Canby invited Wolfe to dinner. Wolfe describes the occasion in a letter to Julian Meade dated 4 May 1936:

> I was over at the Canbys' for dinner last night and of course, made no reference to the article but finally Mr. Canby himself brought it up . . . . said he had got a pretty vigorous letter a few days ago denouncing the article and asking why a man's book should be reviewed by his enemies and so on. So I figured it was your letter he was talking about. I told him that personally I had no hard feelings and that although I read every scrap that was written about me in the way of a review or criticism, provided I saw it, and still took the whole thing very much to heart, it didn't bother me quite as much as it once did. I added that I had my living to earn, and that the only way I have of earning it is through what I write, and that if a reviewer says I am no good, it's just too bad for me and perhaps occasionally for him, but that nevertheless, I was going to keep right on writing. (*Letters* 509–510)

The irony of breaking bread with Canby and his wife in the wake of the DeVoto review seems to have been just too much for Wolfe, however. By fall of 1937, he had drafted an early satire on Canby – playing on the homophonic element in his name, *can be,* which Wolfe changed in the draft to *Wilby*. Wilby, Wolfe notes, had brought joy "to the souls of the correct" by referring to the works of some of the modernist authors as the delayed productions of "a dirty little boy . . . . who scrawls bad words upon the walls of privies." Wolfe continues:

> A pleasing image was thus subtly conveyed to the readers of the Atlantic Monthly, the Boston Evening Transcript, and Dr. Wilby's own Distinguished Thursday Review of Letters. It conveyed to these cultivated readers a comfortable feeling of urbanity – for what could be more comfortable or urbane for a devoted reader of the Thursday Review – than the sense that just as he was squatting comfortably to attend to the most inevitable of the natural functions he might look up and read with an amused and tolerating eye certain words that various dirty little boys like Anatole France, G. B. Shaw, Dreiser, Wells, Sherwood Anderson, and D. H. Lawrence had scrawled up there with the intention of shocking him.
>   Obviously the natural reaction of the well-trained Thursday Afternooner would be to – smile and wipe. (*Notebooks* 882)

Wolfe continues to discuss Dr. Wilby's editorial staff, led by the "celebrated stylist and bon vivant of fine letters, Nicholas Crowthorpe," described by Wolfe as "a whimsical old son of a bitch."

Wolfe's "Portrait of a Literary Critic," which appeared after his death in the pages of *The American Mercury* in April 1939, developed out of this sketch. It was the only work ever written by Wolfe completely dedicated to satirizing a single critic. In 1941, this short story was reprinted in *The Hills Beyond* (150–161). In the story, Canby is depicted as Dr. Hugo Twelvetrees Turner, editor of the *Fortnightly Cycle of Reading, Writing, and the Allied Arts* and the nation's "leading practitioner of middle-of-the-roadism" (*The Hills Beyond* 150). It was Dr. Turner, the narrator continues, "who first made the astonishing discovery that Sex is dull" (152). Turner's triumphs are listed by Wolfe in a seemingly endless roster of his discoveries in *Popular Culture*:

> Charlie Chaplin was discovered to be, not primarily a comedian at all, but the greatest tragic actor of the time (learned adepts of the arts assured the nation that his proper role was Hamlet). The true art-expression of America was the comic strip (the productions of the Copleys, Whistlers, Sargents, Bellowses, and Lies could never hold a candle to it). The only theater that was truly native and worth preserving was the burlesque show. The only music that was real was Jazz. There had been only one writer in America: his name was Twain, and he had been defeated just because he was – American . . . but if he had not been American he could have been – *so* good! (153)

The name *Turner* refers to Canby's predisposition to hedging and possibly to the phrase *to turn*, suggesting the ability to waffle in his judgements. Originally referring to Joyce's *Ulysses* as "that encyclopædia of filth," Wolfe's Turner later refers to Justice Woolsey's famous decision to legally permit its sale in the United States as "a magnificent vindication of artistic integrity." Similarly, Dr. Turner's early review of William Faulkner is entitled "The School of Bad Taste," although after the appearance of Faulkner's *Sanctuary*, Turner likens Faulkner to Edgar Allan Poe, suggesting in the conclusion of his review that Faulkner "may go far" (154–155). Time after time, Turner eats his words. "Among his enemies," Wolfe writes, "there were some who were cruel enough to suggest that he wanted to be all things to all men, that Turner was not only the proper, but the inevitable name for him, that the corkscrew shaped his course" (157).

Dining with Turner and his wife, George Webber, whose second novel has been reviewed by Turner, feels "helpless and confused" (159). During his stay in the "Turnerian haven," Webber, whose physique is anything but lithe, is constantly referred to by the Turners as being "like an Elf!" (160–161). As he listens to the critic and his wife comment on his novel, Webber becomes aware that they are confusing his writing with the work of two other writers, Robert Nathan and Thornton Wilder, and that their evaluation of his writing is based more on their limited stock of comparisons than it is on any real understanding of his work.

Burton Rascoe, quoting heavily from the novel in a lengthy review titled "The Ecstasy, Fury, Pain and Beauty of Life" appearing in the 10 March 1935 issue of *The New York Herald Tribune*, lavishly praises the novel. He writes:

> While reading Thomas Wolfe it is requisite or advisable to suspend one's ordinary critical faculties, trained, sharpened and selective as they may be by familiarity with the hard, clear image, the deft concision, the precise pattern of much of our modern writing; for Wolfe is lush and exuberant, word-drunk like an Elizabethan, with utterable and unutterable music pounding in his brain. To the calm, the phlegmatic, the insensitive, the sophisticated, the disillusioned or the imperturbable reader much of Thomas Wolfe's first and second novels . . . may appear like the rough draft of multitudinous notes from which a novel, in the more ordinary sense of the term, might be selected, edited, polished and builded. But like the novels of Rabelais, Sterne and Fielding these are not novels by any prosaic or academic definition. They are a deluge of intensity. (1)

Continuing, Rascoe comments on Wolfe's ability to catch in words not only beauty, but "the very evanescence of beauty." "If you look for a plot," he writes, " . . . you will not find it." Instead you will find "a hundred stories and five years of life, richly experienced, deeply felt, minutely and lyrically recorded" (2).

In the final paragraph of his review, Rascoe chose to use Wolfe and his novels to counter arguments made by Kenneth Burke and Edmund Wilson, literary Marxists whose critical studies alleged that literature in America, like American civilization, was running down in bulk, vitality, and gusto. "In these days when some of our best writers are tired or short of breath," he writes, "it is thrilling to contemplate and to read the teeming novels of Thomas Wolfe," who "writes as though the Spanish Armada had not very long ago been sunk by Drake and the expansion of the North American continent had just begun . . . "(2).

After chastising Wolfe for writing a novel that is simply too long, A. J. Cronin writing in the *New York Sun* praises Wolfe's *Of Time and the River*, which he favorably compares to the autobiographical novels of English novelists. "How refreshing," he writes, "to turn to Mr. Wolfe's . . . autobiography which bears the colors of storm and sea and sky, the rude virility of the earth, the electricity of the lightning flash itself," after having read the scores of "petunia-tinted, wilted and poetically sad" autobiographical novels of the English writers ("A Book in Which a Man Reveals His Soul").

By the final weeks of March, however, the more critical assessments of the literary critics had begun to appear. Unlike the newspaper reviewers, who were primarily journalists, the reviewers writing for the literary journals were primarily academics. Instead of being concerned with the appropriateness of a literary work for the average American audience of the twentieth century, the academics were concerned in determining the position that that work assumed (if any) within the American literary canon.

One of the earliest of these critical assessments was written by Malcolm Cowley, a high-school classmate of Kenneth Burke. Appearing in the 20 March 1935 issue of *The New Republic*, Cowley's "The Forty Days of Thomas Wolfe" begins by equating his reading of *Of Time and the River* to forty days spent in the wilderness of Outer Mongolia. He summarizes the good passages, the *oases*, in the novel (the depiction of Uncle Bascom, the description of the students in Professor Hatcher's course, the death of Oliver Gant, the comedy of Abe Jones, the tragedy of the Coulson family, the disintegration of Starwick, and the train ride to Orléans) in a single paragraph, relegating the rest of the article to a discussion of the "bad passages" in the novel. These *deserts* (Wolfe's "flabby" prose style, Eugene's reveries about time and death, the drunken brawl in South Carolina, his Orestean flight to the north) are, Cowley suggests, every bit as common in Wolfe's writing as are his good passages (163). Noting the autobiographical elements in the novel (which were emphasized by Scribners failure to replace the "I" of Wolfe's short story "Bascom Hawke" with the "he" of *Of Time and the River*), Cowley concludes that Wolfe writes "like a God-intoxicated ninny" (164).

In a 21 March notebook entry, Wolfe indicates that he has received a number of excerpts from the reviews, all evidently retyped for the purpose of keeping him from getting into a "murderous condition." He continues:

> I can see from the tenor of these excerpts – and they are wonderfully good – what some of the criticism may be – God knows, I could be helped by criticism as much as any man alive – but how much more critical am I, who am generally supposed to be so totally lacking in the critical faculty, than my critics . . . .
>
> I think I can see from these excerpts what the main trend of criticism will be – and how wrong it is! – It is one thing to profit by criticism, but no reasonable man can hope to profit by being torn limb from limb by 27 different people all pulling him apart in different directions . . . . (*Notebooks* 688)

Autobiography and collaboration, the first the result of Scribners error in incorporating sections of "Bascom Hawke" into the novel and the unwillingness of the author to carefully proof the finished text and the second the result of the advertising strategy of Scribners that marketed Wolfe's prolific prose style in its newspaper advertisements and of Wolfe's generous dedication of the book to his editor, Maxwell Perkins, would become the major themes discussed in the literary journals.

Three days after the appearance of Cowley's review, an unsigned article, "Laurels to an Editor," appeared in the *Publishers' Weekly* (the trade journal of the publishing community), praising Wolfe for dedicating his book to his editor but at the same time crediting Perkins with making Wolfe's hundreds of thousands of words "publishable." And in the April 1935 issue of *New Outlook*, Robert Cantwell openly attacked Rascoe's description of Wolfe's writing. Referring to Melville, with whom Wolfe's writings had often been linked by the critics, he argues that it had taken Wolfe five years to write *Of Time and the River*, whereas Melville had written five novels, including *Moby-Dick*, over a space of three years. Next to Melville's inventive resourcefulness, which Cantwell argues enabled him to raise his text to a plane above autobiography, Wolfe's prose-poems seemed to be "confessions of imaginative bankruptcy." Not even Wolfe's rhapsodic descriptions of the American scene escaped Cantwell's criticism. His vision of America, Cantwell write, "is indeed that of a man who looks out upon it from a Pullman window, and lets his imagination race, ungoverned by its realities."

Like Cantwell, Robert Penn Warren in his May 1935 "The Hamlet of Thomas Wolfe" published in *The American Review*, referred back to the blurbs and reviews that had likened *Of Time and the River* to Melville's *Moby-Dick*. But unlike Cantwell who compares Melville to Wolfe on the basis of their productivity, Warren compares Melville's themes and structures to Wolfe's. Warren writes that Melville in *Moby-Dick* "had a powerful fable, a myth of human destiny, which saved his work from the centrifugal impulses of his genius, and which gave it structure and climax. Its dignity is inherent in the fable itself" (206–207). No such dignity, he concludes, is inherent in *Of Time and the River*. While recognizing the *enormity* of Wolfe's talents, he refers to the pretense of fiction in the autobiographical work as "thin and slovenly" (192), pointing out the same confusion of first-person and third-person pronouns in the text mentioned by Cowley in "The Forty Days of Thomas Wolfe."

It is a humbled but still optimistic Wolfe who writes Max Perkins on 23 May 1935. He cautions his editor against pushing the stories intended for publication in *From Death to Morning* too quickly into print. "Please don't go too far with the stories before I get there," he writes. "There are things I can do that will make them much better, and if you will only wait on me I will do them and we will have a fine book of stories." His intention, he adds, is to meet the criticism of his critics by showing them how his writing is improving and how he is learning his "business all the time" (*Letters* 462).

Most of the critics felt that *Of Time and the River* could only have been improved by more judicious pruning. Among these was Edward Hooker Dewey, whose review "The Storm and Stress Period" published in the May 1935 issue of the *Survey Graphic* was also among the first to suggest that Wolfe's novel functioned not only as a literary but as a social document. Wolfe's social philosophy is implicit, Dewey notes, in a discussion of the sterility of modern society and the division between classes. Wolfe concludes, at last, that man is his own worst enemy.

Writing in *The Yale Review* in a column subtitled "Outstanding Novels" in the summer of 1935, Helen MacAfee in a short but stimulating review begins to explore the questions of *structure* raised by earlier critics and reviewers but never fully discussed by them. She writes:

> The novel is a conveniently loose term lending itself to much variation of shape and size, pace and temper. It will be as impossible to say just what a good novel is as to say just what a good human being is until the last person on earth (who will, I assume, write autobiographical fiction) has delivered the last copy. Then perhaps some visiting Martian will decide. It is easier, and safer, to say now what a good novel does. For one thing, it strikes and holds the imagination of a reasonably well intentioned reader of suitable mental age. In any novel there are pretty sure to be passages that one such reader or another will consider weedy or arid, but a skilled writer will carry him over these by main force. Mr. Wolfe has plenty of force. *Of Time and the River* shows this force, I think, as still undirected through the book as a whole. (vii)

Unlike Cowley, Cantwell, and Warren, who deal with the autobiographical element in the novel as a reflection of Wolfe's major weakness as a novelist, MacAfee attributes the weakness of sections of that book to "a faulty conception of the best means to emphasis" (vii). Wolfe creates emphasis, she suggests, in three ways: through expansion, variations on a theme, and reiteration of key words. *Expansion*, which she loosely defines as the creation of dramatic scenes, is she feels one of Wolfe's strengths but, when stretched by the author to cover the American scene, seems "strained to the breaking point." She also charges his writing with redundancy, a use of repetitive themes and key words which extends beyond the musical model on which it is based to create instead of a willing suspension of disbelief, a genuine resistance to the narrative. MacAfee concludes, as Cowley, Cantwell, and Warren, that *Of Time and the River* is not really a very good novel, although, like these earlier critics, she maintains that Wolfe is probably quite capable of producing *good* novels in the future (vii-viii).

In an even more interesting review appearing in the June 1935 issue of *The North American Review*, John Slocum suggests that many of Wolfe's problems in *Of Time and the River* are the result of his inability to escape the influence of the critics. The "critics," he writes, congratulated themselves on having discovered an author who was capable of portraying "the American Scene" in their reviews of *Look Homeward, Angel*. This unfortunate demand for national consciousness in creative writing, he concludes, put undue pressure on Wolfe, who then succumbed to geographical "jingoism" (175). Referring to the extended rhapsody to America which stretches from page 155 to page 160 in *Of Time and the River*, in which Wolfe covers the country from Maine to California and back again, Slocum insists that Wolfe's purple prose depiction of America in this passage is a "gigantic hoax." Should Wolfe be able to rise above the critical praise of his American descriptions and become less self-conscious, Slocum concludes, there is no reason why he cannot produce work that comes closer to expressing the romanticism of America "than [that of] any novelist living today" (177).

By 21 June, Wolfe was writing Perkins from Copenhagen. "I have a letter," he begins, "from a New York publisher – with quoted excerpts which informs me that *Scribners* last month carried *3 printed attacks* on me" (*Letters* 468). Wolfe had every right to expect that *Scribner's Magazine*, the house organ of his publisher, would support his work – and his confusion, in the face of a negative review of his novel by Evelyn Scott, statements made about him by Hemingway in an installment of *The Green Hills of Africa*, and a put-down by William Lyons Phelps, all appearing in the June 1935 issue of that magazine, is understandable. Evelyn Scott had reviewed *Of Time and the River* under the title "Colossal Fragment," arguing that Wolfe had come close to remaking the universe "in his image" but, because of his inability to order his amorphous sensations and emotions, succeeded only in mingling "platitude with poetry" and "banality" (4). Meanwhile, Hemingway had questioned whether exiling Wolfe to Siberia or the Dry Tortugas would make a better writer of him, providing him with "the necessary shock to cut the over-flow of words and give him a sense of proportion" (340). Williams Lyons Phelps, although he included *Of Time and the River* in a list of the best one hundred novels of 1935, then admitted that it had been too long for him to read (380).

Although Wolfe's purposeful courting of the Marxist critic V. F. Calverton, editor of *The Modern Monthly*, in the hopes of providing himself with a positive review, resulted in a few difficult social engagements for

Wolfe, it ultimately proved successful.[4] In a review titled "Thomas Wolfe and the Great American Novel" which appeared in the June 1935 issue of *The Modern Monthly*, Calverton not only compared Wolfe to Herman Melville, but referred to him as a "greater genius" and a greater writer than the author of "Benito Cereno," *Typee*, and *Moby-Dick*.

Listing the novelists of his generation who had failed to produce a second novel equal to the promise of their first (Frank Norris, Ernest Poole, Theodore Dreiser, and Sherwood Anderson), Calverton suggests that Wolfe may well succeed where others have failed. Although neither of Wolfe's two novels qualifies for the title of *The Great American Novel*, each suggests that in the future Wolfe could well produce a novel which deserves that description. "Wolfe," he writes, "is haunted, as have been and still are all sensitive, imaginative minds, by the tragedy of being human, the tragedy of a world destined for death, of men and women caught within its maw and ground into nothingness without even a chance to struggle or escape" (249). Once again, however, Wolfe's rhetorical powers, his lack of discipline, and his autobiographical subject matter are seen to betray his potential. But Wolfe's weaknesses, Calverton concludes, are not the weaknesses of a weak writer, but the weaknesses of a strong one, "who when he overcomes them will be stronger and more powerful still." Even with his weaknesses Wolfe is one of the finest novelists America has produced; without them he could well become the greatest American novelist.

The old-school Marxist Joseph Freeman, referring to Wolfe's second novel in an article printed in the July/August issue of the *Partisan Review* ("Mask, Image and Truth"), complains about those critics who ballyhoo the productions of their friends (an obvious reference to Calverton) and then launches into an extended discussion of Wolfe's anti-Semitism in the novel. Although Freeman defines the novel as "extraordinary . . . rich in narrative, observation and feeling," he expresses some concern about Wolfe's treatment of Abe Jones, whom Wolfe describes as bearing "The

---

[4]Wolfe's letters to Calverton dated 3 and 9 April 1936 indicate the kind of misunderstandings to which Wolfe was susceptible when "courting" a critic. Asked by Nina Melville, Calverton's wife, to attend a cocktail party, Wolfe was astonished to find that the party was really a dinner for the Marxist publication edited by Calverton, the *Modern Monthly*. In addition, after accepting Melville's cocktail-party invitation, he was told that he had been placed on the program as a featured speaker. When Wolfe tried to bow out of the engagement, Calverton fired off a Special Delivery letter explaining that the announcements of his speech had already been sent to the press and the programs printed. Wolfe reworked his Boulder, Colorado, speech, which later became the basis for *The Story of a Novel*, and delivered it at the *Modern Monthly* dinner on 17 April (*Letters* 497–500).

whole flag and banner of his race . . . in the enormous putty-colored nose" (*Of Time and the River* 457). "And they say that Communist writers abuse people and call them names," Freeman crows(4).

Had he written his descriptions of the Jewish community in an article, Freeman suggests, he would have been "damned" by everybody from *The New Masses* to *The New York Times*. "Under the corrupt standards of current bourgeois aesthetics," he continues, using Wolfe's novel to exemplify his text, "the 'creative' artist may slander workers, Negroes, Jews, anyone he likes; he may give way to his most reactionary impulses, yet not be called to account as he would be if he spoke directly . . . . He is treated as a priest who speaks from on high, the sacrosanct oracle whose god is 'art'" (6). In concluding his article, Freeman writes passionately of the need for the Marxist critic to "expose the propagandist behind the poet." "Without the Communist," he prophesies, "the propertied classes would unrestricted *bamboozle* the masses with their 'democratic' images. Without the Marxist critic the 'faustian' creative writer would *unhampered* propagate his poisonous ideas in obscure, false but effective images" (8–9).[5]

A year later, in a 20 May 1936 letter to Margaret Roberts, Wolfe expresses the naive belief that his working-class background will provide him with a defense against the Marxist charges that his writing lacks "social consciousness." Many of the Marxists, he counters, are young gentlemen "whose fathers provide them with a comfortable allowance which enables them to indulge their political fancies without knowing a great deal about some of the things or people of whom they write" (*Letters* 519). He sees them to be ideologically opposed to, but essentially the counterparts of the wealthy young members of the "New Confederacy," the Agrarians, who also had attacked him. He argues:

> My whole spirit and feeling is irresistibly on the side of the working class, against the cruelty, the injustice, the corrupt and infamous privilege of great wealth, against the shocking excess and wrong of the present system, the evidences of which are horribly apparent I think, to anybody who lives here in New York and keeps his eyes open. I think that the whole thing has got to be changed, and I'll do everything within the province of my energy or talent to change it for the better, if I can,

---

[5]Freeman's dogmatism is best described by Frank Lentriccia in his 1983 study *Criticism and Social Change* (Chicago: U of Chicago P), pp. 22–25. Lentriccia describes Freeman's confrontation with Kenneth Burke at the first American Writer's Congress, an attempt to extend the reach of the John Reed Clubs. According to Burke, Freeman, a moving force in the Marxist Congress, responded to Burke's suggestion for changing the Party language to refer to "people" rather than "workers" by rising up and saying, "We have a traitor among us." This confrontation took place in the same year that Freeman wrote his review of *Of Time and the River*.

but I am not a Communist, and I believe that the artist who makes his art the vehicle for political dogma and intolerant propaganda is a lost man . . . . although I am myself the son of a working man, I go so far as to say that an artist's interest, first and always, has got to be in life itself, and not in a special kind of life. (520)

His notebook entry dated 13 September 1936 (a draft of an early manuscript version of his short story "I Have a Thing to Tell You" originally published in the 10 March, 17 March, and 24 March 1937 issues of *The New Republic* and later incorporated into *You Can't Go Home Again*) discusses Wolfe's categorizing of the Agrarians with the Marxists more fully. In response to a statement made by Count Orlovski (Adamowski in the novel) about France's being the only place where there is any *freedom* left, Wolfe's unnamed narrator (later George Webber) responds:

> Let us examine this statement: – It is a familiar one, and has been uttered to me by various people at many various times during the past fifteen years. – In the 1920's the Malcolm Cowleys, the Allen Tates, the Bunny Wilsons, the Harry Crosbys, etc., of the Left Bank were uttering it very often. They lived in France they said, because it was the only place where there was any freedom left – and they loved freedom.
>
> Now, I think their love for freedom has somewhat abated. The Malcolm Cowleys and the Bunny Wilsons want the Revolution, the World Union of the Soviets, etc. They do not want freedom. I believe that is now sometimes called "a bourgeois ideal" – and the Allen Tates, etc. want a form of high-toned fascism which bears the high-toned name of Southern Agrarianism. (*Notebooks* 836)[6]

Wolfe returned to the United States on 4 July 1935, which he would later describe as the *best* day of his life. Reporters met him as the boat docked, there were pieces about him in the newspapers, and he and Perkins wandered through the streets of New York, climbing tall buildings to watch the fireworks, which, Wolfe could almost have believed from the nature of his reception, were being shot off in his honor. Every one seemed to be excited by his book. He had left the United States in March a one-book novelist; by the time of his return he had been lionized by the press. In a 10 July 1935 letter to Martha Dodd, the daughter of the United States ambassador to Germany, who had taken a good deal of interest in Wolfe during his stay in Germany, he revealed that he had stayed up until five o'clock in the morning the night before reading "hundreds and hundreds of reviews." "They took some nice, cheerful, wholehearted pokes at me," he conceded, "but they seemed to love me,

---

[6]This passage was not included in the final text of the story printed in *The New Republic* or in *You Can't Go Home Again*. "Bunny" was Edmund Wilson's nickname.

and the total effect is overwhelming." He confessed that he felt happy, but a little guilty and ashamed. "If they think this book is good, I know I am going to beat it forty ways with the next two." He continues:

> I failed in this book, not in the ways the critics said I did, but in another way that Max and I know about. In spite of their talk about its tremendous energy and so forth, I wrote it in less than a year before it was published, at a time when I was horribly tired and when I had exhausted myself in writing the two books which are to follow. Perhaps I should have taken another year, but so much time had gone by without publication that I agreed with Max that it was more important to get it out and to go on to all the work that awaits me than to spend more time perfecting this one. (*Letters* 477–478)

Included in the mail waiting for him was an invitation to deliver a lecture at the Writer's Conference in Boulder, Colorado, from Edward Davidson, the program director at the University of Colorado. Davidson had originally asked Bernard DeVoto to speak at the conference, but at the last moment, DeVoto, concerned with political entanglements in his own academic career at Harvard and heading off to a new post at *The Saturday Review of Literature*, had declined the offer. In his place, Wolfe, in August, presented a speech in which he described the writing of *Of Time and the River*. In the company of Robert Frost and Robert Penn Warren, Wolfe felt comfortable and at home. Acknowledging Warren's negative review of *Of Time and the River*, Wolfe was sufficiently graceful to turn that potential "enemy" into a friend. In Colorado, he felt "anonymous"; they did not know whether he had written "King Lear or The Face on the Barroom Floor" (*Notebooks* 784). In front of this congenial audience, his speech, which began with the same uncomfortable stammering that marked his brother Fred's speech, developed into an oratorical triumph. He was so well received that, returning to New York, he asked Elizabeth Nowell to edit and market it. In December of 1935 an expanded version of the speech titled *The Story of a Novel* was published in three installments in the 14, 21, and 28 December 1935 issues of *The Saturday Review of Literature*; on 21 April 1936 Scribners published it as a small clothbound book.

Four days later, on 25 April, Bernard DeVoto, not yet permanently appointed to "The Editor's Easy Chair" at *The Saturday Review of Literature* but eager to create the kind of impression that might win him that post, published his punishing review of Wolfe and *The Story of a Novel*, "Genius Is Not Enough." Although Wolfe's letters suggest that his initial response to DeVoto's review was philosophic, after the publication of this review, Wolfe's life and literary career were never the same.

Bernard DeVoto never published a formal review of Wolfe's second novel, although he referred to that novel repeatedly in "Genius Is Not Enough." His earliest reference to Wolfe appears instead in a 27 April 1935 review of James Boyd's *Roll River*, also published by Scribners. Titling his review "A Novel Hammered Out of Experience" (as Wolfe's novels were supposedly not), he compares Wolfe's *Of Time and the River* to Boyd's *Roll River*, concluding that *Roll River* wins by a number of "Mormon blocks" over Wolfe's novel. He writes:

> There are a number of ways to write that undefined entity, the American novel. Mr. Wolfe has recently exhibited one way: to print the word "America" ten thousand times, to depict young Faustus as a victim of manic-depressive insanity, to fill the stage with Mardi Gras grotesques who suffer from compulsion neuroses and walk on stilts and always speak as if firing by battery, to look at everything through the lens of infantile regression . . . . Mr. Boyd now exhibits another way . . . . His book is only 600 pages long, it contains not a single goat-cry, and no one beats his head or knuckles to a bloody pulp on any wall within its covers.

DeVoto concludes that Boyd, unlike Wolfe, is "one of the very few first-rank novelists of his generation and one of the foremost technicians." Scribners, DeVoto snidely suggests, must have held up the publication of *Roll River* to provide the public with an opportunity to compare the gigantism in *Of Time and the River* to the profundity of a truly fine work of fiction.

Wolfe and Bernard DeVoto never met — they could scarcely have been considered enemies; yet, they stood at opposite poles in their perception of the writing process. When DeVoto wrote his famous review "Genius Is Not Enough," he was fresh from what he perceived to be a resounding defeat at Harvard, where the temporary position he held had not been made permanent. The political process that denied him continuity at Harvard, inadvertently, impugned DeVoto's integrity — as a result of some confusion as to whether he had actually been offered the position at *The Saturday Review of Literature* or had used the offer merely to bolster his candidacy at Harvard (*The Uneasy Chair* 171).

A study of DeVoto's annotated copy of *Of Time and the River* reveals two things: 1) that he was a careful reader, copiously marking the text; and 2) that the response to the book described in "Genius Is Not Enough" was an honest one. DeVoto did find much in *Of Time and the River* to value, although far more of the criticism than the praise found its way into his review article. Brought up in Ogden, Utah, DeVoto, the grandson of pioneer Mormon farmers and inevitably a cultural outsider at Harvard, approves of Wolfe's initial description of Francis Starwick, "the youngest

of a middle-western family of nine children, small business and farming
people in modest circumstances [who] gave the impression of wealth because . . . [he had been] endowed with wealth by nature." He drew a ver-
tical line next to the entire passage and wrote, "Good stuff. He catches it
here" (100). He finds Wolfe's depiction of the Boston Irish "damn good"
(161), "much better . . . than O'Neill's" (164). He thinks the scene in
which Eugene visits the Simpsons on pages 208 and 209, a "good scene,"
writing beneath it with an arrow directed to several lines and without apparent sarcasm, "This is how you write the Great American Novel." He
labels Wolfe's characterization of Dr. McGuire "great" (238) and notes
that the chapter in which McGuire collapses in a drunken stupor, simultaneously the object of Luke Gant's appeals for miracles and Nurse
Creasman's contempt is "A hell of a good scene" (234). It seems of great
importance to him that Eugene's notebook jottings (pages 661–680) come
"closer to inspiring respect . . . than [anything] else," and he marks it with
a star. But he does not mention it in his review.

It would be misleading to imply that DeVoto's annotations are uncritical; more often his responses are negative – notes on what he perceives to
be technical problems – and incredulous, occasionally coarsely phrased,
epithets in the face of what seemed to him to be prose that exaggerated
simple human acts. He catches nearly every error in pronoun reference in
the book, noting the failure to translate "A Portrait of Bascom Hawke"
into the third person but interpreting it as evidence of Wolfe's inability to
disguise the autobiographical substructure of the novel. In addition, he
pinpoints a chronological inconsistency (corrected prior to the fifth printing) on page 886, when Eugene, who earlier claims to have seen the last
of Ann, comes across her in a Marseilles cafe. Commenting on Eugene's
escape from the scene, DeVoto characterized it "Another casual orgasm of
violent feeling with no reason."

He comments in other places that the dialogue is "lousy" (251), that
much of the book is "Romantic nonsense," that the novel creaks "like an
O'Neill play" (382), is "worse than Lewis's worst" (291), and more
"heavy handed" than Dreiser (313). "Infantile voyeurism," he adds,
"marks his whole book" (581). "Somehow," he writes on page 609 next to
a burlesque of Queen Victoria, "naivete is not enough." This was, in all
likelihood, the seed for the title of his review article – a title that might
never have been used had the Scribners campaign not so successfully focused on Wolfe's genius.

Wolfe, DeVoto argues in his review, "Genius Is Not Enough," is an
astonishingly immature artist totally dependent on his editor, and his description of the writing of his second novel in *The Story of a Novel* suggests

that his writing is more the product of the Scribners "assembly line" than the product of a single writer. DeVoto writes,

> The most flagrant evidence of his incompleteness is the fact that, so far, one indispensable part of the artist has existed not in Mr. Wolfe but in Maxwell Perkins. Such organizing faculty and such critical intelligence as have been applied to the book have come not from inside the artist, not from the artist's feeling for form and aesthetic integrity, but from the Office of Charles Scribner's Sons . . . . But works of art cannot be assembled like a carburetor . . . .(4)

DeVoto's own, well-disciplined novels, patterned after his writing philosophy, achieved little critical success. Somewhere in this fact lies a clue to his perplexity in handling Wolfe as a novelist. Throughout his copy of *Of Time and the River* there are points of confusion, a confusion seemingly based on an inability to understand why a novel "intolerably bad" in so many places should also be "intolerably good" (147). He writes, for instance, on page 769 beneath the scene in which Eugene takes leave of Ann and returns to Paris with Starwick, "An utterly senseless scene, unaccounted for, without motive or meaning. And yet a truly dramatic situation handled with much force." It would have been difficult for Milton to have justified the ways of Thomas Wolfe to Bernard DeVoto, difficult to explain the raw, frenzied, and often-undisciplined phrases of the young writer to the seasoned editor who valued discipline and craftsmanship. DeVoto defined his predicament best in an anonymously written article printed in *Harper's Monthly Magazine* some four months after the publication of "Genius Is Not Enough." "Age," he wrote of the mature novelist, "may have given you confidence in your material and skill, so that you know you will avoid many of the pitfalls and most of the torment that are your professional risks; but also it has taught you your limitations, deprived you of a young novelist's fine carelessness, given you obstinacy and vigorousness and a respect for your job that have their satisfaction but also take their toll" ("On Beginning to Write a Novel" 179).

Within a week of the publication of "Genius Is Not Enough," Wolfe, dining with Henry Seidel Canby, the editor of *The Saturday Review of Literature*, was shown a letter from Julian Meade written to Canby protesting the review. Wolfe's earliest recorded response to the DeVoto attack suggests that he has not yet fathomed the impact that DeVoto's charges were to have on his literary career. In a lengthy 4 May 1936 letter to Meade, he thanks him for his support and describes for him the condition of criticism in America:

> I think really my only objection to the *Saturday Review* piece was that it didn't review the book. It seems to me that it was hardly a review at all,

but rather a kind of general denunciation of all my deficiencies as a writer, some of which, of course, I am prepared to admit and have done so already. I don't think a writer has any right to dictate to the editors of a literary review who shall review his book or what form the review should take, but I do think he has a right to expect a *review* of his book, whether hostile or favorable, rather than a mass assault on every other book he has ever done . . . . I have found out that a man who writes anything, no matter what it is, or where he gets it published, whether in *Scribner's Magazine* or in book form or in the Oregon Fur Traders' Quarterly, lays himself open to almost any form of attack or personal abuse known . . . . Moreover, as you yourself should know by now, if the aspiring young author has any illusions concerning the temperate, reasonable and coolly impartial tone in which the matter of book-reviewing and literary criticism is carried on, it won't take him long to have this pleasant daydream kicked out of him. Under the guise of high-toned criticism and impartial literary judgment, he must be prepared to hear himself described as a manic-depressive, a pathological item of the specialist in criminal psychology, a half-wit, or the grandson of Wordsworth's idiot boy, the bird that fouls its nest, a defiler of the temple of religion, a political reactionary, or a dangerous red, or a traitor to his country. (*Letters* 510–511)[7]

"I have lived through it all, I have known it all," Wolfe continues (in a passage that closely echoes Whitman's crucifixion image in *Song of Myself*, "I am the man, I suffer'd, I was there").[8] "I have had it all happen to me, and although as you may infer from this letter, I am not yet exactly resigned to it, in a state of philosophic benevolence, I am at least a little prepared for it and not google-eyed with astonishment when it happens" (*Letters* 511).

Wolfe concludes his letter to Meade by citing from a review of some of William Wordsworth's poetry. The review begins, he notes: "It is now apparent that young Mr. Wordsworth's malady is incurable. We had hoped for a while that the disease might be checked and controlled before it spread to dangerous proportions, but since it is evident that this is now impossible, we can only do what we can to prevent the malady from spreading further" (511–512).

Holding to the mistaken belief that only the *truth* could hurt him, Wolfe writes Kent Greenfield the following month about the influences that the critics have on him: "Well, what is there to say? . . . I still take it hard; I still get mad about it; but if there is anything true in what they say,

[7] DeVoto's tenure in the Editor's Easy Chair at the *Saturday Review of Literature* did not formally begin until late in the Fall of 1936.

[8] See Whitman's "Song of Myself," l. 832.

I have got a good memory and I don't forget it; and if what they say is not true, then how can a man be hurt by it?" (*Letters* 529). Wolfe felt that the only criticism that *hurt* was the *truth*. The DeVoto review had not *hurt* him (yet) because it was not true, it had only made him mad (528).

Still, writing about Foxhall Edwards (a character he based on Maxwell Perkins) in *You Can't Go Home Again*, Wolfe proceeds to describe him by referring to what he is not, and what Foxhall Edwards is not is a "little Pixy of the Aesthetes." In the process of describing George Webber's editor, Wolfe demonstrates the animosity that he and George Webber have come to feel toward the critics.

> Fox did not go around making discoveries nine years after Boob McNutt had made them. He didn't find out that Groucho was funny seven years too late, and then inform the public *why* he was. He did not write: "The opening *Volte* of the Ballet is the historic method amplified in history, the production of historic fullness without the literary cliché of the historic spate." He had no part in any of the fine horse-manure with which we have allowed ourselves to be bored, maddened, whiff-sniffed, hound-and-hornered, nationed, new-republicked, dialed, spectatored, mercuried, storied, anviled, new-massed, new-yorkered, vogued, vanity-faired, timed, broomed, transitioned, and generally shat upon by the elegant, refined, and snobified Concentrated Blotters of the Arts. He had nothing to do with any of the doltish gibberings, obscene quackeries, phoney passions, and six-months-long religions of fools, joiners, and fashion-apes a trifle brighter and quicker on the uptake than the fools, joiners, and fashion-apes they prey upon. He was none of your little franky-panky, seldesey-weldesey, cowley-wowley, tatesy-watesy, hicksy-picksy, wilsony-pilsony, jolasy-wolasy, steiny-weiny, goldy-woldly, sneer-puss fellows. Neither, in more conventional guise, was he one of your groupy-croupy, cliquey-triquey, meachy-teachy devoto-bloato wire-pullers and back-scratchers of the world. (485–486)

Wolfe's trivialization of the magazines and the journals in which he had been reviewed (*The Hound and Horn, The Nation, The New Republic, The Dial, The American Spectator, The Mercury, The New Masses, The New Yorker, Vogue, Vanity Fair*, and *Time*, among others) and the critics by whom he had been reviewed (Waldo Frank, George Seldes, Malcolm Cowley, Allen Tate, Granville Hicks, Edmund Wilson, E. Jolas, Gertrude Stein, and Michael Gold) is merciless. By turning the names of magazines into simple and compound verbs he makes use of the alliterative and onomatopoeic opportunities afforded him, as well as suggesting that their critical approaches are childishness.

Some of the references are obvious: *broomed* may refer to Louis Bromfield; *Franky-panky* is a play on *hanky-panky*, an indication of the critic's *underhandedness*; *hicksy-picksy*, a reference to that critics *pickiness*; *devoto-bloato*, a reference to that critic's verbal flatulence or possibly *hot air*. The others are nonsense syllables, added to the critics' names, but not having any real significance. By *groupy-croupy*, Wolfe was probably referring to the *coarseness* of their critical prose style as well as to the fact that they tended to be defined in literary groups (Agrarians, Marxists, etc.), and by *meachy-teachy*, he was probably referring to their position in society as literary pedants: those who *can't do* so they *teach*.

It is evident from Wolfe's notebooks that in September 1936, at least, he was considering writing a political and literary satire in the manner of Jonathan Swift's "A Modest Proposal," but based on what he had observed of Fascism in Nazi Germany and what he perceived as its advocacy in the American critical community. Under Wolfe's projected *program*, freedom of speech and freedom of the press would be suppressed, "but so would freedom of Press-Filth" and "Press-Lies." "Let us consider some of the probable benefits of such a system," Wolfe writes. "I should be suppressed, which would be a national loss and a loss to art, but the Malcolm Cowleys, the Mike Golds, the V. F. Calvertons, the Bunny Wilsons, etc., etc., would also be suppressed which would be a gain to everyone and everything." He concludes his fragment with the depiction of great armored trucks cruising through the "bleak, gaunt, almost deserted streets of lower New York." The first haul has been thorough and exact, containing "3,642 of the city's leading murderers, gangsters, vice promotors, and crime-monopolists" (*Notebooks* 832).[9] Extrapolating from Wolfe's notes, it is likely that the second haul will be the roundup of the literary criminals he describes at the beginning of the fragment.

By December 1936, eight months after the appearance of the DeVoto review, Wolfe had come to recognize the nature of the literary entanglements created by the critics' persistent discussion of his relationship to his editor, Maxwell Perkins. In lionizing Perkins's influence on Wolfe, they denied Wolfe the authority of his own prose. In an undated letter to Perkins, which was never mailed, Wolfe describes his dilemma:

> The editorial relation between us, which began, it seems to me, so hopefully, and for me so wonderfully, has now lost its initial substance. It has become a myth — and what is worse than that, an untrue myth — and it seems to me that both of us are victims of that myth. You know the terms of the myth well enough — it was venomously recorded by a man named De Voto in *The Saturday Review of Literature* during this past summer — and the terms of the myth are these: that I cannot write my books

---

[9]Wolfe uses a similar number, 3,264, in a 31 March 1935 letter to Maxwell Perkins. In that letter, this number refers to the faults in Wolfe's writing that the critics have indicated need correction (*Letters* 450).

without your assistance, that there exists at Scribners an "assembly line" that must fit the great dismembered portions of my manuscript together into a semblance of unity, that I am unable to perform the functions of an artist for myself. How far from the truth these suppositions are, you know yourself better than anyone on earth. There are few men – certainly no man I have ever known – who is more sure of *purpose* than myself . . . .

And I am writing therefore now to tell you that I am, upon the date of these words, dissolving a relationship that does not exist, renouncing a contract that was never made, severing myself and of my own accord a bond of loyalty, devotion and self-sacrifice that existed solely, simply and entirely within my own mind, and to my own past grief of doubt, my present grief of sorrow, loss, and final understanding. (*Letters* 556–557)

Six months later, Wolfe severed his relationship with Maxwell Perkins, his editor, and the house of Scribners, which had published his first two novels; the track of Wolfe's literary career took a whole new direction.

The English and German Reviews

The first Heinemann printing of *Of Time and the River*, published in August 1935, varies from the first Scribners printing in 313 substantive readings, most of which reflect the corrections of the simple typographical mistakes made by Scribners, corrections which were incorporated into the American edition by the sixth American printing in April 1935. Several of these changes, however, were intended to make the novel more palatable to an English audience. Wolfe's use of the word *balls* (Scribners edition 73.16 and 299.7) is variously eliminated or replaced by the less offensive *Bosh* (Heinemann edition 73.16 and 299.17), *gas* (Scribners edition 349.28) is replaced by *p-p-p-petrol* (Heinemann edition 349.27), *cobbler* (Scribners 357.36) by *pie* (Heinemann 357.36), and *whores* (Scribners 755.35, 771.11, 792.11, and so forth) by *wretches* (Heinemann 791.36) and *prostitutes* (820.7). Many of the changes resulted in eliminating from the English edition the obscenities and profanities in the American edition. The most extensive of these is a four-line emendation made in the text appearing on page 598 of the American and English editions. The American edition reads:

> "Yuh f——kin' Kikes! . . . Yuh f——kin' Jews! . . . I'll kick duh f——kin' s——t outa duh f——kin' lot of yuh, yuh f——kin' bastards, you . . . . Hey-y! You! . . . Yuh f——kin' dummies up deh talkin' on yer f——kin' fingers all duh time . . . . Hey-y! You! Inches! You f——kin' bastard, I don't give a s——t for duh whole f——kin' lot of yuh."

The English edition reads:

"Yuh------ Kikes! . . . Yuh------ Jews! . . . I'll kick duh------ s----t
outa duh------ lot of yuh, yuh------ bastards, you . . . . Hey-y! You! . . .
Yuh------ dummies up deh talkin' on yer------ fingers all duh time . . . .
Hey-y! You! Inches! You------ bastard, I don't give a s----t for duh
whole------ lot of yuh."

The most interesting of the changes is a change made in a passage that
appears on page 609 of both the American and the English edition soften-
ing a burlesque of Queen Victoria. In this passage an Englishman, Old
Fenton, is described imitating the Queen sitting down to read *The Times*.
The American edition reads: "He insisted on doing an imitation of Queen
Victoria sitting down to read *The Times* upon her w.c. just after modern
plumbing was installed – Ow! he cried exultantly . . . ." The English edition deletes the phrase "upon her w.c."

On the whole, however, the English edition of *Of Time and the River*
was treated with far more respect by Wolfe's English editors than *Look
Homeward, Angel* had been treated in 1930. In 1930 Wolfe had been a relatively unknown writer; by 1935, however, he had attained an interna-
tional reputation. The same Heinemann editors who had ravaged the text
of *Look Homeward, Angel*, felt no such compunction to meddle with *Of Time
and the River*.

By the time the English edition of *Of Time and the River* was published,
Wolfe had left England and returned to New York. There is no evidence
in either his published letters or notebooks that he saw the English reviews. Most of the reviews appeared between 20 and 24 August 1935.
The earliest of these, the "Saga of American Life," which was printed in
the 20 August issue of the *London Times* (7), and "Of Time and the River,"
which appeared in the 22 August issue of the *Times Literary Supplement*,
were both unsigned. The *London Times* reviewer likened Wolfe to Whitman and noted that the work was part of what was to be a six-book set;
the reviewer for the *Times Literary Supplement* referred to the
"Brobdingnagian" element in the novel, comparing Wolfe to Swift as well
as to Whitman. The signed reviews by Seán O'Faoláin and Peter Quennell appearing in *The Spectator* and *The New Statesman and Nation* on 23 and
24 August 1935, respectively, were far less complimentary. O'Faoláin argued that Wolfe showed only a "slight" talent, and he referred the reader
to the "wild Whitmanesque bellowing" of his nine hundred-page novel.
Peter Quennell describes the novel as a "vast, emphatic, violent yet curiously vacuous book." Quennell questions what Wolfe, who could go on
for pages describing a single moment, would have made out of World
War I. He describes for his readers the "sprawling paragraphs that would

have multiplied beneath his pen, the leaden volumes that would have thundered from the press."

Wolfe's second novel was published in Germany as *Von Zeit und Strom* by Rowohlt Verlag in Spring 1936. Once again the translator of the text was the often-praised Hans Schiebelhuth. Translated into German, *Of Time and the River* ran to eleven hundred pages and was printed in two volumes. In the course of his lifetime, Thomas Wolfe took seven trips to Europe, and on each of these trips he traveled to Germany: one in 1924, one in 1926, one in 1927, one in 1928, one in 1930 (on a Guggenheim Fellowship), again in 1935 (just before the publication of *Of Time and the River*), and finally in 1936. He describes his communion with the German countryside and its people in his 1934 *Scribner's Magazine* story, "Dark in the Forest, Strange as Time" (273–278).

Rushing through Bavaria on a wintry afternoon in a great train, the narrator comments on the "gray," the "impenetrable" sky, and the "cold mountain air." He continues:

> Within an hour the train had entered Alpine country; now there were hills, valleys, the immediate sense of soaring ranges, and the dark enchantment of the forests of Germany, those forests which are something more than trees – which are a spell, a magic, and a sorcery, filling the hearts of men, and particularly those of strangers who have some racial kinship with that land, with a dark music, a haunting memory, never wholly to be captured. (171)

He refers to it as his "father's country."[10] The scene is an enchanted one, a homecoming for a stranger – for whom the countryside was strange but vaguely familiar – a racial memory inherited from his father's past.

As he writes in his notebook in a draft of a letter, known as "The Spanish Letter," written but never sent to Donald Ogden Stewart, he believed that no man or woman in the world was not in one way or another richer for the unbroken line of German spirit passed down from the eighteenth century in art, literature, music, and philosophy. The evidence of this spirit was manifest everywhere during his visits in the twenties, and in 1935, during his first trip to Germany after the publication of *Look Homeward, Angel*, he entered Berlin – and discovered that he was famous. Wolfe writes:

> It is said that Byron awoke one morning at the age of twenty-four to find himself famous. I had to wait ten years longer. I was thirty-four when I

---

[10]Even though Wolfe was of Dutch, not German, descent, the German critics, reading that W. O. Gant had lived with the Pennsylvania Germans, assumed that Wolfe was of German descent.

reached Berlin, but it was magic just the same. I suppose I was not really very famous. But it was just as good, because for the first and last time in my life I felt as if I were. A letter had reached me from America telling me that my second book had been successful there, and my first book had been translated and published in Germany a year or two before. The German critics had said tremendous things about it, my name was known. When I got to Berlin people were waiting for me. (*Notebooks* 905)

During his 1935 trip to Germany, Wolfe began to feel a sense of the oppression of the growing Nazi regime, but his love for Germany and its people was so great – their acceptance and love for him and his work so palpable – that the political realities of the Third Reich only slowly dawned on him. When he left Germany in June 1935, many of his conceptions were wavering.

German commentators had been almost unanimous in acclaiming Wolfe's *Look Homeward, Angel* in 1933. The reception of *Of Time and the River* (*Von Zeit und Strom*) was even more impassioned. Most of the German critics awarded Wolfe an important place in American literary history, likening his texts to the poetry of Whitman and the fiction of Faulkner and Wilder in America, to the works of Galsworthy, Bennett and Walpole in England, and to the writings of Proust and Joyce. Writing in the scholarly *Die Neuren Sprachen* in an article titled "Neue Entwicklungstendzen in der amerikanischen Literatur der Gegenwart" ("The New Evolution in American Literature of the Present") Hans Effelberger referred to Wolfe as "one of the greatest talents of American literature" (158–159). While in an extended article reviewing *Von Zeit und Strom* in the Catholic journal *Die Christliche Welt*, Detta Friedrich compared Wolfe and Faulkner, concluding that although both reflect America, Faulkner depicts it more surely in the spirit of his writing that Wolfe does in the realism of his. Still, Friedrich writes, "Nobody should approach these books who is not strong enough to go through a 'thunderstorm' with all its energy, with thunder and lightening and all the terrors of nature and at last the redeeming rain that softly embraces everything and washes away the dark, dull and shuddering." Quoting briefly from *The Story of a Novel* to demonstrate Wolfe's creative method and to demonstrate the inaccuracy of American critics who focused on his writings as being "too" autobiographical, Friedrich describes Wolfe as a creator "responsibly standing above his work. He despises those who do not dare to show life the way it is, but instead euphemize and conceal it." In conclusion, Friedrich's comments are particularly sensitive and perceptive. He writes,

But what is Wolfe himself in the sublimity and loneliness of his creation and the glow out of which he forges the past of life? He is a new, contemporary novelist, remote from the powerful but cold picture of reality drawn by Dreiser, remote from the satirical narration of Sinclair Lewis. He is something new, something that neither he nor the world knows where it will lead. As a reader, though, one only needs the spark that jumps over to do justice to the moods and madnesses, the disorders and beauties, the hundred-fold characters, the sketched landscapes, the whole meaning of the book that constitutes life itself. How good it is for us Europeans to have a mediator between the old and the new world, on which arch of a bridge we can reach the foreign world safely and seeing it, understand it for the first time . . . . (1117–1121)

Writing that modern life finds its artistic counterpart no longer in the epic but in the novel, Gert H. Theunissen reviews Wolfe's second novel in *Der Bücherwurm*. For Theunissen the importance of Wolfe's second novel lies in its redefinition of the "novel" as the means of commenting on modern life rather than *epos*. In this restructuring, he argues, "Thomas Wolfe is the one to forge the way." Praising the Transcendental and spiritual element in the work that "elevated the novel to a point from which the horizons of life reach over the death zone into a transcendental state that bestows time and man with the sign of lost and found mercy," he concludes that the *epos* focused on events, whereas the novel focuses on the essence made manifest in the event. "Wolfe," he concludes "has exchanged the scientific aspects for the theological ones." Out of the violence of America, Theunissen continues, Wolfe creates "the New Man." "If time is the mask behind which the abundance of being hides," Theunissen notes, "Man is thrown into the abyss of time and above the abyss there is a light shining into the dark." *Von Zeit und Strom*, he argues, is both a Christian and a political work in which "Wolfe forms the unity of theological reflection on being and political responsibility out of a creativity that leads far into the future." Wolfe's characters, he writes, cross the nothingness or perish in it, but they do not avoid it (194–195).

The important German critic and translator Wolfgang von Einseidel also reviewed the novel, in the *Europäische Umschau*, examining its importance from the "European, not the American, point of view." In comparing Wolfe's first novel to his second, von Einseidel compares *Schau heimwärts, Engel!* to a mountain stream which widens into a river in *Von Zeit und Strom*. The essence and form of the novel, he continues, is contained in the parable of its title:

Like a river, the plot flows past the reader. We see neither its origin nor its goal. All we see is a continuous motion, all we hear is an endless roar. The surface of the river glows from the reflection of numberless lights, it darkens under shadows from the clouds and over bottomless depths. Carried by the river, threatened by it, boats full of people rush by, of whom we get a glimpse but whose faces, nonetheless, stay in our memory forever . . . . This book, born out of the element, connected with the element, is boundless and shapeless. But in a deeper sense it is not deformed. (841–844)

The novel, he concludes is "Hymnic-rhapsodic," "epic-descriptive," "dramatic," and at the same time "analytical." Its unifying structure is the "monstrous, roaring of life itself." Comparing Wolfe to Proust, Einseidel notes that both deal with the issue of memory. But, Proust stood at the end of a long social and literary development, and the shadowy picture of the "I" in his writing loses its power. With Thomas Wolfe, on the other hand, functioning in a younger nation, the "I" becomes a point of emphasis. "For Proust," he argues, "there is only past . . . . For Wolfe there is only a present, as everything that has happened in the past is always rising to the surface of the present." *Von Zeit und Strom*, he writes,

> deals with nothing else than the fate of the basic, the natural, the creative 'I' in the modern world in general – the world being America or Europe. And the reassuring and warming aspect of his novel lies within the experienced and shaped experience, that helps the 'I' not only to resist the impersonal dragging powers of the modern world, but in the end to triumph over them by repelling everything that is foreign to its essence . . . . (841–844)

In a phrase that painfully foreshadows the political movements that had begun by 1936 in Germany and would reach their fruition in World War II, von Einseidel praises Wolfe's protagonist, Eugene Gant, who he writes, quoting Wolfe, is among the few chosen ones to realize that "one day, he would overcome and swallow the masses, that one man was more than a million men, stronger than a wall, bigger than a portal, higher than a tower of ninety floors" (844).

Only Hans Franke writing in the pro-Nazi *Die Neue Literatur* found fault with Wolfe's second novel. Although it was well written and interesting, he did not perceive it to be a good representation of America. Formless, nihilistic, and confusing, this novel was not a positive role model, he concluded.

Embittered, Wolfe escaped to Germany in the summer of 1935 to protect himself from the American "literary community." By 23 May 1935, despite his warm reception by the German people, he could write to Perkins expressing his confusion. He writes:

> I want to tell you that I do not see how anyone who comes here as I have come could possibly fail to love the country, its nobel Gothic beauty and its lyrical loveliness, or to like the German people who are I think the cleanest, the kindest, the warmest-hearted, and the most honorable people I have met in Europe . . . .

Now I so much want to see you and tell you what I have seen and heard . . . because one feels they are so evil and yet cannot say so justly in so many words as a hostile press and propaganda would, because this evil is so curiously and inextricably woven into a kind of wonderful hope which flourishes and inspires millions of people who are themselves . . . certainly not evil . . . . But more and more I feel that we are all of us bound up and tainted by whatever guilt and evil there may be in this whole world and that we cannot accuse and condemn others without in the end coming back to an accusal of ourselves . . . . This nation today is beyond the shadow of a vestige of a doubt full of uniforms and a stamp of marching men – I saw it with my own eyes yesterday in one hundred towns and villages . . . . all filled beyond a doubt with hope, enthusiasm and inspired belief in a fatal and destructive thing – and the sun was shining all day long and the fields the greenest, the woods the loveliest, the little towns the cleanest and the faces and the voices of the people the most friendly of any I have ever seen or heard . . . .[11]

[11]Quoted in Roger Burlingame's *Of Making Many Books* (New York: Scribners, 1946), pp. 325–326.

5: The Concept of the "Enemy"

"WHAT NO CRITIC seems to have realized," Thomas Lyle Collins comments in the October/December 1942 issue of *The Sewanee Review*, "is that the appearance of Thomas Wolfe may have been an event of the utmost significance in the history of American literature . . . . There is even a possibility that future generations will come to regard him as the author of The Great American Novel" (489).

Collins's argument that Wolfe was the author of *Great American Novels* but not of The Great American Novel, focuses on four main problems in the encounter of the American critics with the modern novel: the problem of *scope*, the problem of *greatness*, the problem of *significance*, and the problem of *form* (489). In defining the problem of *greatness*, Collins likens Wolfe's novels to the writings of Homer, Dante, Shakespeare, and Goethe. Like these authors, Wolfe was capable of synthesizing the universal and the particular. In addition, Collins concludes moving on to a discussion of the *significance* of Wolfe's writing, although Wolfe did not enter into the discussions of the important sociological and political issues of twentieth-century America until the publication of *You Can't Go Home Again*, his earlier novels focus incessantly on the poverty of tradition, the blind materialism, and the barrenness of middle-class life in America. All four novels catch "that strange and unique combination of brilliant hope and black despair which is the quintessence of the American spirit" (500–501). Critical condemnations of Wolfe's writing based on its lack of *form* are, Collins continues, both "foolish and unprofitable." Critics making these arguments are confused by a tendency to view the novel as a "fixed and immutable *genre*." Using Kenneth Burke's definition of form as "the creation of an appetite in the mind of the auditor, and the adequate satisfying of that appetite," Collins argues that Wolfe's works are structured on three basic and interdependent forms: the episode, the complete work, and the novel.

Collins concludes his essay by discussing the problem of *scope*. Although Wolfe wrote "*great* American novels . . . great *American* novels, and . . . great American *novels*," he did not write The Great American Novel. That term, Collins argues, implies that the novel should summarize and epitomize the promise of America's becoming one of the great ages of man. Wolfe's novels fail to do this because, Collins adds, this is impossible. Unlike the periods that produced Homer's *Iliad*, Dante's *Divine Com-*

edy, and the plays of Shakespeare, present-day America contains so many forces of disunity and skepticism that no work of literature could bring them together into a "coherent and comprehensible pattern" (504).

Collins's essay is a particularly sensible and logical assessment of Wolfe's writing and its position in the American literary canon, based on the understanding of language, symbol, and structure provided Collins in 1942 by critics such as Kenneth Burke and the advocates of the New Criticism. Using these arguments, Collins is as successful in undercutting the evaluations of Wolfe's writings made by DeVoto and Robert Penn Warren in the 1930s as he is in analyzing the importance of Wolfe's novels.

In his "Genius Is Not Enough," Bernard DeVoto, Collins argues, betrays his own critical judgment because he needs to make a show of being "hard-headed and commonsensical" (490). When he attacks Wolfe for writing lyrical poetic passages in novels, rather than undiluted dramatic narrative, DeVoto is demonstrating a critical *dogmatism* which "attempts to keep poetry and fiction and comedies and tragedies and ballet and opera set completely apart from each other in neat little compartments" (490). When DeVoto argues that Wolfe's writing is not great because it does not fulfill the standard definitions of novels, he makes this dogmatism even more evident. Writers create *genres* and are not responsible for structuring works according to those genres. As Collins so aptly notes, the problem of *genre* is of secondary importance to the decision about how great Wolfe's writing is (492). In terms of DeVoto's impugning of Wolfe's artistic integrity, Collins argues that DeVoto confuses structural emphasis and form. "No editor," Collins writes, "can by the wielding of a blue pencil, impart *form* to a work of art; he can only lay bare the form which is somewhat obscured by surplus material . . . .every dramatic scene, every colorful characterization was *formed* by Wolfe, not by his editor" (492–493).

Turning to Robert Penn Warren's "A Note on the Hamlet of Thomas Wolfe," Collins deals with Warren's criticism of the lack of objectivity in the autobiographical novel. Warren, Collins charges, is guilty of focusing his review of *Of Time and the River* on the novelist, not on the novel. "*Hamlet*," he concludes, " . . . would be no less great if Shakespeare actually had been a prince of Denmark" (494).[1]

_____

[1]Collins's article is a wonderful demonstration of the values of the New Criticism. His only error is in his dating of Warren's "A Note on the Hamlet of Thomas Wolfe," which was originally published in May 1935, before DeVoto's "Genius Is Not Enough" (published in April 1936) and not after it. Because of this Collins's argument that Warren "follows the critical line laid down by DeVoto" (493) is anachronistic. Collins's error arises from his use of the 1937 reprint of Warren's review which appears in Morton

As comforting as Collins's argument is, it too is flawed. Certainly, *Hamlet* would retain its own sweet perfection regardless of the identity of its author; but it is unlikely, were its author anyone but Shakespeare, that any play, written at the beginning of the seventeenth-century, would continue to be widely read and performed into the 1990s. Had the author of that play been the historical Hamlet instead of Shakespeare, it would be equally as unlikely that the modern audience would respond to the work in quite the same way as it does. Given Hamlet as author, an audience might respond to his interior monologues as self-serving rationalizations of criminal acts (of which, in the course of the drama, he commits several – including the murder of Polonius), more like the sensationalized confessions of the protagonists of Capote's *In Cold Blood*[2] than Shakespeare's "noble Dane."

Wolfe's novels are read as "thinly disguised autobiography," somewhat differently than they would be read were they completely fictional. However, it can be argued that almost all great literature, whether it is recognized as such or not, is at least in part *autobiographical*. This autobiographical element, for instance, is what Hawthorne is referring to at the beginning of *The Scarlet Letter* when he writes about "the inmost ME behind its veil." Yet, it is also evident that a reading of *The Scarlet Letter* is less dependent on recognizing the similarities between Hawthorne (the artist whose artistic talents seem to have been betrayed by his work in the Customs House) and his protagonist, Hester Prynne (the artist whose ability to love seems to have been betrayed by Chillingworth and Dimmesdale), than a reading of *Of Time and the River* is on the reader's recognition of the similarities between Thomas Wolfe and Eugene Gant.

Several of the critics analyzing *Of Time and the River* in the forties and the fifties focus on the theme of "the enemy" as it was treated in Wolfe's fiction, letters, and journals – using the private documents produced by Wolfe in the course of his lifetime to illuminate the published documents. One scholar in particular, Floyd Watkins, focuses on the scene in *Of Time and the River* in which W. O. Gant dies. After 1960, critical assessments of this novel focused on Wolfe's attitudes toward the South, questions of form and genre, and the Faustian element in his writing.

Zabel's *Literary Opinion in America* instead of referring to the original publication of that review in the May 1935 issue of the *American Review*.

[2]Truman Capote. *In Cold Blood* (New York: Random House, 1966; London: Hamilton, 1966).

The 1940s and the 1950s

Many of Wolfe's frequently cited "enemies" were, in the light of day, his friends. Both Nowell and Donald describe Wolfe's "black moods" at length in their biographies of him. Donald describes Wolfe's turning on Perkins in a drunken rage that only by serendipity failed to result in a fist-fight (*Look Homeward: A Life of Thomas Wolfe* 413); Nowell describes the angry call she received from Wolfe at three in the morning charging her with *willing* his novel to failure (*Thomas Wolfe: A Biography* 12). It seems that it was often difficult for Wolfe, suffering from the exhaustion of his routine, to tell the difference between friends and enemies or, as Melville would have phrased it, to distinguish between *Typee* and *Happar* or *clam* and *cod*.

It is unwise, however, to confuse Wolfe's "black moods" and intemperate acts of physical violence with his response to his critics. Wolfe may have chastised Canby and DeVoto in his private journals and even depicted them satirically in his fiction, but he did not go out of his way physically to confront or professionally to malign them. He was no stalker. The joy he felt in receiving good reviews and the frustration and pain he felt in receiving negative reviews were always vented in the personal, not the public, arena, and attacks made in his fiction were always "veiled"; an in-group of readers may have recognized the real counterparts of the figures he satirized, but most readers would have read those figures as humorous or eccentric *fictional* characters.

Was Wolfe *paranoid*? Was he incapable of forming close relationships without feeling *suffocated*? Was he *oversensitive* to criticism? Were his moments of *despair* the results of chemical imbalances or emotional instabilities? Was he *manic-depressive*? There really is no answer to any of these questions; neither is there significant evidence of *emotional instability* or *irrational behavior* in his letters and journals. There are, however, descriptions of gigantized moments of intemperance (generally occurring when Wolfe was under the influence of alcohol or when he was frustrated in his writing) described in his private documents and in the reminiscences of his friends and in his fiction. Had Wolfe been less "open" to life and less adept at analyzing his own emotional experience, it is likely that few of these incidents would have become a matter of record. In fact, it does seem a bit hypocritical to praise Wolfe's prose style for its *sensitivity* while denying the author of that *sensitive* prose style an occasional emotional outburst.

Still, it is disturbing to see Wolfe's constant references to his "enemies," whether these references appear in his depictions of Starwick (Wolfe's friend Kenneth Raisbeck) in *Of Time and the River*, of Esther Jack

(Wolfe's mistress, Aline Bernstein) in *The Web and the Rock* and *You Can't Go Home Again*, or of Jerry Alsop (John Skally Terry) in *The Web and the Rock*. The concept of the "enemy" *is* an issue in Wolfe's fiction, as three of his critics, Herbert Muller, Martin Maloney, and Malcolm Cowley, point out.

In his 1947 study, *Thomas Wolfe*, Herbert Muller fails to recognize the importance of Eugene's rejection of Starwick (Muller writes, "The only apparent basis for the mortal enmity is that Starwick got the girl" [57]) as the rejection of a mediocre artist by an original artist, but he does recognize that in *Of Time and the River* Wolfe displays his primary gift as a mythmaker, providing the reader with a sense of "the wonderful strangeness of the familiar, the enchantments of routine modern experience" (72). The creation of myth is, Muller argues, more difficult for Wolfe than it was for Homer, simply because America in the 1920s and 1930s is more complex and ironic than ancient Greece had been. It is a sign of Wolfe's growing maturity, Muller concludes, that the triumphant ending of *Of Time and the River* in which Eugene Gant returns from Europe is neither forced nor shrill. "The wanderer," Muller notes, "returns from Europe, more enthralled by the homecoming than was Ulysses . . . . Wolfe is mythicizing, in the heroic manner; and good Americans may be embarrassed. Yet if this grandiloquence is 'against reason and knowledge,' Wolfe by now does have the reason and knowledge . . . . He has not come by his enthrallment easily or cheaply" (71–72).

But, as Muller notes, in order to create the heroic myth of Eugene Gant/George Webber, it is necessary for Wolfe (like Milton in *Paradise Lost*) to create an *enemy* or *demon* for his protagonists to overcome. Out of this need Wolfe creates the myth of the "enemy." In *Of Time and the River* this enemy was Starwick; in Wolfe's letters and notebooks it is at first his Asheville persecutors (sometimes his family) and later the critics who seem to lie in wait for him; at the time of his break with Scribners, it seems to be Maxwell Perkins. In his third novel, *The Web and the Rock,* that demon materializes as Esther Jack and the circle of flawed aesthetes who surround her; in *You Can't Go Home Again* the demon becomes social injustice. The complexity of that fear of being undone by the "enemy" that marks Wolfe's protagonists as well as his private writings is best summarized in Wolfe's *The Story of a Novel* in which he writes about the dreams that "murdered" his sleep. Ironically, his greatest fear is not of his antagonists but of the "passivity" that would result from his loss of these antagonists. Wolfe writes:

> There was a kind of dream which I can only summarize as dreams of
> Guilt and Time. Chameleon-like in all their damnable and unending fe-
> cundities, they restored to me the whole huge world that I had known,

the billion faces and the million tongues, and they restored it to me with
the malevolent triumph of a passive and unwanted ease. My daily conflict with Amount and Number, the huge accumulations of my years of
struggle with the forms of life, my brutal and unending efforts to record
upon my memory each brick and paving stone of every street that I had
ever walked upon, each face of every thronging crowd in every city,
every country with which my spirit had contested its savage and uneven
struggle for supremacy – they all returned now – each stone, each
street, each town, each country – yes, even every book in the library
whose loaded shelves I had tried vainly to devour at college – they returned upon the wings of these mighty, sad, and somehow quietly demented dreams – I saw and heard and knew them all at once, was
instantly without pain or anguish, with the calm consciousness of God,
master of the whole universe of life against whose elements I had con-
tended vainly for all-knowledge for so many years. And the fruit of that
enormous triumph, the calm and instant passivity of that inhuman and
demented immortality, was somehow sadder and more bitter than the
most galling bitterness of defeat in my contention with the multitudes of
life had ever been. (*The Story of a Novel* 62–63)

At this stage of his life, the frustration of the young writer had developed
into a feeling of persecution. "All around him," Muller notes, "he saw not
merely indifference but hatred, malice, venom – a calculated plot to destroy him. He had to have enemies; nothing else could explain his frustra-
tions" (Muller 103).

Martin Maloney in his 1955 essay "A Study of Semantic States: Thomas Wolfe and the Faustian Sickness" develops Muller's idea of the enemy in Wolfe's writing more fully. "The enemy" is a product, Maloney
argues, of Wolfe's endless Faustian hunger, his need to consume all of
life – and "the enemy" is anyone or thing that keeps him from consuming
all of that life. Maloney quotes an early letter from Wolfe to his mother:

I know this now: I am inevitable. I sincerely believe The only thing that
can stop me now is insanity, disease or death . . . . I want to know life
and understand it and interpret it without fear or favor . . . . For life is
not made up of sugary, sticky, sickening Edgar A. Guest sentimentality,
it is not made up of dishonest optimism, God is *not* always in his
Heaven, All is *not* always right with the world . . . . It is savage, cruel,
kind, noble, passionate, selfish, generous, stupid, ugly, beautiful, painful,
joyous, – it is all these, and more, and it's all these I want to know and,
By God, I shall, though they crucify me for it. (*The Letters of Thomas Wolfe
to His Mother* 42)

The undefined, but obviously "inimicable 'they,'" Maloney argues, was a
defense mechanism for the young Wolfe. His sense of the "enemy" provided him with protection from the failure he anticipated and against

which he struggled. As he grew older and dealt with the more legitimate concerns of the artist, he kept the "paraphernalia of martyrdom" close at hand, as a means of protecting himself and his alter egos.

It is the "Faustian" element in Wolfe's writing, conclude Muller and Maloney, that generates the powers and energies of his prose and characterization, a release of energy prompted by his passion to succeed in the face of all obstacles and all enemies. When Wolfe turned away from this "Faustian" madness and tried to write more sane and temperate literature (as he did in *The Web and the Rock* and *You Can't Go Home Again*) his work became pedestrian.

In his 1957 *Atlantic Monthly* article, "Thomas Wolfe," Malcolm Cowley, on the other hand, charges that later in life Wolfe developed paranoid symptoms that included delusions of persecution and grandeur. Most critics, Cowley notes, quote Wolfe's 15 December 1936 letter to Perkins, in which Wolfe writes that he will wreak out his vision "of this life, this way, this world and this America . . . with an unswerving devotion, integrity and purity of purpose that shall not be menaced, altered or weakened by any one." These same critics, Cowley argues, slur over the less eloquent passages of that same letter that read:

> I will go to jail because of this book if I have to . . . . I will be libelled, slandered, blackmailed, threatened, menaced, sneered at, derided and assailed by every parasite, every ape, every blackmailer, every scandalmonger, every little Saturday Reviewer of the venomous and corrupt respectabilities. I will be exiled from my country because of it, if I have to . . . . But no matter what happens I am going to write this book. (*Letters* 587)

Wolfe, Cowley argues, came to recognize this "Dr. Jekyll" element in his personality and became aware that he was losing touch with reality – but also recognized that his paranoia was not the result of unsolved emotional conflicts, but of the romantic artist's need to stretch the limits of his emotions and energies. Cowley concludes by quoting Wolfe's letter to Alfred Dashiell:

> The effort of writing or creating something seems to start up a strange and bewildering conflict in the man who does it, and this conflict at times almost takes on physical proportions so that he feels he is struggling not only with his own work but also with the whole world around him, and he is so beset with demons, nightmares, delusions and bewilderments that he lashes out at everyone and everything, not only people he dislikes and mistrusts, but sorrowfully enough, even against the people that he knows in his heart are his friends.
>
> I cannot tell you how completely and deeply conscious I have been of this thing and how much bloody anguish I have sweat and suffered

when I have exorcised these monstrous phantoms and seen clearly into what kind of folly and madness they have led me. ("Thomas Wolfe" 212; this letter also appears in a slightly different form in Nowell's *Letters* 374)

"Don't be afraid of going crazy – ," Wolfe wrote Mabel in 1929, "I've been there several times and it's not at all bad" (*Letters* 180). Wolfe's depiction of his "madness" and his need to confront his enemies is probably best described in chapter 36 of *The Web and the Rock* in which he writes about George Webber:

> Sometimes the wave of death and horror came upon the insane impulses of a half-heard word, a rumor of laughter in the street at night, the raucous shout and gibe of young Italian thugs as they passed by below his window in the darkness, or a look of mockery, amusement, curiosity from some insolent face at a restaurant table, some whispered, unheard communication. And sometimes it came from sourceless depths, from no visible or tangible cause whatever. It would come as he sat quietly in a chair at home, as he stared at the ceiling from his cot, from a word in a poem, from a line in a book, or simply as he looked out of the window at that one green tree. But whenever it came, and for whatever cause, the result was always the same: work, power, hope, joy, and all creative energy were instantly engulfed and obliterated in its drowning and overwhelming tide . . . .
>
> And always now, when the convulsion of pain and horror drove him mad, he sought again the spurious remedy of the bottle . . . . His brain burned slowly and literally like a dull fire smouldering in a blackened, rusty brazier, and he would sit numbed and silent in the sullen darkness of a slowly mounting and murderous rage until he went out in the street to find the enemy, to curse and brawl and seek out death and hatred in dive and stew, among the swarms of the rats of the flesh, the livid, glittering dead men of the night. (546)

Clearly, Wolfe, like his protagonists Eugene Gant and George Webber, was obsessed with the process of writing and, clearly, that obsession was a little *crazy* – as almost all obsessions by definition must be. Still, it was a *productive* obsession, one that focused his energies on his work and protected him from the multitudinous distractions that life threw in his path. Had Wolfe not been *maddened* by his need to write, he would never have had the energy necessary for composing the millions of manuscript pages that he produced during his lifetime, would never have become an important published writer and, as a result, would never have been subjected to the somewhat morbid emotional analysis prevalent in a number of the articles written about him. The assumption of Wolfe's *normalcy* then would reside not in the question of whether he suffered from moments of possessed madness, but in the fact that in his conformity to the mores of society he had failed to produce anything that would make an in-depth study of the nature of his mental states of any importance.

One of the most interesting analyses of Wolfe's theme of the "enemy," both in his fiction and in his life, appears in a reminiscence written by Wolfe's friend Belinda Jelliffe, wife of the eminent neuropsychiatrist Dr. Smith Ely Jelliffe. Jelliffe believed that Wolfe's concept of the "enemy" had developed out of the pattern of power struggles he had experienced in his own family as a boy, in which angry argument yielded to respect and, ultimately, to a kind of reconciliation that stressed the unconditional acceptance of one family member for another. This *pattern* became the basis for relationships Wolfe established outside of his family. In New York, for instance, Scribners became a kind of family for Wolfe, and he transferred the behavioral pattern that had enabled him to survive in his family to his relationship with his publisher. In describing the break-up between Perkins and Wolfe, Belinda Jelliffe writes:

> The conflict between his great love for Max, his sincere appreciation of Scribners, became exhausting. His naturally suspicious nature led him to extravagances of imagination concerning their financial integrity, while his heart told him how wrong he was, and that made him confused and sick.
>
> Scribners came to be his family all over again, with his love, his fears of disapproval, his frustrated desire to be really free. He himself could not understand that the iron bars which held him prisoner were within him, not in Scribners or anyone else. (*Wolfe and Belinda Jelliffe* 57–58)

Jelliffe continues, "I told Max: 'Can't you see that you've simply got to have a fight with him, a real emotional disturbance, and then make up? His whole pattern of life is established upon that procedure, and his personality demands and needs it'" (*Wolfe and Belinda Jelliffe* 58). The "enemy," for Wolfe, was anyone who would force or manipulate him into being other than he was: as a young man this included family and friends; as a young writer it included his editors; as a mature writer it included his critics. His procedure for dealing with these "enemies" was to deny their power over him by creating a real or imaginary "emotional outburst" which would, so to speak, clear the air, and enable him to reestablish his sense of self.

The concept of the "enemy" is an important part of Wolfe's transcendent prose style. Prose cannot be *transcendent* if it has nothing to transcend. It is also clear that this sense of transcendence over an enemy is uniquely tied to the epiphanies that appear in his work. Many of his passages are stylistically reminiscent of Whitman and Melville. One passage from *Of Time and the River* is equally as reminiscent of the cadences of the Old Testament.

Who has seen fury riding in the mountains? Who has known fury strid-ing in the storm? Who has been mad with fury in his youth, given no rest or peace or certitude by fury, driven on across the earth by fury, un-til the great vine of the heart was broke, the sinews wrenched, the little tenement of bone, blood, marrow, brain, and feeling in which great fury raged, was twisted, wrung, depleted, worn out, and exhausted by the fury which it could not lose or put away? Who has known fury, how it came? (27–28)

The reader is not surprised to find that this passage, which extends over five paragraphs, concludes in a depiction of the young Eugene's fight against wind and storm as he delivers papers on his appointed route. Wolfe continues,

he leaned down against the wind's strong wall towards Niggertown, blocking his folded papers as he went, and shooting them terrifically in the wind's wild blast against the shack-walls of the jungle-sleeping blacks, himself alone awake, wild, secret, free and stormy as the wild wind's blast, giving it howl for howl and yell for yell, with madness, and a de-mon's savage and exultant joy, up-welling in his throat! (28–29)

It is evident in comparing this description of the "fury" to Wolfe's de-scription of the "passivity" that he finds so galling in *The Story of a Novel* (62–63), that Wolfe found bursts of emotion to be liberating, and "passivity" to be an acceptance of defeat.

Floyd Watkins in his 1957 study, *Thomas Wolfe's Characters*, describes the death of Gant, depicted in chapters 30 through 33 of *Of Time and the River*, as the most "effective" segment of that novel. Compared with Wolfe's treatment of the sordid family squabbles when Ben died in *Look Homeward, Angel*, Watkins concludes, "the account of old Gant presents a much more favorable view of the family" (58–59). Still, Watkins over-looks the way in which the dream scene at the center of this segment is built on Robert Frost's famous 1916 poem, "The Road Not Taken," and the way in which the death of Gant is built on one of the premier death scenes in American literature, James Fenimore Cooper's description of the death of Natty Bumppo in *The Prairie*. In Frost's poem, a traveler encoun-ters two roads and chooses to follow one because it seems less traveled. The final two verses of the poem read:

> And both that morning equally lay
> In leaves no step had trodden black.
> Oh, I kept the first for another day!
> Yet knowing how way leads on to way,
> I doubted if I should ever come back.

> I shall be telling this with a sigh
> Somewhere ages and ages hence:
> Two roads diverged in a wood, and I –
> I took the one less traveled by,
> And that has made all the difference.

In chapter 33 of *Of Time and the River*, as Gant lies at the point of death, "his great hands of living power quiet with their immense and passive strength beside him on the bed" (258), he falls asleep and begins to dream of his youth in Spangler's Run. He finds himself in a graveyard, beside the white frame church of the United Brethren, where his friends and family have been buried. On one of the tombstones, he has carved his own name, W. O. Gant. Admiring the fullness of the Pennsylvania landscape, Gant provides the "idiot boy" Willy Spangler with a plug of tobacco because he "saw that he might never come this way again." Wandering further and further into the forest, he comes upon a child and upon "a place where the path split away into two forks." "Which one shall I take?" he asks. But the child is silent. Looking down the path, Gant sees that someone has been there before him. He sees a footprint on the earth; Wolfe continues,

> then, with the bridgeless instancy of dreams, it seemed to him that all of the bright green-gold around him in the wood grew dark and sombre, the path grew darker, and suddenly he was walking in a strange and gloomy forest, haunted by the brown and tragic light of dreams . . . . And again he stopped and listened, the footsteps faded, vanished, he shouted, no one answered. And suddenly he knew that he had taken the wrong path. (260–261)

Unlike Frost's traveler, who chooses the road "less traveled by," Gant chooses the road where he seems to hear footsteps. But, as in the Frost poem, the condition of choice in matters of life and death is, at best, an illusion, for both paths lead to death. The scene as depicted by Wolfe is, however, far less somber than his allusion to Frost's poem suggests.

Echoing the last words of Cooper's Natty Bumppo in *The Prairie*, Gant cries out "Here" at the moment of his death, "'Here, Father, here!' and heard a strong voice answer him, 'My son!'" (268). As Natty dies, Middleton and Hard-Heart each extend a hand to support him, only to find that he has already died. Similarly, in Wolfe's narrative of the death of the stonecutter Gant, Gant is held at the moment of his death "supported in two arms." Implicit in the allusion to the Cooper novel is a sense of the grandeur and dignity in the passing of a heroic larger-than-life figure that Wolfe hoped to capture in his depiction of the death of Eugene's father, and also, possibly, a reference to the family line (that according to family tradition stretched back on Julia Wolfe's side of the family to Davy

Crockett). The death of Natty Bumppo additionally provides Wolfe with a means of alluding to Eugene's father's profession, since the final passages of *The Prairie* deal with the inscription on Natty's headstone: "May no wanton hand ever disturb his remains!"

The 1960s and After

One of the earliest treatments of Wolfe's *Of Time and the River* to appear in the 1960s was C. Hugh Holman's "'The Dark, Ruined Helen of His Blood': Thomas Wolfe and the South," published in 1961 by Louis Rubin and Robert Jacobs in their *South: Modern Southern Literature in Its Cultural Setting*. Although Holman analyzes all four of Wolfe's major texts in this essay, he focuses significantly on *Of Time and the River*, in which he sees Wolfe's attention centering on (as Tocqueville suggested) the common man as the center of a patriotic art intent on capturing the American experience as epic. Holman quotes from Wolfe's *The Story of a Novel*:

> . . . in the cultures of Europe and of the Orient the American artist can find no antecedent scheme, no structural plan, no body of tradition that can give his own work the validity and truth that it must have. It is not merely that he must make somehow a new tradition for himself, derived from his own life and from the enormous space and energy of American life, the structure of his own design; it is not merely that he is confronted by these problems; it is even more than this, that the labor of a complete and whole articulation, the discovery of an entire universe and of a complete language, is the task that lies before him. (*The Story of a Novel* 92)

Comparing Wolfe to Whitman, Holman concludes that whereas Whitman believed that the writer should see in himself the microcosm of the American experience, Wolfe believed that the writer "as artist" derived out of his sensitivity to the common family of man, an understanding of all of the anguish, error, and frustration that any man could have experienced. Whereas Thoreau, like Wolfe, saw himself as the proper subject for a national art, Wolfe, unlike Thoreau, depicted not only his own experience but also his observations of his fellow men.

In his regionalism, Holman argues, Wolfe is essentially Southern. The mammoth scope of his work (the six-book set outlined at the beginning of *Of Time and the River*) matches the work of other Southerners such as James Branch Cabell, Ellen Glasgow, and William Faulkner, who distrust the abstraction of Northern romanticism and feel the need to design their works out of solid details and facts. Holman believes Wolfe, like these Southern writers, to have been attuned to the complex reality of the nature of time, in which past and present exist side by side. Wolfe, Holman comments, also delighted in the use of folk speech, dialect, and speech mannerism, indicative of his Southern origins. Had he known more about the Southern Agrarians, Holman concludes, Wolfe would have recognized that their concerns with the danger of *progress* and *industrialism* and their sense of the need for the South to emerge into the modern world were concerns that they shared with him.

It is unlikely that Holman writing in the early sixties would have had access to the satirical material written by Wolfe on the Agrarians in his notebooks, which remained in untranscribed manuscript form in the vaults of the Houghton Library until published by Richard S. Kennedy and Paschal Reeves in 1970. In claiming that Wolfe's concerns echoed those of the Agrarians, Holman may have had in mind a congenial meeting between Wolfe and the Agrarians that occurred during the 1936 Modern Language Association meeting in Richmond, Virginia; however, had he referred back to *The Web and the Rock*, Holman would have found Wolfe continuing to satirize the Agrarians even after that meeting.

As Thomas A. Underwood, in his carefully documented essay "Thomas Wolfe's Trip to Richmond: Détente at the 1936 MLA Meeting," describes it, Wolfe set out on his first visit to the South after the publication of *Look Homeward, Angel* on the day after Christmas in 1936. Informed by Henry Seidel Canby that the aristocratic Virginia novelist, Ellen Glasgow, was throwing a holiday party for some literary critics and southern writers in Richmond, Wolfe (who during the same period was courting the Marxist critic V. F. Calverton in an attempt to create the kind of bridges that might result in better reviews of his work) decided to stop there on his way to New Orleans.

Probably *not* by coincidence, Wolfe registered at the Hotel Jefferson, where the Modern Language Association was holding its fifty-third annual meeting. There Wolfe might have encountered several of his old New York University colleagues, a den of literary critics – including Bernard DeVoto and Mark Van Doren, and the core of the Southern Agrarian movement from Vanderbilt. The Agrarians present included Donald Davidson, who had negatively reviewed *Look Homeward, Angel* in 1930; Alan Tate; Robert Penn Warren, who had negatively reviewed *Of Time and the River*; and John Crowe Ransom, who had made some negative comparisons of Wolfe to the authors of other "horrible" novels.

Wolfe had charmed Warren at the 1935 Writer's Conference in Boulder, and after that conference the two men had spent a few enjoyable days exploring San Francisco together. When Wolfe saw Warren in Richmond, Wolfe insisted on their getting together. The two men were joined by the literary critic Cleanth Brooks, a coeditor with Warren of *The Southern Review*, and later by their wives, by John Crowe Ransom, and by Alan Tate and his wife, Caroline Gordon. Wolfe seemed to enjoy being surrounded by the Agrarians, charming everyone except for Caroline Gordon, who found Wolfe "drunk and dumb and extremely amiable." Wolfe later reported to Dixon Wecter in a letter dated 5 March 1937 that he had spent a "pleasant evening with the Warrens, the Tates, the Brooks and Mr. Ransom" and had done almost everything "except become a Southern Agrarian" (*Letters* 615).

In the manuscript of what ultimately became *The Web and the Rock*, however, Wolfe left a devastating attack on the Agrarians, whom he charged with rejecting the reality of the city for a rural landscape that they had never tilled. Wolfe writes:

> So the refined young gentlemen of the New Confederacy shook off their degrading shackles, caught the last cobwebs of illusion from their awakened vision, and retired haughtily into the South, to the academic security of a teaching appointment at one of the universities, from which they could issue in quarterly installments very small and very precious magazines which celebrated the advantages of an agrarian society. The subtler intelligences of this rebel horde were forever formulating codes and cults in their own precincts – codes and cults which affirmed the earthly virtues of both root and source in such unearthly language, by such processes of æsthetic subtlety, that even the cult adepts of the most precious city cliques were hard put to it to extract the meaning.
>
> All this George Webber observed and found somewhat puzzling and astonishing. Young men whose habits, tastes, and modes of thought and writing seemed to him to belong a great deal more to the atmospheres of the æsthetic cliques which they renounced than to any other now began to argue the merits of a return to "an agrarian way of life" . . . . Moreover, as one who was himself derived from generations of mountain farmers who had struggled year by year to make a patch of corn grow in the hill erosions of a mountain flank, and of generations of farm workers in Pennsylvania who had toiled for fifteen hours a day behind the plow to earn a wage of fifty cents, it now came as a mild surprise to be informed by the lily-handed intellectuals of a Southern university that what he needed most of all was to return to the earthly and benevolent virtues of the society which had produced him. (242–243)

The narration continues, suggesting that Agrarianism was established out of Southern fear and failure: "its fear of conflict and of competition in the greater world; its inability to meet or to adjust itself to the conditions, strifes, and ardors of a modern life; its old, sick, Appomattoxlike retreat into the shades of folly and delusion, of prejudice and bigotry, of florid legend and defensive casuistry, of haughty and ironic detachment from a life with which it was too obviously concerned, to which it wished too obviously to belong" (243). The Agrarians, Webber comments, infiltrating the rhetoric of the Confederacy, were the "defeated ones."

Unlike Herbert Muller, who concludes in his 1947 study of Wolfe that *Of Time and the River* is inferior to *Look Homeward, Angel*, Richard S. Kennedy, in *The Window of Memory* (1962), argues that despite its structural difficulties, Wolfe's second novel represented an advance beyond the first novel. "However loose," he writes, "its grasp embraces more; however unsteady, its aim is loftier" (272). In addition, Kennedy concludes, the scope of the novel has widened from the purely autobiographical themes of *Look Homeward, Angel* to themes of the national consciousness.

By 1971, in his essay "Thomas Wolfe's Fiction: The Question of Genre," Kennedy could write about how in the second novel Wolfe was moving toward the solution of his problem of form. *Of Time and the River*, Kennedy writes, "was like nothing else that had ever appeared on the American literary scene – vast in scale, over 900 pages long, in scene ranging up and down the Atlantic coast of America and all over England and France, with more than a hundred characters passing before the observant eye of the narrator" (18). Although the work incorporates elements of both the epic and the *Bildungsroman*, it is neither. Unlike the epic, it drops down to realistic dialogue and satire; unlike the *Bildungsroman*, it reflects the national life. "What kind of work can we call it?" Kennedy asks, before launching into a remarkably detailed analysis of the first Book of *Of Time and the River*, in which Wolfe introduces the principal characters; makes clear the initial situation of Eugene's escape to the north; develops themes of wandering and the home, the yearning for the father, the hunger of youth, and the question of time and mortality; and sweeps the regional contrast in America, depicting regional politics, games, and dialog.

The mixture of genres in pages 1 through 86, Kennedy suggests, is even more remarkable. In less than one hundred pages, the author demonstrates his mastery of the novel, the essay, the choral ode, the descriptive travelogue, oratorical discourse, dramatic vignette, and cinematographic montage.

In attempting to define Wolfe's lyric fiction, Kennedy coins the phrase *fictional thesaurus*, which he defines as a "long literary work made up of short units in prose or verse in which the parts are joined together by association of ideas rather than by probable and necessary development . . . . It achieves unity by its association with the actions of a single character or a closely-related group of characters and . . . may rise to epic dignity by an elevation of style and by a heroic stylization of character" (29). Given this definition, Kennedy concludes, Wolfe's *Of Time and the River* need no longer suffer from its inability to be squeezed into the boxlike definition of the *novel* used by the critics. It can instead be grouped with works like Waldo Frank's *City Block,* Joyce's *Ulysses,* Dos Passos's *U.S.A.,* Cummings's *Eimi,* Huxley's *Ape and Essence,* Jean Toomer's *Cane,* Steinbeck's *Grapes of Wrath,* Whitman's *Song of Myself,* and Norman O. Brown's *Love's Body.*

As calculated as Kennedy's purposes were in defining the *fictional thesaurus,* thirty-five years have passed since he discussed that phrase at a University of Georgia symposium on Thomas Wolfe, and it has not yet caught on; and, of course, Kennedy never meant that it should. Kennedy's purpose in using the phrase was *exemplificative* not *definitive.* It was a dramatic demonstration meant to show that human beings arbitrarily create literary *terms,* which in the best of all possible worlds adequately enable them to communicate about and analyze literature, but in the real world are often taken to be evaluative. Kennedy's point, of which the concept *fictional thesaurus* is an excellent example, is an important one in the study of literature. Readers and critics, especially if they are unaware of the all-too-human source of literary definition and classification, tend to assume that the definitions of genres such as "lyric," "drama," and "novel" are immutable, especially if they appear in one of the standard dictionaries of literary terms. The designation of *genres,* which for practical purposes determines the fashion in which anthologists organize their texts and in which colleges and universities organize their literature courses, can then assume inappropriate power in literary study – generating reader *expectations* which can result in the critical and popular success or failure of a variety of literary works. The power of the literary term to *include* or *exclude* a literary work from the field of study on the basis of its conformity to the arbitrary tenets of its definition is, as Kennedy argues, a dangerous one.

As any phrase, including the phrase *the novel,* becomes entrenched in literary discussion over time, it comes not only to define but also to modify literary apprehension; it serves as a paradigm, focusing the reader's vision by opening the reader's perception to some element in the text, while at the same time denying the reader access to some other element of the text. Kennedy's suggestion that the structure of Wolfe's fiction is not understood because it fails to fit neatly into one of the little "boxes" of critical theory is an important one. It is derived from an understanding of the nature of language – that is, that language facilitates but also biases perception – and it responds to those earlier criticisms of Wolfe's works that charged his writings with being *formless* – on the basis of preconceived notions of what a novel *should be.* Literary terms are, however, only tools for textual analysis; when appropriately used, they *describe* the elements of literature in a way that fosters analysis; when they *prescribe* the elements of literature they tend to prematurely truncate discussion of new and innovative literary forms. Literary terminology thus, is almost inevitably *conservative*. It lags behind the narrative and structural innovations of new literary forms which cannot be adequately perceived through the lenses of terms contained in a *literary thesaurus* – which is inevitably a dictionary of definitions of what *has been* and not of what *is* or *will be*.

The comprehension of the literary craftsmanship of an author such as Thomas Wolfe, who, as Kennedy so successfully shows was highly innovative in his prose style and structure, will at first almost inevitably be negative (as Robert Penn Warren's and Bernard DeVoto's reviews were) because the available thesaurus of the critic does not yet include the terms necessary for adequately perceiving or discussing the manner in which his works function.

The sophistication of Kennedy's scholarship over the past three decades has been based largely on his success as a historical/biographical and textual critic, but in his study of Wolfe, Kennedy demonstrates an awareness of language that suggests his familiarity with the linguistic studies of the postwar generations. It also suggests his concern with the means by which literary *power* is generated in the 1990s. Tucked away in the innocuous little volume, Paschal Reeves's *Thomas Wolfe and the Glass of Time*, never reprinted (possibly because Wolfe critics were put off by Kennedy's use of the term *literary thesaurus*, which on the surface appears to be a bit naive), Kennedy's essay on genre remains one of the finest and most important defenses of Wolfe against those critics who charge that his work lacks form and structure.

Margaret Church in her 1963 essay "Dark Time," like Kennedy, responds to *Of Time and the River* as a more fully realized text than *Look Homeward, Angel*. *Of Time and the River* is a kind of time epic, she suggests, in which Wolfe inquires into the nature of time and its properties. Whereas in *Look Homeward, Angel* Wolfe's attitudes toward time seem to be influenced by James Joyce, in *Of Time and the River* the influence of Proust is more evident. Church develops her argument by comparing the famous Madeleine of Proust's *Remembrance of Things Past* to Wolfe's use of the watch that Ben gives Eugene on his twelfth birthday (*Of Time and the River* 52).

The significance of the title of the novel, she continues, becomes evident in light of a series of passages: the passage on page 510 in which Wolfe writes of "the moving tide of time as it flows down the river"; the passage on page 245 in which Wolfe likens life to "a river . . . fixed, unutterable in unceasing movement and in changeless change as the great river is, and time itself"; and the passage on page 492 in which Abe Jones's mother reflects upon seven thousand years as "yesterday, tomorrow, and forever, a moment at the heart of love and memory." The mythical section headings of the novel, obviously inspired by *Ulysses*, she surmises, are less indicative of the content of those sections than they are reminders that the author was aware of the recurrent nature of reality.

Leo Gurko's 1975 study of Wolfe, *Thomas Wolfe: Beyond the Romantic Ego*, like Church's discussion of time as a unifying element in the novel and like Kennedy's discussion of genre, makes several statements that shed significant light on *Of Time and the River*. Gurko argues that Wolfe's last three novels were never meant to be novels, "but murals" (80). They lack plot and continuity and defy outlining. "Unlike," he notes, "the intricately detailed, labyrinthine constructs of Henry James, they can easily be broken up into separate sections. It did not fundamentally matter where Max Perkins ordered *Of Time and the River* brought to a halt or on what basis Edward Aswell hacked out the texts of *The Web and the Rock* and *You Can't Go Home Again* after Wolfe's death. Almost any arrangement would have served since these works do not depend on structural arrangement in usual fictional terms" (80). Wolfe's novels, like Utrillo's Parisian street scenes, Gurko concludes, are not counterparts of literary romanticism, but counterparts of the expressionist works of authors such as Frank Wedekind, Stefan George, Ernst Toller, Elmer Rice, and John Dos Passos. Describing Dos Passos as "the guerrilla raider of letters" because of his displacement of character in his fiction in favor of "extrafictional" techniques borrowed from the movies, newspapers, history, art, and modern technology, Gurko describes Wolfe's writing as an analogous "disengagement" from conventional fiction.

Gurko continues:

> If read as a standard novel, *Of Time and the River* is a busted-up, every-which-way sort of book, quite awful. But it is quite wonderful if taken as a pursuit of the far perspective of time, as a thrilling first stage in which Wolfe is shucking off his original trappings and, snakelike, struggling to create a new skin . . . .
>
> In the grandiosity and bulk of this swelling ambition, Wolfe recalled the universe-swallowing Whitman, Eugene O'Neill with his unfinished eleven-play cycle . . . and naturalists like Theodore Dreiser with their compulsively documentary recording of every last detail . . . .
>
> *Of Time and the River* is not a finished piece of work. Its genius lies precisely in the fact that it is not finished, that in its deep internal division between the old form of narrative and the new it emerges as a book of strikingly separable sections, of gigantic fragments. Its interest is thus intensely dramatic. It is the salient crossroads, the great battleground of Wolfe's emerging art. (106–107)

Reversing the clichés of those critics of Wolfe's writing who continually referred to it in "GarGANTuan" terms, Kenneth Seib, in an intriguing 1978 essay, "Thomas Wolfe in Miniature," suggests that it is not "magnification" that is central to Wolfe's writing, but "miniaturization" (224). What most critics see to be Wolfe's stylistic excesses, Seib suggests, are "more accurately large metaphysical concepts miniaturized into insufficient tropes." In *Of Time and the River* this "miniaturization" occurs in Wolfe's incorporation of the Orestean myth into his fiction. In the first section of the novel, for instance, "Orestes: Flight Before Fury," Eugene is driven from his home town as in the *Oresteia* Orestes is driven by his personal furies. The parallels are even more obvious, however, to the depictions of Orestes in Aeschylus's *Eumenides*, for in *Of Time and the River* the railway station of Altamont represents Delphi, Eliza Gant represents the oracle, and Helen represents Clytemnestra. Wolfe's method, here again, Seib argues, involves "miniaturization, the reduction of Olympian legend to human proportion, and of tragic passion to melodramatic self-pity" (228). He continues:

> Wolfe, who is too often presented as an author unaware of what he is about, clearly intends a subtle parallel between past and present, legend and reality, Greek and modern culture. Delphi has been reduced to a small-town railroad station, the depot its temple; Mt. Olympus to an insignificant mountain range; and the tragic coming of the Furies to the arrival of a steam locomotive.... Genuine oracular mysteries of the Delphic priestess have become "Pentland spooky stuff" muttered by a wearisome old lady; the tragic utterances of Clytemnestra have become the whining complaints of a jealous sibling; the flight of Orestes has become the frenzied escape of a confused youth. (228)

Wolfe's satire, Seib suggests by referring to Northrup Frye's *Anatomy of Criticism* (234), exposes the ridiculous by showing us "society suddenly in a telescope as posturing and dignified pygmies, or in a microscope as hideous and reeking giants" (228).

In his "Thomas Wolfe and T. S. Eliot: The Hippopotamus and the Old Possum," which appeared in the Spring 1981 issue of *The Southern Literary Journal*, John Idol, Jr., provides an illuminating discussion focusing on Wolfe's berating of T. S. Eliot. Ironically, just as he was satirizing the Wastelanders ("the futility boys and girls, the stealthy lasses, the elegant mockers, the American T. S. Elioters") in a November 1930 letter to Alfred Dashiell (*Letters* 275), Wolfe also was attempting to mold his second novel, *Of Time and the River*, on the identical mythical method described by Eliot in his "*Ulysses*, Order and Myth," which appeared in the 1923 issue of *The Dial*. Although Wolfe ultimately failed to incorporate this mythical method into his writing of his second novel, he did not give up the names and the mythic relevance these names (Antæus, Faust, Helen, Telemachus, Jason, and Orestes) bore to Eugene Gant.

Idol sees in the "dry bones" passage of *Of Time and the River* (148–149) a reflection of the Wastelanders ideology in the defeatist attitude of Bascom Pentland. Later in the novel, Eugene describes the young Rhodes Scholar Sterling, whom he encounters in the room of his friend Johnny Park, as "a virtual Prufrock." Sterling, he notes, was

> a most precious, a most subtle, elegantly sad, quietly bitter and disdainful fellow: he was quietly, subtly a devoted follower of Mr. T. S. Eliot . . . .
>
> He wore about him always this air of elegant, cold, and slightly disdainful restraint, and he had the habit of looking across his thin arched hands with a faint disdainful smile, and listening coldly, saying nothing, while the others talked, as if the waste-land chatter of their tongues, the waste-land vacancy of their lost waste-land souls was something that he knew he must endure . . . . (*Of Time and the River* 630–631)

Wolfe's list of American rivers (*Of Time and the River* 868 – 869), Idol suggests, is a parody of Parts I and IV of *The Waste Land*, as is his narrative of the death of a Greek lunchroom operator who had drowned in the July 1916 flooding of the French Broad River in Asheville. From here, Idol notes, Wolfe plunged headlong into the criticism of Eliot, which would be more fully developed in *You Can't Go Home Again* (especially in the chapter titled "The Hollow Men").

Richard S. Kennedy's 1983 collection of papers which had been presented at the third annual meeting of the Thomas Wolfe Society at Harvard University in Cambridge, Massachusetts, *Thomas Wolfe: A Harvard Perspective*, contains two essential discussions of Wolfe's *Of Time and the River*: John Hagan's "Thomas Wolfe's *Of Time and the River*: The Quest for Transcendence" and Klaus Lanzinger's "Thomas Wolfe's Modern Hero: Goethe's Faust."

Hagan argues that by the 1980s critics had come to largely ignore *Of Time and the River*. Wolfe's reputation, he suggests, had come to rest almost exclusively on *Look Homeward, Angel*. Although the critical preference for Wolfe's first novel over his second is to some extent a result of shifting taste and academic fashion, its deeper cause is the critical attacks made on its "formlessness." Hagan, on the other hand, sees *Of Time and the River* as structured on four overlapping quests: 1) the quest for *adventure*, motivated by a "Faustian" desire to race against death (Hagan sees *time* and *change* as the *enemies* confronted by Eugene Gant in Wolfe's second novel); 2) the quest for *knowledge* in books that will enable Eugene to overcome time and death by providing him with the "answer to the riddle of this vast and swarming earth" (*Of Time and the River* 137); 3) the quest for *security*, for the lost paradise of his youth; and 4) the quest for *art*, which Hagan suggests becomes Eugene's "surrogate religion" (10–11).

The significance of the novel, Hagan continues, resides in three crucial discoveries that Eugene makes about *art*. The first of these is that there is no *ideal* place to write, the "place to write" is anywhere – as long as the artist has the stuff of his art *inside* him. The second discovery is that the subject matter of art is not found in *fantasy* or *romance*, but in drawing heavily upon memory. Finally, the third and last discovery leading to his maturation as an artist comes when he recognizes that art alone can overcome time and death. During his reading of his play to Joel and Rosalind, Eugene comes to recognize in "one blaze of light" the reason why the artist works and lives and has his being – the reward he seeks – the only reward he really cares about, without which there is nothing . . . is to snare the spirits of mankind in nets of magic . . . . that from life's clay and his own nature, and from his father's common earth of toil and sweat and violence and error and bitter anguish, he may distill the beauty of an everlasting form, enslave and conquer man by his enchantment, cast his spell across the generations, beat death down upon his knees, kill death utterly, and fix eternity with the grappling-hooks of his own art . . . .

> He is at once life's monstrous outcast and life's beauty-drunken lover, man's bloody, ruthless, pitiless and utterly relentless enemy, and the best friend that mankind ever had . . . . (*Of Time and the River* 550–551)

As the novel ends, Eugene finds the central subject of his art, like Whitman's, to be America and the life he has lived there. This begins, Hagan notes, a series of creative outbursts that moves Eugene closer to achieving his task of producing a work of art that will impart a "radiant immortality" to his past ("Thomas Wolfe's *Of Time and the River*: The Quest for Transcendence" 18).

Klaus Lanzinger's treatment of the "Faustian" element in Wolfe's second novel is both historical and thematic. Lanzinger finds the key to Wolfe's understanding of Faust as a modern hero in a performance of Goethe's *Faust* that Wolfe attended on 25 November 1928 in Vienna. Wolfe, Lanzinger argues, was tormented by the Faustean predicament, the desire to know and experience everything on earth. The last chapter of Book II of *Of Time and the River*, "Young Faustus," Lanzinger notes, is an adaptation of the *Osterpaziergang* (Easter Sunday Walk) in *Faust*. As Eugene and Starwick stroll along the banks of the Charles River on their Sunday walk, their relationship takes on the characteristics of the relationship between Faust and Mephistopheles. Eugene and Starwick meet Ed and Effie Horton, and Starwick points out to Eugene that Horton's father still writes his son "begging him to repent and mend his ways before his soul is damned forever." The warning given to Eugene, is that he may risk losing his soul if he does not resist the Bohemian enticements of the artist's life. The entire Paris section of the novel, Lanzinger concludes, is

Wolfe's version of the "Walpurgisnacht" in *Faust*. Once again the relationship between Starwick and Eugene parallels that of Mephistopheles and Faust. Starwick tries to divert Eugene from his work, just as Mephistopheles tries to lure Faust into inertia. As Faust turns from Mephistopheles in disgust in the scene "Trüber Tag.Feld," so Eugene physically attacks Starwick at the end of the Paris section, ridding himself of his "seducer, tempter and tormentor" ("Thomas Wolfe's Modern Hero" 28).

Another of Perkins's authors, Marjorie Kinnan Rawlings, recognized the importance of the artistic *angst* in Wolfe's creative process, as John Idol successfully demonstrates in his 1988 essay, "Thomas Wolfe and Marjorie Kinnan Rawlings." Even though Rawlings envied Wolfe the attention their editor, Max Perkins, paid to his writing, she admitted that her reading of *Of Time and the River* had been painful and emotional. Later, when she read Wolfe's account of how he had wrestled with the novel, Rawlings recognized a kindred spirit. She wrote Perkins,

> Wolfe's "Story of a Novel" is unbearable. I have just finished it. It's unbearable – its honesty, – its fierceness, – its beauty of expression. And for another writer –
> There is no damnation for such a man. Don't be concerned – I know you are not – that he goes "completely off the reservation." He is his own torment and strength.
> He is so young! When a little of the torment has expended itself, you will have the greatest artist America has ever produced.[3]

But, of course, finally Wolfe did not have the time to *expend* his artistic *angst*.

In 1938, Wolfe traveled west and rented an apartment in Seattle, where he planned to settle for several months. After a brief trip to Vancouver, he developed pneumonia, and that illness led to complications. When his condition became increasingly serious, he was transferred from Providence Hospital in Seattle by train to Johns Hopkins Hospital in Baltimore. Exploratory surgery showed that he had tuberculosis of the brain, and Wolfe died in Baltimore only a few short weeks before his thirty-eighth birthday. In his will, he named Maxwell Perkins, from whose editorial advice he had fled following DeVoto's publication of the infamous review "Genius Is Not Enough," the executor of his estate. His manu-

---

[3]Selected Letters of Marjorie Kinnan Rawlings, ed. Gordon Bigelow and Laura V. Monti (Gainesville: U Presses of Florida, 1983), pp. 107–108.

scripts were held, however, not by Perkins, but by Wolfe's editor at Harper's, Edward Aswell. Between them, they carved the two posthumous novels, *The Web and the Rock* and *You Can't Go Home Again*, out of the manuscript material that Wolfe left at the time of his death.

6: The Posthumous Novels

RESPONDING TO RICHARD S. Kennedy's suggestion that Wolfe's fiction be labeled a *fictional thesaurus*, C. Hugh Holman suggested that a better and more descriptive classification would be *fictional anthology* (*The Loneliness at the Core* 81). It is probably best – considering the means by which Wolfe's posthumous novels were carved from the million-or-so-word manuscript that Wolfe left at Harper's with his editor, Edward C. Aswell, before Wolfe's fatal trip west – to apply that label to Wolfe's *The Web and the Rock* and *You Can't Go Home Again*. The sequences and basic structures of the novels are almost inevitably Wolfe's, but the "connective tissue" between sequences and the arrangements of the sequences are largely Aswell's. Taken as *novels*, *The Web and the Rock* and *You Can't Go Home Again* are hybrids. Because they are the product of not only the author's intent, but also the intent of his editor (more blatantly than either *Look Homeward, Angel* or *Of Time and the River*), they tend to be more uneven, less rhetorical, more sequential, and somewhat more simplistic than the earlier novels. Taken as *fictional anthologies*, however, these books contain some of Wolfe's strongest writing.

Although *The Web and the Rock* is close to seven hundred pages long, nearly every critic reviewing that novel spends a few lines discussing a small four-paragraph segment of that work, the "Author's Note" prefacing the volume. The note, supposedly a statement about Wolfe's purpose in writing his last manuscript, is dated May 1938; it indicates that Wolfe believed himself to be turning away from the introspective themes that had dominated his earlier work. It reads:

> This novel is about one man's discovery of life and of the world – discovery not in a sudden and explosive sense as when "a new planet swims into his ken," but discovery through a process of finding out, and finding out as a man has to find out, through error and through trial, through fantasy and illusion, through falsehood and his own foolishness, through being mistaken and wrong and an idiot and egotistical and aspiring and hopeful and believing and confused, and pretty much what every one of us is, and goes through, and finds out about, and becomes.
>
> I hope that the protagonist will illustrate in his own experience every one of us – not merely the sensitive young fellow in conflict with his town, his family, the little world around him; not merely the sensitive young fellow in love, and so concerned with his little universe of love that he thinks it is the whole universe – but all of these things and much

more. These things, while important, are subordinate to the plan of the book; being young and in love and in the city are only a part of the whole adventure of apprenticeship and discovery.

This novel, then, marks not only a turning away from the books I have written in the past, but a genuine spiritual and artistic change. It is the most objective novel that I have written. I have invented characters who are compacted from the whole amalgam and consonance of seeing, feeling, thinking, living, and knowing many people. I have sought, through free creation, a release of my inventive power.

Finally, the novel has in it, from first to last, a strong element of satiric exaggeration: not only because it belongs to the nature of the story — "the innocent man" discovering life — but because satiric exaggeration also belongs to the nature of life, and particularly American life. (v)

As most of the reviewers of *The Web and the Rock* recognized, there was no "turning away" in his third novel from the stance taken by Wolfe in his earlier novels. Except for a few physical changes, even Wolfe's protagonist George Webber was a clone of Eugene Gant, and both seemed to be merely fictional surrogates for Wolfe himself. How could Wolfe have been so wrong about his own work? Was DeVoto right in suggesting that Wolfe could only write novels based on the "placental" nature of his own youth? The answers lie in our understanding of the sequence of events just preceding and following Wolfe's death, leading to the publication of his third novel. Wolfe *had* written the paragraphs contained in the "Author's Note" — but in a dramatically different form and context than Aswell and Harpers suggested. In them he was referring to the entirety of the manuscript left at his death, which incorporated text that would later become *You Can't Go Home Again* as well as *The Web and the Rock*.

Less than two weeks before his trip, Wolfe wrote Aswell describing the state of the manuscript. It was, Wolfe indicated, in about the same "state of articulation" that *Of Time and the River* had been in December 1933, when Perkins first saw it. It had taken almost a full year more for Wolfe and Perkins to ready that book for publication; and it is implicit in Wolfe's letter that he believes it will take a similar amount of time to get the new manuscript into a publishable state (*Letters* 758). When Wolfe headed west in May 1938, he left a wooden crate full of his manuscripts in the offices of Harpers. After Wolfe's death in September 1938, however, it was up to Aswell to make the practical decisions about the manuscript material, arranging, cutting, and adding to the manuscript to salvage something for publication. Harpers recouped whatever losses Aswell feared it might sustain (specifically, the unauthorized ten thousand-dollar advance that Aswell had given Wolfe when he signed with Harpers) when the two novels salvaged by Aswell, *The Web and the Rock* and

You Can't Go Home Again, appeared in print in June 1939 and September 1940, respectively. But when these novels appeared, Aswell and Harpers were less than forthright about the conditions under which the manuscript had been prepared. They insisted in a "Publisher's Note" appearing on the verso opposite the copyright page of *The Web and the Rock* that Wolfe had completed both novels and delivered them to his publishers a "few months" before his untimely death.

Both the "Publisher's Note" and "The Author's Note" appearing in *The Web and the Rock* are misleading. The "Author's Note" (supposedly written by Wolfe in May 1938), printed on the recto following the copyright page in *The Web and the Rock*, was actually the third of a series of avatars of a 14 February 1938 letter to Aswell written by but never posted by Wolfe. The first and second versions of this document appeared in Nowell's *Letters* and in the Marxist journal *The Daily Worker*, respectively. The letter was originally discovered by Elizabeth Nowell among Wolfe's papers after his death. She passed it on to Aswell, but also chose to print it on pages 710 through 719 of her collection of Wolfe's letters. The document closest to Wolfe's intent is clearly the one printed in *The Letters of Thomas Wolfe*, but the earliest version to appear in print is the excerpt from this letter printed on 15 May 1939 in the New York *Daily Worker*. As it appears in *The Daily Worker*, the letter is titled "An American Author's Testament: Unpublished Letter of the Late Thomas Wolfe Reveals a Changed Outlook." In Nowell's *Letters*, the document is over thirty paragraphs long, leading into a synopsis of Wolfe's book; in *The Daily Worker*, it is thirteen paragraphs long (there is no statement in either the "Author's Note" version or *The Daily Worker* version indicating that the text is an excerpt); in the "Author's Note" to *The Web and the Rock*, it is four paragraphs long. The brief editorialized introduction to *The Daily Worker* printing reads:

> The promise of maturing literary genius was stopped short by the death of Thomas Wolfe a year ago at the age of 37. The author of "Look Homeward, Angel" and "Of Time and the River" has been hailed as one of the greatest literary figures America has produced.
>
> The Daily Worker presents today an important document. It is a letter which Wolfe sent to one of the editors of Harper Brothers, his publishers, shortly before his death. Here Wolfe speaks of the significance of the million-word manuscript which he left behind him and which Harper will publish soon as two volumes, "The Web and the Rock" and "You Can't Go Home Again."
>
> Chief importance in the letter is that it reveals his awakening social consciousness before his untimely death.

The long list of things to which the young author feels he cannot go back further defines that "social consciousness": "The whole book might almost be called 'You Can't Go Home Again' – which means back home to one's family, back home to one's childhood, back home to the father one has lost, back home to romantic love, to a young man's dreams of glory and of fame, back home to exile, to escape to 'Europe' and some foreign land, back home to lyricism, singing just for singing's sake, back home to aestheticism, to one's youthful ideas of the 'artist,' . . . back home to the escapes of Time and Memory."

Each of the three incarnations of this document demonstrates that Wolfe saw the writing of his last manuscript as a pivotal point in his development as a writer; his protagonists would no longer function as subjective Romantic heroes, but as objective instruments by which the events of life would be ordered and explored. By comparing the three versions of this document, however, several points in the discussion of the publication of Wolfe's posthumously published novels become clear: 1) that Aswell could, when he chose to, play fairly loose and free with Wolfe's texts – even to the point of altering the dates of documents if he felt that was necessary; 2) that Aswell perceived Wolfe's posthumous novels not only to represent the mature work of that author and his developing "social consciousness" but to represent a movement in his writing toward a broader and more liberal philosophy (based on a recognition of the need for social change) which he felt would appeal to a Marxist audience; and 3) that by publishing "An American Author's Testament" in *The Daily Worker*, Aswell was actively attempting to frame what he believed *should be* the response of the Marxist critics to these novels. Each of these elements would be addressed by Wolfe's reviewers and critics as they struggled to make sense of the last two of Wolfe's novels.

The American Reviews

The sentiments expressed by Wolfe in his 14 February 1938 letter to Aswell more accurately described the "socially conscious" stance he took in *You Can't Go Home Again* than it did the "quasi-autobiographical approach" of *The Web and the Rock*. Had Aswell been a little more experienced as an editor, he might have recognized that using this note as a preface to *The Web and the Rock*, a novel which did not *really* reflect any major change in Wolfe's approach to the writing of fiction, would open up a can of *critical* worms. The "Author's Note" did (as Aswell hoped) provide reviewers with a framework for perceiving *The Web and the Rock*, but that framework was a negative one – one that by contrasting what appeared to be Wolfe's intent (to write "socially conscious" fiction) with his "autobiographical" text led reviewers to believe that he was limited in the scope of his writing – unable to produce work in more than a single key.

The speed with which Harpers retreated from this position is documented in that firm's advertising campaign for *The Web and the Rock*. The first major blurb for the book appears in the 25 June 1939 issue of *The New York Times Book Review*. It reads:

> Only superlatives can describe this magnificent novel, which Thomas Wolfe completed before his untimely death. Its love story is one of the most tempestuous and moving in literature. Its writing its passion and its poetry rank it with the best and truest that Wolfe has written – but with a new candor, a more realistic and more revealing attitude toward life. (13)

Within days of its publication the book reached the best-sellers lists. Despite a large first printing of over thirty thousand copies (twenty thousand more than the first printing of *Of Time and the River*), there was still a call for three more printings in the month of June alone. As overwhelming as its popular reception was, its critical reception was disappointing; and, all of the succeeding advertisements appearing in *The New York Times Book Review* (9 July 1939, 16 July 1939, 23 July 1939, 30 July 1939, 6 August 1939, 13 August 1939, and 27 August 1939) focused on the power of Wolfe's prose style, quoting Clifton Fadiman, Burton Rascoe, George Stevens, and J. Donald Adams. None of these advertisements repeated the assertion made in the 25 June 1939 advertisement that Wolfe had written *The Web and the Rock* "with a more realistic and more revealing attitude toward life."

Of the fifty reviews of this novel located, no more than one or two fail to refer to or quote from what the critics were led by Aswell and Harpers to believe was an "Author's Note" specifically written by Wolfe for insertion at the beginning of his third novel. Most of the critics, even those favorably reviewing the novel, make a point of focusing on Wolfe's failure to fulfill the intent expressed in the "Author's Note" in *The Web and the Rock*. A series of the most significant reviews of *The Web and the Rock* suggest the disappointment the critics felt in Wolfe's inability to live up to what they had been led by Aswell and Harpers to perceive to be his authorial intent.

Paul Fisher, writing in the *Kansas City Star*, calls *The Web and the Rock* the "most disappointing book Wolfe ever wrote." After quoting from the "Author's Note" he asks, "How has he turned away?" Concluding his review, Fisher comments on Wolfe, "So much was expected from him and he accomplished so much. But in 'The Web and the Rock' he has repeated himself, whether tragically we may tell when his final novel is published next fall" ("Wolfe's Last Look Homeward"). Clifton Fadiman, writing in *The New Yorker* on 24 June, also began his review by quoting several lines from the "Author's Note." Writing about the strong resemblance between Monk Webber, his creator, Thomas Wolfe, and that author's earlier protagonist, Eugene Gant, Fadiman concludes that the novel did not mark the "spiritual" or "artistic" change in Wolfe's writing that readers had hoped for. It is, he argues, "simply more of the same Wolfe" (69). Writing in the *Buffalo Evening News*, a reviewer with the initials R. E. M. echoes Fisher and Fadiman. "The Wolfe of 'The Web and the Rock,'" he writes, "is not different from the Wolfe of 'Of Time and the River' or of 'Look Homeward, Angel.'" And George Stevens in *The Saturday Review of Literature* referred to the question of objectivity in the novel promised in the "Author's Note" as a "red herring." "'The Web and the Rock,'" he continues, "is Wolfe exactly as we have known him since 'Look Homeward, Angel' was published in 1929; it represents no positive development of his ability," though it does reveal the power and intensity of his talents. Stevens makes an interesting supposition, suggesting that had *The Web and the Rock* been published as two separate novels, the first half would have been Wolfe's best novel and the second half his most disappointing. Meanwhile, Charles Angoff, in *The North American Review*, in a review that confused Wolfe's brother Ben with Faulkner's Benjy Compson, reported that Wolfe "neither progressed not retrogressed. After fifteen years of writing he remained almost exactly where he started from: a perennial adolescent emotionally and intellectually, extremely shaky in his feeling for words and even more so in the matter of form."

Two of the most important reviews of the novel, the J. Donald Adams review appearing in the 25 June issue of *The New York Times Book Review* and Malcolm Cowley's "Thomas Wolfe's Legacy" published in the 19 July 1939 issue of *The New Republic* also seem to pivot on the misleading "Author's Note." Subtitling his review, "'The Web and the Rock' Is, Like its Predecessors, Autobiographical," Adams writes, "If Wolfe believed what he wrote, and there is no reason to think that he did not, he deceived himself." He concludes his essay by arguing that the novel is a real disappointment: it shows Wolfe "as distant as ever from that selectivity which a mature art must practice." Cowley, calling the novel "the weakest" of Wolfe's works, still praises the stories of Baxter Lampley, the butcher's son; Jim Randolph, the football hero who never got over it; Dick Prosser, the Negro who ran amok; Seamus Malone; and Esther Jack – before devoting half a column of print to the worst passages in the book. He concludes his list with Wolfe's description of Esther:

The sight of her face, earnestly bent and focused in its work of love, her sure and subtle movements, and her full, lovely figure – all that was at once both delicate and abundant in her, together with the maddening fragrance of glorious food, evoked an emotion of wild tenderness and hunger in him which was unutterable. (*The Web and the Rock* 444)

Cowley concludes by suggesting that even though Wolfe's editors have worked with care to produce *The Web and the Rock*, he doubts that they have done the best that they could have for Wolfe's posthumous career. In retrospect, it is clear that despite its good intentions, Harpers bungled the publication of Wolfe's third novel.

Only Charles Lee, in a review titled "Thomas Wolfe in Tempestuous Novel About Art, Love, and Genius" printed in the 24 June 1939 issue of *The Boston Herald*, questioned whether it was really all that important to have a *new* Wolfe when the *old* Wolfe was so good. He writes:

Such a revolution cannot now be, and doubtless never would have been. It is to be questioned whether he could have whipped his charging, rolling, tumblingly rapturous prose into anything like orthodoxy, and, on reflection, though I think the blue-pencil might effectively have been used on incidents, I would rather have Wolfe Wolfe than anything else when it comes to style.

Another issue that concerned the critics reviewing *The Web and the Rock* was the subjective element in the novel, the lack of definable distance between the author, Thomas Wolfe, and his protagonist George Webber. Critics had been making this charge against Wolfe since the appearance of his first novel in 1929. However, by 1939 several of the reviewers were redefining this issue, noting that Wolfe, as author, intruded in the text in a way that provided readers with an additional character who challenged George Webber's position as the hero of the text. Allen W. Porterfield, reviewing the novel on 22 June in the *New York Sun,* writes that although the novel is the most heavily "padded" that he has ever read, even the padding is interesting. "There are," he continues, "a few long sentences but not an involved, uninteresting, or obscure one in the whole three hundred thousand words." However, as his review continues it becomes more negative. "It requires unquestioned genius," he concludes, "to move an ugly case up into the family of belles lettres, and do it in such a way that every sentence points to the fertile difference between the weakness of the characters created and the strength of the man who created them."

The tendency of the narrator to assume the heroic proportions in the novel which should have been assumed by his protagonist was also noted by Mary-Carter Roberts in the *Washington Sunday Star* in a 25 June 1939 review titled "Writer and Hero Merge in 'Discovery of Life.'" "Mr. Wolfe," she writes, "takes the stage himself much oftener than the young man about whom he is ostensibly writing a book . . . . The final effect is as of a pallid and perfunctory play presented in a number of scenes, after every one of which a violent picturesque knave of a scene shifter curvets out upon the uncurtained stage and whoops and shouts . . . . The scene shifter would be Mr. Wolfe, the actor his hero, and there simply is not room for both of them in this book."

Other critics focused their attention on the raw satire and parody in the novel. One of the earliest reviews of *The Web and the Rock*, Charles Poore's discussion of the novel appearing in the 22 June 1939 *New York Times*, noted that one of the most common critical responses to Wolfe's writing (the charge that his work was autobiographical) was answered by Wolfe in his satiric depiction of the eccentric publishing firm, Rawng and Wright (alias Boni & Liveright) parodied in chapters 32 and 34 of *The Web and the Rock*. Boni and Liveright had rejected Wolfe's *Look Homeward, Angel* just as Rawng and Wright (which Wolfe depicts as being notable for never actually reading a manuscript) reject George Webber's *The End of the Golden Weather*. In chapter 32 of the novel, "The Philanthropists," the firm is pictured as misrepresenting its philanthropic interest in new writers. Mr. Hyman Rawng chortles that he cares nothing for money, labeling one young author an ingrate for requesting his share of the royalties for his book. Magnanimously, Rawng wipes away the young writer's debt to the publishing firm, but not before they argue at length – the young writer claiming his royalties, the cagey old publisher claiming that it has all been used up in the advance. Wolfe finishes the chapter with a ringing parody of Joyce Kilmer's "Trees":

> Poems are made by fools who write,
> And books are published by Rawng and Wright;
>
> Poems are made by flame and song,
> But God knows who made Wright and Rawng!
>
> Whenever I see the two of them
> I'm glad there are so few of them.
>
> Whenever Rawng doth to me nod,
> I'd rather be Wright than Rawng, by God!
>
> Until Wright comes, and I see light
> And know I'd rather be Rawng than Wright! (496)

James N. Wright's dull-witted letter rejecting Webber's novel is printed in the thirty-fourth chapter of the *The Web and the Rock*, "Glory Deferred." Even though these publishers have not read the manuscript (they claim to be able to smell publishable material from yards away), Rawng and Wright reject the novel because it is "autobiographical" in the way that all first books by young men are. "We published at least a half dozen books just like this last year," Wright writes, "and lost money on all of them, we don't see how we could risk money on your book, particularly since the writing is so unskillful, amateurish, and repetitive" (514).

Later in the novel, in a thinly disguised parody of the Irish critic Ernest Boyd, Wolfe depicts the "remarkable" Seamus Malone. Bitter because his talents have been overlooked by a "moronic populace," Malone launches into an envenomed diatribe attacking the writings of Sinclair Lewis, T. S. Eliot, Thornton Wilder, Theodore Dreiser, Edna St. Vincent Millay, Edwin Arlington Robinson, Elinor Wylie, Sherwood Anderson, Carl Sandburg, Edgar Lee Masters, Ring Lardner, Ernest Hemingway, Robert Frost, Eugene O'Neill, Robinson Jeffers, Ellen Glasgow, Julia Peterkin, Willa Cather and F. Scott Fitzgerald, "the Kansas Tolstois, the Tennessee Chekhovs, the Dakota Dostoevskis, and the Idaho Ibsens," before he can utter a single kind word to George Webber about his novel (528–536).

Like Poore, Arthur Rhodes, writing in the *Brooklyn Eagle*, and Charles Lee, writing in the *Boston Herald*, praise Wolfe's satiric depictions of Rawng and Wright and Seamus Malone. Rhodes calls the novel, "the greatest thing Wolfe has left for posterity" ("Stormy Struggle for Life's Secret"); Lee suggests that the humor in the novel is "worthy of Dickens," the prose style worthy of Whitman, and the satire comparable to that of Edgar Lee Masters ("Thomas Wolfe in Tempestuous Novel"). The reviewer for *The Saturday Review of Literature*, George Stevens, however, refers to the "elephantine satire on literary life in the twenties" as embarrassingly bad ("Always Looking Homeward").

Perhaps the most touching of all of the reviews was the one written by Burton Rascoe appearing in the 26 June 1939 issue of *Newsweek*. Wolfe, he writes, "left a monument to truth about human beings." "I am too humble to express anything except to doff my hat and kneel and pray God his soul will rest peacefully," Rascoe concludes, "because his books have given me nourishment of the heart and mind." Similarly, Fanny Butcher writes in her 24 June 1939 review in *The Chicago Daily Tribune*:

> There will be – there already are – many readers who cannot give themselves to the slow, heavy rhythm of Thomas Wolfe's method. They will find "The Web and the Rock" too turgid. Others will feel, almost from its beginning, the impressive thoroughness, the ponderous strength of Thomas Wolfe's genius. However, few, and those only Wolfe devotees, will find the book living up to Mr. Wolfe's hero's avowed dream of a book which "in the end, as the strands increased, extended, wove, and crossed, would take on the denseness and complexity of the whole web of life and of America."

Meanwhile, May Cameron in the 22 June issue of the *New York Post* urged her readers to run, not walk, to their local bookstores to purchase a copy.

The unfortunate, premature use of the material in the "Author's Note" biased a number of the reviewers who found it difficult to praise Wolfe's prose style when he, himself, seemed to be so blind to what he was doing. The critical perception nurtured by the "Author's Note" in *The Web and the Rock* — that Wolfe was incapable of writing anything other than auto-biographical fiction — was, however, misleading. In writing his manu-script, Wolfe did experience a change in his sense of what he should be doing as a writer; but this change was evident in the material that Aswell used to develop *You Can't Go Home Again*, which was not published until September 1940. This sense of a broadening perspective in Wolfe's fiction is best expressed in what is now frequently referred to as Wolfe's Purdue Speech, "Writing and Living." This speech was delivered at Purdue University's annual Literary Awards banquet. However, it is clear that as Wolfe prepared his speech, he was thinking less about his Purdue presen-tation than about the conclusion of the lengthy manuscript on which he was working. He wrote Elizabeth Nowell on 3 May 1938:

> For months now, it has occurred to me that I would conclude the tre-mendously long book on which I am working with a kind of epilogue that takes the form of personal address — to be called, "You Can't Go Home Again" or "A Farewell to the Fox," or perhaps by still another ti-tle. That epilogue, as I have conceived it, would be a kind of impas-sioned summing up of the whole book, of everything that has gone before, and a final statement of what is now . . . . Anyway, that is what I am doing now: transforming the material for the simple Purdue state-ment into the terms of poetic and imaginative fact — into the truth of fic-tion — because it seems to me that is really my essential job. (*Letters* 751)

Wolfe spoke off the cuff at Purdue and did not use the manuscript — al-though reports suggest that what he did say followed fairly closely along the lines of that manuscript. After his death, when Elizabeth Nowell was collecting material for his biography, she found the typescript of the speech, parts of which Wolfe had removed and worked into the manu-script of *You Can't Go Home Again*. Edited by William Braswell and Leslie A. Field and published in 1964 as *Thomas Wolfe's Purdue Speech: "Writing and Living,"* the document is essentially Wolfe's last statement about the pivotal change in his attitude toward life and writing that he believed would be evident once the unfinished manuscript material stored at Harpers was published.

Because in *The Story of a Novel* he had focused on the process by which artists create their work, Wolfe chose to focus his Purdue speech on what he referred to as "shop" talk, that is, on the nuts-and-bolts process by which writers craft their careers. His intention seems to be to compare the work he accomplished in his "shop" at the Chelsea Hotel in New York to that produced in his father's stonecutting shop in Asheville. This discussion may have been generated by his letter to Margaret Roberts in which he discussed his "working-class" background (*Letters* 520) or by his recognition that his mother was incapable of perceiving that his writing was "real work," or perhaps by a combination of both. In describing his work as a writer, he talks about going through progressive stages of development: the stage of aesthetic preciosity in which he talks about "beauty" and "art"; the stage of accomplishment in which he first publishes a book; and the stage of social consciousness that he suggests began early in May 1930, when he went abroad to Europe (*Thomas Wolfe's Purdue Speech* 46–54). There, although fame had made the "world his oyster," something happened for which he had been unprepared:

> Too much gray weather had soaked through into my soul, and I could not forget. The memory of unrecorded days, the renaissance of brutal weathers, the excavation of the jungle trails – it all came back to me again insensibly, soaked through the shining brightness of that air, came through the latches of those clacking tongues, forced through at last its grim imponderable into the contours of those shining surfaces, the sense of buried meanings which not even May and magic and the Kurfurstendamm could help.
>
> Sometimes it came to me with a desperate pleading of an eye, and the naked terror of a sudden look . . . . Sometimes it just came and went as light comes, just soaked in, just soaked in – words, speech and action, and finally in the mid-watches of the night, behind thick walls and bolted doors and shuttered windows, the confession of unutterable despair, the corruption of man's living faith . . . .
>
> And then day would come again, the cool glow of morning red . . . but none of it was the same as it had been before. For I had become aware of something else in life, as new as morning, and as old as Hell . . . . (*Thomas Wolfe's Purdue Speech* 114–115).

Much of this speech is worked into pages 708 to 730 of *You Can't Go Home Again*, in which Wolfe/Webber continues to describe what he sees to be the pivotal distinction between the subject matter of the first two novels, *Look Homeward, Angel* and *Of Time and the River*, and the manuscript on which Wolfe was working at that time.

> . . . I began to be conscious of the submerged and forgotten Helots down below, who with their toil and sweat and blood and suffering unutterable supported and nourished the mighty princelings at the top.
>
> Then came the cataclysm of 1929 . . . . Through those years I was living in the jungle depths of Brooklyn, and I saw as I had never seen

before the true and terrifying visage of the disinherited of life ... of man's inhumanity to man, and as time went on it began to blot out the more personal and self-centered vision of the world which a young man always has .... I was coming more and more to feel an intense and passionate concern for the interests and designs of my fellow men and of all humanity. (*You Can't Go Home Again* 724–725)

The critics, who *did* find Wolfe "turning away" from the subjectivity of his earlier work in *You Can't Go Home Again* were far more positive in their reviews of Wolfe's last novel than they had been in reviewing his third novel. Claude Simpson writing in the Autumn 1940 issue of the *Southwest Review* commented that "The seemingly ill-advised preface to *The Web and the Rock*, if applied to the entire sweep of the two novels, is not so wide of the mark." Although the Wolfe of *You Can't Go Home Again* is not a new Wolfe, Simpson argues, he is a more mature Wolfe. Referring to two of the more successful sections of the text, the revision of "I Have a Thing to Tell You" and "The Party at Jack's," Simpson calls the first one of the most successful sections of the book and the second both "tedious" and "flatulent." Fanny Butcher more eloquently expressed her attitude toward the novel in an 18 September 1940 review appearing in the *Chicago Tribune. You Can't Go Home Again*, she writes, "is an authentic work of art .... A great book vivifies its readers as inevitably as a flaming match ignites dead wood. Such a book is 'You Can't Go Home Again,' and thousands of readers who will never be able to tell you why it is great will know that they have met greatness within its cover." Writing in *The New York Mirror*, Charles Wagner's praise echoed Butcher's. "Thousands" of Wolfe's readers, he argues, will be fed by the novel "a surfeit beyond anything they have read for years ... even ... 'The Grapes of Wrath.'" The full-length page-one review of the novel written by J. Donald Adams and appearing in the 22 September 1940 issue of *The New York Times Book Review* summarizes the sentiments of most of the critics: "Thomas Wolfe's Last Novel," the title reads, " ... Is a Work of Mature Power."

Writing in *The Saturday Review of Literature* that same month, Stephen Vincent Benét was among the first to define Wolfe's relationship to his critics. The critics, he notes, were always asking Wolfe to "stand off from himself, be more objective, tame and order the extravagances of his power." It was, Benét notes, the kind of criticism good for nine writers out of ten, but not for Wolfe: Wolfe had to write as he wrote. With its discussion of Webber's relationship to an older woman and his disenchantment with fame, the novel, Benét notes, sounds like a study in disillusionment – but is not. Although it contains some heavy-handed satire on literary life in New York (notably in the chapter, "The Party at Jack's"), it is "written with all Wolfe's furious energy, with his devouring

zest for all sorts of different human beings, with his amazing gift for suck-
ing the very last drop of juice out of a character or a scene." Milton
Rugoff, writing in *The New York Herald Tribune Books* for 22 September
1940 also depicts "The Party at Jack's" as one of the most remarkable
scenes in Wolfe. "It is an extravaganza," Rugoff writes, "grotesque and
satiric, pointing up the thin line which divides secure power from chaos,
doubly symbolic in that the only ones who suffer in the end are two ele-
vator men who die, like slaves, in their cages." Rugoff hits on a telling
truth about Wolfe's writing in the final paragraph of his review. He
writes:

> The weaknesses of "You Can't Go Home Again," as of all of Wolfe's
> books, are, so to speak, functions of its virtues. On the one hand its
> power and on the other its excesses both stem from his unexampled
> exuberance, his floodlike richness, his epic intentions . . . . whatever the
> weaknesses in this book, there is in it more than ever that range which
> made Wolfe seem the most variously gifted American novelist of our
> time.

Even the Marxist critic Henry Hart found something to praise in
Wolfe's last novel. In a review appearing in the 22 October 1940 issue of
The New Masses, Hart referred to the last thirty-six pages (Webber's farewell letter to the Fox) as a major event in American literature. In those
pages, he argues, Wolfe "lay bare, with a lucidity unattainable in any pre-
vious decade, the distinction between literature as a mature writer would
have it and literature as the owning class desires and wills it to be" (25).

Critics such as Harry Sylvester, writing in the 25 October 1940 issue
of *Commonweal*, argue that in his fourth novel Wolfe demonstrated a social
awareness which had not been apparent in his first three novels. Much of
the novel, Sylvester concludes, is just straight commentary and criticism
on his times and their people, all of which is "interesting," "accurate," and
"penetrating." At least one critic, Desmond Powell, writing in the Winter
1941 issue of *Accent*, noted that in his last novel Wolfe finally seemed to
take the criticism of his critics and reviewers to heart.

The German Reviews

Wolfe made his last visit to Germany in 1936, after the publication of *Von
Zeit und Strom*. He was greeted even more warmly by the Germans than in
1935, but as time went on the taint of the Third Reich sank in on him. It
was the time of the 1936 Olympics, and Wolfe contrasted the spectacle of
the multinationalism espoused by those games to the growing preemi-
nence of Nazi militarism in Germany. He wrote in his notebook of the

... great displays of marching men, sometimes ungunned but rhythmic, great regiments of brown shirts swinging through the streets; again, at ease, young men and laughing, talking with each other, long lines of Hitler's bodyguards, black-uniformed and leather-booted, the Schutz-Staffel men, stretching in unbroken lines from Leader's residence in the Wilhelmstrasse up to the arches of the Brandenburger Tor; then suddenly the sharp command, and instantly, unforgettably, the liquid smack of ten thousand leather boots as they came together, with the sound of war. (*Notebooks* 913)

Returning to America, Wolfe wrote the story of his last days in Germany, a train ride to the border of that country, during which a small Jewish man was arrested by the Gestapo. The story, "I Have a Thing to Tell You," was published in *The New Republic* in three installments appearing on 10, 17, and 24 March 1937; later the story was incorporated into pages 634–651, 655, 663–704, and 743 of *You Can't Go Home Again*. Wolfe was well aware that *The New Republic* was one of those American journals "gutted" by Goebbels and his staff at the Propaganda Ministry in Berlin. In writing his story, he was aware of its political ramifications: he would never be able to return to Germany again. He writes about this decision in a 5 March 1937 letter to Dixon Wecter:

> *The New Republic*, beginning with this week's issue, is publishing three installments of a long story that I wrote about Germany. They are advertising it rather lavishly as "a new short novel," but it is not a novel, long or short, and I never said it was. I think it may be pretty good. At any rate I've crossed the Rubicon as far as my relations with the Reich are concerned. It cost me a good deal of time and worry to make up my mind whether I should allow the publication of the story because I am well known in Germany, my books have had a tremendous press there, I have many friends there, and I like the country and the people enormously. But the story wrote itself. It was the truth as I could see it, and I decided that a man's own self-respect and integrity is worth more than his comfort or material advantage . . . . (*Letters* 614)

As a result of the serialization of his short story, Wolfe's books were banned in Germany for a few months. When Wolfe's posthumous novels appeared in 1939 and 1940 as Ernst Alker notes in his 1948 review, "Thomas Wolfe und die neue amerikanische Dichtung" ("Thomas Wolfe and the New American Literature"), George Webber's sexual liaison with his Jewish mistress, Esther Jack, was enough to keep the books from being published in Germany. Alker comments that *The Web and the Rock* had to be published in Switzerland. Hitler's literary bureaucracy, which had tolerated those earlier books written by Wolfe published at Rowohlt because of the strong criticism of American conditions in them, considered George Webber's erotic relationships a threat to the Third Reich.

Because the German rights for the posthumously published novels were contracted not by Rowohlt Verlag in Germany, but by Alfred Scherz Verlag in Bern, Switzerland, Hans Schiebelhuth did not prepare the translations of these texts. Frau Tonnemacher's translation of *The Web and the Rock* was, in William Pusey's opinion, timid but adequate. The work was retitled, confusingly, *Strom des Lebens*. The translation of *You Can't Go Home Again* rendered by either Ernst Reinhard or Dr. Rudolf Frank (the title page credit and the publishing house records are not in agreement on this point) was unimaginative and inaccurate. In this translation, the Great Smoky Mountains are transformed into a river and moved to Kansas, the phrase "thinker of base thoughts" is interpreted as "Denker von Baseball-Gedanken," and "in his flivver" is rendered as "im Paddelboot und im Schilf" ("The German Vogue of Thomas Wolfe" 135, note 36).

Few reviews were written on these translations of the novel. Otto Koischwitz refers briefly to *You Can't Go Home Again* in a 1941 essay printed in *Die Literatur*, "Echo des Auslands" ("The Foreign Echo"). He writes: "A novel by Thomas Wolfe has been published posthumously. Again a volume of over 700 pages. Judging from the extracts, it is just as endless and dissolutely poetic as his earlier novels, that are known also in Germany. The title 'You Can't Go Home Again' sounds like a mystical foreboding of the dying poet. This novel is one of the highest bookselling successes of the year" (240). Referring to Wolfe as half German and half Scottish as so many critics did, Ernst Alker calls him as "Homer of America." Alker's article, printed in *Wort und Wahrheit*, notably appears in November 1948, well after the fall of the Third Reich. Writing of *You Can't Go Home Again*, he notes that in Wolfe's final novel nihilistic individualism is overcome by a new relationship between the individual and humanity. In this novel Alker sees Wolfe's dealing with several possibilities for human existence in Brooklyn and with the problems of literary fame. Alker notes that in this novel "the tempting, flattering Germany (noticed by George Webber as such) has already become the realm of demons" that Wolfe fears will infiltrate the United States "through dark paths, which find good nourishing grounds in a world disappointed by the continuous progress and the catastrophe of an economic depression." It is not a surprise, however, that Alker in reading the German translation in the Alfred Scherz Verlag text with its multiple inaccuracies should still find the book "disappointing" (852–857).

By 1950 Rowohlt Verlag contracted with Wolfe's American publisher (Harpers) for the German rights to *You Can't Go Home Again*. This translation by Susanna Rademacher titled *Es führt kein Weg Zurück* was published in 1950; three years later Rademacher also translated *The Web and the Rock* into German for Rowohlt Verlag which published the novel under the title *Geweb und Fels*.

7: The Authority of the Text

WOLFE'S FRIEND HAMILTON Basso perhaps best understood the importance of Wolfe's work and its position in the American literary canon of the first half of the century. Writing in the 23 September 1940 issue of *The New Republic*, Basso commented at length about Wolfe's relationship to his critics. Wolfe, he notes, "disliked the critics as much as any creative writer." Their charges that his novels were overly autobiographical resulted ironically in the very conditions that caused Wolfe to create his last protagonist in the image of his first. Basso quotes an unidentified document written by Wolfe referring to his response to the critics:

> In another way as well, our love of neat definitions in convenient forms, our fear of essential exploration, may be the natural response of people who have to house themselves, wall themselves, give their lives some precise and formal definition . . . . Anyway, all of these things have seemed to me to be worth thinking of, and I know that we still have to fight to do our work the way we want to do it – not only against the accepted varieties of surveyordom, that is book publishers, most of the critics, popular magazines, etc. – but against even deadlier and more barren forms; deadlier because they set up as friends of exploration when they are really betrayers and enemies; I mean little magazinedom, hound and horners, young precious boys, esthetic Marxians and all the rest of it.

Wolfe, Basso argued, never became a "terse" writer, because he was not the least bit interested in becoming one. "So, what of it?" Basso continues, "It also became obvious that he would never bring the tremendous engine of his creative ability under full control and that he would be forever loose and sprawling and sometimes windy enough to blow your hat off . . . .The fact remains that when he gets hold, when he digs through to what he is after, he is magnificent in a way few American writers ever have been – making his detractors seem puny and feeble by comparison."

The 1940s and 1950s

In his 1942 *Sewanee Review* article, Thomas Lyle Collins refutes the arguments made by Wolfe's critics that in his last novel Wolfe had turned away from the Romanticism of his youth to a more mature concern with "social issues." "One does not have to read *You Can't Go Home Again*," he writes, "to find 'significance'" in Wolfe's writing. "There is significance a-plenty in Wolfe's first three novels if one will but read carefully some of the passages of 'dark substance' therein." The death of the father, the rejection of Starwick, the protagonists' love affairs, all depicted in Wolfe's early novels, Collins suggests, are all symbols of Wolfe's "social themes." These themes find their best expression in the prefatory poem to *Look Homeward, Angel* (" . . . a stone, a leaf, an unfound door") and in the chapter "Time Is a Fable" in *The Web and the Rock*, in which Wolfe writes:

> We are small grope-things crying for the light and love by which we might be saved, and which, like us, is dying in the darkness a hand's breadth off from us if we could touch it. We are like blind sucks and sea-valves and the eyeless-crawls that grope along the forest of the sea's great floor, and we die alone in the darkness, a second away from hope, a moment from ecstasy and fulfillment, a little half an hour from love. (*The Web and the Rock* 627)

In *You Can't Go Home Again*, however, the social concerns of the author became "explicit" rather than "symbolic." In his "Credo," in the chapters "Boom Town" and "The Company" and in his description in "Piggy Logan's Circus," Wolfe achieves "an effect of single selfishness and compulsive greed . . . an effect of strange and gripping horror of a decadent aristocracy." In defining Wolfe's position in the national literature, Collins concludes that he stands "very close to the top" (496–500).

For Herbert Muller, Wolfe's *The Web and the Rock* is largely an unsatisfying novel, which only becomes satisfying when read in conjunction with *You Can't Go Home Again*. Despite the strengths of individual chapters such as "Child by Tiger," which treats the wild shooting spree of a normally quiet and religious black man in the South, and a more highly defined sense of the theme of the quest for a father, and Wolfe's contrast of the romantic mythology of the decadent aristocracy (and the Southern intellectuals and aesthetes) with the squalid realities of Negro bondage, tenant farmer, and child labor, *The Web and the Rock* cannot successfully stand on its own (*Thomas Wolfe* 117–121). In *You Can't Go Home Again*, on the other hand, Wolfe reached an exceptionally full sense of the American scene which he demonstrated in his treatment of the social issues presented in the chapters titled "The Party at Jack's" and "I Have a Thing to Tell You." Had Wolfe lived in a simpler time, Muller suggested, he might have become the American Homer. "Given 'the billion forms of America' and 'the dense complexity of all its swarming life,'" Muller concludes, Wolfe's writing comes closer than that of any other writer to being a true "American epic" (189).

Like Muller, Pamela Hansford Johnson finds Wolfe's depiction of George's affair with Esther Jack in *The Web and the Rock* to be particularly unsuccessful. "The writing of this section," Johnson concludes, "is blustering and hysterical, at best like the worst of Emily Brontë, and at worst (which is more frequent) like third-rate Victorian melodrama." As an example she quotes from the scene in which George throws Esther out of his apartment. Overcome with remorse, he "struck his fist into his face, a wild and wordless cry was torn from his throat, and he rushed from his room and from the house, out in the street to find her." Johnson writes:

> The picture of George smashing himself in the face, giving a "wordless cry" and plunging for the street does not merely approach the ludicrous; it overruns it. The whole chronicle of these quarrels and reconciliations is prolonged, repetitive and tedious, narrowing down the interest to two persons who are already overfamiliar and have little more to reveal concerning themselves. (*Hungry Gulliver* 79)

Of all of Wolfe's novels, Johnson argues (contradicting most of Wolfe's critics), *The Web and the Rock* is the most "egotistical." In *Look Homeward, Angel* the character of Eugene Gant reflects his family; in *Of Time and the River*, he reflects Starwick, Elinor and Ann; but in *The Web and the Rock* Eugene-George is the entire play. Johnson notes, "We see Esther only as he saw her, through his dark and distorted mirror" (107). Johnson recognizes that although Wolfe chose to change the name of his protagonist in his third novel, he projects the woman with whom Eugene falls in love at the end of *Of Time and the River* into his third novel. Not only the object of Eugene Gant's love interest, Esther Jack also becomes the object of George Webber's love interest. "Wolfe," she writes, "created George Webber not because he was growing closer to men and women, was seeing them with a greater objectivity, but because, without realising it, he was drawing away from them" (110).

Unlike those critics who praised *You Can't Go Home Again* for its demonstration of "social consciousness," Johnson sees Wolfe in the spring of 1938 in full political retreat. Although he recognized the evils of society and was filled with noble rage and disgust by the inhumanity of man to man, he felt incapable of dealing with any of the significant social issues of the day. He did not admire the energy writers engaged in political controversy injected into the community; he feared becoming like them because he dreaded the loss of creative artistic time that would result from him moving beyond his passionate isolation.

"With all his gigantic faults, his prolixity, his ranting, his stupefying absurdities," Johnson notes, "Wolfe is incomparably the most significant figure in three decades of American literature" (155). Next to Wolfe, Faulkner appears neurotic and obscure, Hemingway appears overly sophisticated, and Steinbeck appears recessive. She writes:

His tremendous pride, the pride that vented itself in hostility towards the friends of Esther Jack, towards the English, and towards the publishers 'Rawng and Wright,' is counteracted by an even greater joy of being young . . . . Alone among the writers of his generation he understands that the indigenous culture of his country today is as young as England's was when Chaucer struck open the great way of modern English letters." (164)

The grand renunciation at the end of *You Can't Go Home Again* is, as Oscar Cargill argues in his 1949 essay, "Gargantua Fills His Skin," the highpoint of both George Webber's and Thomas Wolfe's careers. Whereas Johnson suggests that Wolfe is incapable of any real political action, Cargill recognizes that in writing novels in which a young American Christian becomes involved with an older Jewish woman and in writing social commentary such as "I Have a Thing to Tell You," which focused on the brutality of Nazism, Wolfe was aware that he would be heavily penalized. He had been lionized in Germany, and his books had sold well there. The enthusiasm with which he describes the German population is unmistakable in both of his last books. Still, this loss did not deter him from taking a just position.

Although, as Cargill notes, the author of *Look Homeward, Angel* and *Of Time and the River* was often denounced for the apparent anti-Semitism of his protagonist, in denouncing the Third Reich and casting a miserable Jewish refugee as the instrument of Webber's conversion, he emerged from *You Can't Go Home Again* "a bigger person than we have known before" (30).

Henry Steele Commager, writing in *The American Mind* in 1950, described the effect that the American Depression had on American authors. "The depression," he writes, "made everything that was merely plaintive and precious and whimsical seem dated. It tore the novelists away from satire that was often an expression of superciliousness, and disillusionment that was often too personal, and brought them back to the main current of protest and reform" (267). Among those writers who emerged in the twenties and the thirties, Hemingway, Dos Passos, Fitzgerald, Steinbeck, and Farrell, Wolfe's quarrel with his society remained the most personal and consistent. All of Wolfe's novels, Commager argues, indict the society in which Wolfe was so "articulately uncomfortable" (268). None of these writers, however, was successful in documenting the changes in the American economy.

Walter Fuller Taylor, writing three years after the publication of Commager's *The American Mind*, argued to the contrary in his essay "Thomas Wolfe and the Middle-Class Tradition." Large areas of Wolfe's fiction, Taylor argues, "are in the truest sense *social* . . . his middle-class

Weltanschauung affords . . . a door that opens on an understanding of much that might be carelessly judged anomalous or just rhetorically turgid" (543). Those elements in Wolfe's writings, Taylor concludes, which have been dubbed "provincial," are, in actuality, "national and American" (547). Like William Dean Howells, Wolfe's core concern is with the people of the middle-class. Rather than aiming his work deliberately at any social criticism, that criticism rises implicitly out of Wolfe's gallery of portraits of middle-class men and women, each an "uncalculated reply to the charges of dulness and standardization with which Lewis, Mencken, and others were fond of belaboring the American bourgeoisie" (548).

Taylor's point is well taken; the middle class (or working class), even when depicted by realists such as Wharton and Howells, is generally drawn as drab, inarticulate, and crude. Wharton's Lily Bart, disenfranchised by her own economic impoverishment from the "upper class" and rendered unmarriageable by the scandalous lies circulated about her by her "upper class" friends, chooses to commit suicide rather than to make her living as a milliner. In Howells's *Imperative Duty*, a young girl is horrified at the prospect of learning not only that she is one-sixteenth black, but that she is descended from working people. Faulkner's world seems divided between fallen aristocrats and white trash; Fitzgerald's world seems devoted to the very rich. Only Wolfe focuses on middle-class characters, depicting, in ways that are occasionally crude and violent, their energy and complexity.

Wolfe's treatment of the speculative boom of the twenties and its catastrophic collapse into the Great Depression in his last novel seems to be written a decade late, but this is not the case. Eugene/George reaches the age that Wolfe was during this period of his life only in the novel *You Can't Go Home Again*. It would have been inappropriate for Wolfe to foist a mature sense of "social consciousness" on the protagonists of any of the first three novels, all of whom exist in a prelapsarian (predepression) state.

Wolfe talked at some length about the relationship between his work and the Great Depression in his Purdue speech of 19 May 1938. He explained:

> It has seemed to me for some time that there is a kind of significance in the fact that my first book appeared in October 1929. For me, it seemed that in a way my life – my working life – had just begun; but in so many different ways I did not know about, or even suspect at that time, so many things that I believed in, or thought that I believed in, were ended. Many people see in the last great war a kind of great dividing line in their own lives – a kind of great tale of two worlds . . . but in my own experience . . . I think I should be more inclined to use 1929 as the dividing line. (*Thomas Wolfe's Purdue Speech* 47)

The "boom and bust" metaphors of Wolfe's *You Can't Go Home Again* (the fire in the House that Jack Built; the pasteboard sadism of a Piggy Logan; the fall of the Citizen's Trust Bank; the triumph of the Federal Weight, Scales, and Computing Company over the individual; and the suicide leap of C. Green – who at last was not a "hollow man") have been adequately explored and documented by perceptive critics such as William Kennedy in his "Economic Ideas in Contemporary Literature" and Richard S. Kennedy in *The Window of Memory*. There seems, however, to have been significantly little interest in the dramatic rhetorical change in Wolfe's prose style in his last novel, which abandons the romantic rhetoric of his early works and replaces that rhetoric with an intriguing web of journalistic fact and novelistic fiction. Like a string of beads, the allegories of Libya Hills, Frederick Jack, and C. Green seem to stand only in a linear relationship to one another as variations on a means of exploring a single theme, the spiritual and economic impoverishment of a nation. In retreating from analyzing these narratives, Wolfe's critics have overlooked an important parallel in the novel between the "boom and bust" of 1929 and the spiritual "boom and bust" which Wolfe himself experienced between 11 March and 13 March 1935, days immediately following the publication of *Of Time and the River*.

Wolfe discusses his plans for his unfinished novel in several letters he wrote to Jack Westall in February 1938. In the first, dated 14 February, Wolfe asks Westall to send him a complete run of the *Asheville Advocate*. "I am writing a very long book," he writes. "All I can tell you here is that the book is not about any one town nor any specific individual or persons, but it is a book about America, and what happened here between 1929 and 1937." He continues in his second letter to say: "the truth that I am trying to get at in this book is imaginative and fictional truth, and not historical truth – in other words, actual dates do not matter so much – the real thing that matters is what really happened – the spinning of that terrible and gigantic web – political, financial, economic, social, touching, as you say, every element of my life, every man, woman and child, influencing and controlling the press – constituting in the end something more than the mere history of one town – really a kind of history of mankind, a terrific human drama" ("Eleven More Letters of Thomas Wolfe, 1929–1938," 23–29).

The trick for Wolfe was to create a structure that supported the synchronicity of human experience in the late twenties. In this way, the Great Depression in America became for Wolfe not the subject of his book, but a tool for examining a cross-section of American society.

The advertisements for *You Can't Go Home Again* quoting *The New York Times* review of J. Donald Adams read: "this is a book of a man who had something profoundly important to say . . . the story of a man who found himself, in relation to life, in relation to his time." These blurbs are misleading. Wolfe's literary career was never out of touch with social and economic issues; throughout his career he concerned himself not with social or economic matters in their own right, but with their effect on human values and behaviors. Wolfe's 1919 Worth Prize-winning essay, *The Crisis in Industry*, discusses the conflicts between labor and capital, addressing the American dilemma, the need to reconcile the needs of the many (in a nation in which "all men are created equal") to the needs of the individual. "The problem that once to me was economic," Wolfe concludes in this essay, "is now plainly and undeniably human." Wolfe's first novel, *Look Homeward, Angel*, published on 18 October 1929, 11 days before the stock-market crash, discusses with acuity the emotional and personal sacrifices made by a family dominated by an entrepreneurial matriarch. His last novel, *You Can't Go Home Again*, rounds out a literary career concerned with the bifurcation of the American dream, the conflict between the spiritual and the economic in a nation built both on Puritan hopes and the values of Yankee traders.

One of the more interesting experimental techniques used by Wolfe for exploring the human drama at the center of social and political issues is the incorporation of news articles into his writing. At several points in the narrative of *You Can't Go Home Again*, he juxtaposes the point of view of the narrator with the cold, objective, and often ruthlessly shallow and corrupted voice of the journalist. In almost every instance in which he uses this technique in the novel, the journalistic temperament is fictive, and the fiction is based on fact. With the Great Depression as a subtext for his narrative, Wolfe could write on two levels of meaning simultaneously. The total experience in reading the book, and Wolfe had every reason to believe that his audience would be a group of Americans who had actually experienced the Depression, would then derive from a simultaneous grasping of the fiction of the narrative and the corresponding historical fact. The two areas operating on the reader would prevent him from having a one-dimensional response to the book, prevent him from reading it either as social history or as a string of anecdotes. The allegorical structures in *You Can't Go Home Again* take as their basis news stories from *The New York Times* which literalize Thoreau's belief that "if men would steadily observe realities only, they would realize that reality is fabulous."

In *You Can't Go Home Again*, Wolfe refers to four newspaper articles. Wolfe incorporates them into the narrative in a way that not only adds veracity and density to his fictional reality, but enables him to endow that narrative with dimension and make it seem continuous with life without

resorting to his own autobiographical experiences. The first of these occurs in the chapter "Boom Town" in which George Webber is interviewed by the local newspaper in Libya Hill. George's stammerings are
transformed by the writer into a glowing tribute to Libya Hill, one appropriate for a real-estate sales brochure. "In your opinion," the interviewer
asks, "does this section of the country compare with other places you
have seen?" George's response, a simple "good," is then transformed by
the journalist into lugubrious praise for Libya Hills, "the most ideal place
in the whole world to live." The second of these juxtapositions occurs in a
twelve-chapter section of the book, "The World That Jack Built." As William Kennedy points out, the term "jack" has economic connotations,
rendering the title of that section essentially "The World that Money
Built." Escaping from the fire in Frederick Jack's building, George
Webber listens to a journalist describe the fire over the phone to his city
editor. The reporter, described as "fascinated by his own journalese," uses
the word *cordon* which the City Desk misinterprets as *squadron*. The subtext to this discussion is the actual *New York Times* report of the fire at the
Marguery Hotel on 3 January 1930, "Two Die as Blast Rocks the Mar-
guery and Routs Guests." The article repeats the word *cordon* twice. The
third of these juxtapositions occurs in the twenty-fifth chapter of the book,
"The Catastrophe," which describes the ruin of the Citizen's Bank and
Trust Company of Libya Hill, and in which an article supposedly read by
George Webber in the 12 March 1930 issue of *The New York Times*, "Bank
Fails in the South," is reproduced. The actual article treating the closing of
the banks in Asheville appeared in the 21 November 1930 issue of *The
New York Times* and was titled "8 Carolina Banks Fail As Boom Ends."
The fourth point of journalistic reference occurs in chapter 29, "The Hollow Men," which takes as its subtext not only Eliot's famous poem, but
two articles: "Brooklyn Man Falls to Death" (*The New York Times* 30 April
1938) and "Mythical Estates in England" (*London Times* 27 February
1933).

At the beginning of chapter 25, "The Catastrophe," George Webber
opens *The New York Times* to find his hometown, Libya Hill, the dateline
of a 4-inch article dated 12 March, "Bank Fails in South." The original for
this is the *New York Times* article, "8 Carolina Banks Fail As Boom Ends"
which extends slightly more than one full column on the financial page of
that newspaper. The *New York Times* article deals with the failure of the
Central Bank and Trust Company which Wolfe transforms for the purposes of his novel into the Citizen's Trust Company, the name of a bank
established in Asheville in 1906 that had been purchased by the Citizen's
Bank in 1924, six years before the crash. The success of the Central Bank
and Trust Company of Asheville, which boasted that it held accounts for

fully "one-fifth" of the entire population of the county in which it was located, was the subject of several newspaper articles in *The Asheville Citizen.*
One of the earliest, printed on 31 July 1927, accompanied an article on
Wallace Davis, the original for Jarvis Riggs, with a full-page spread advertising the Central Bank. "Central-ized Banking," the advertisement reads,
"the Basis of Asheville's Financial Stability." Davis is quoted as saying,
"While business in the United States as a whole increased 27 percent during the years between 1919 and the present time, Asheville business increased 213 percent."

Wolfe's interpretation of the real-estate frenzy that precipitated the
folding of the Central Bank and Trust Company may well have been
gleaned from firsthand experience; but it also may well have been gleaned
from a second article appearing in the 21 November 1930 issue of *The
New York Times* entitled "Bank Examiner Blames Boom." In that article,
the chief state bank examiner, in a statement at Raleigh, attributes the
closing of the Central Bank and Trust Company to "the collapse of a
highly inflated plane of real estate values." His explanation states,
"Immediately preceding the collapse of the Florida real estate boom, a
large number of high-powered real estate operators transferred their activities from Florida, concentrating largely in Asheville and Henderson-
ville. The result of their activities was to produce an inflated plane of real
estate values. The collapse of real estate, as well as other values, made it
impossible for the failed banks to liquidate their receivables in sufficient
volume to meet demands of depositors."

Since so much of Wolfe's description of the boom and bust in
Asheville, including the suicide of Mayor Baxter Kennedy, is based on recorded fact, it is interesting to speculate why Wolfe would have chosen to
change the date of the Asheville crash from 20 November to 12 March.
Had he reason to change the date at all (in an attempt to make the local
failure mirror the national one), he should have changed the date to October 1929. The date, 12 March, however, had personal significance for
Wolfe. It was one of three days Wolfe spent in Paris following the publication of *Of Time and the River* that were ultimately lost in what Andrew
Turnbull refers to in his biography, *Thomas Wolfe,* as a psychotic depression. It was one of the three *lost* days Wolfe spent in Paris responding to
his fears that the critics had negatively reviewed his second novel.

Wolfe's letter to Westall describes a work that would deal with "what
really happened . . . the spinning of that terrible and gigantic web – political financial, economic, social, touching as you say, every element of my
life, every man, woman and child, influencing and controlling the press."
It is possible that in writing the section on the fall of the bank at Libya
Hill, Wolfe found a metaphor not only for the national experience, but

also for the emotional dread he experienced in the wake of the publications of his books, while he awaited the critical responses to his work.

In chapter 29 of *You Can't Go Home Again*, "The Hollow Men," Wolfe deals with two newspaper accounts, one supposedly appearing in *The New York Times* on 30 April 1938 describing the death of an unidentified man and the other supposedly appearing in the *London Times* on 27 February 1933. As Foxhall Edwards consumes his morning *Times*, "ink fresh . . . with orange juice, waffles, eggs and bacon, and cups of strong hot coffee" (460), his attention is arrested by a nine-line article that coldly and objectively describes the death of one C. Green: "An unidentified man," it reads, "fell or jumped yesterday at noon from the twelfth story of the Admiral Francis Drake Hotel, corner of Hay and Apple Streets, in Brooklyn. The man, who was about thirty-five years old, registered at the hotel about a week ago, according to the police, as C. Green. Police are of the opinion that this was an assumed name. Pending identification, the body is being held at the King's County Morgue."

Although several New York suicides covered by the *The New York Times* could qualify as the original of this text, its similarity in wording clearly identifies it as originating in the snippet of an article, no more than an inch and a half in length, appearing in the lowermost left-hand corner of the sixteenth page of the 30 April 1938 issue of the *The New York Times* describing the death of an unknown man at the Capitol Hotel in Brooklyn. The article, titled "Brooklyn Man Falls to Death," reads:

> A man who registered under the name of "Jack Cohen" of Brooklyn yesterday afternoon plunged to his death from a room on the eleventh floor of the Hotel Capitol, Fifty-first Street and Eighth Avenue. A note addressed to "Hymie" was found by the police. It read: "I'm sorry to do this, but I can't stand it any longer. I am an innocent fool. Good-bye and God bless you."

Is this the whole story? Wolfe asks, responding "no" to his own rhetorical question before going on in the chapter to recreate Green's final days, the grotesque details of his suicide, "brains exploded like pink sausage meat." The points held in common by the two articles, the factual one and its fictional counterpart, are obvious – the unidentified man, about thirty-five years of age, registered under an assumed name, falls to his death from a Brooklyn Hotel. Both articles are about of equal length and adopt the same cold, objective journalistic tone. Still, the points that are not shared by these articles make the comparison even more interesting. For Jack Cohen, Wolfe substitutes C. Green – evoking the fresh green seas on which explorers came to the New World in an image that also successfully evokes the referent of "C" notes – green one hundred-dollar bills. Where Jack Cohen "plunges," a word that implies either accident or suicide, C. Green falls or jumps. Where Jack Cohen's life ends at the Capitol Hotel, C. Green's ends on the sidewalk in front of the Admiral Francis Drake Hotel.

Wolfe's decision to change the Capitol Hotel to the Admiral Francis Drake Hotel may well tie in with his image of Green and Drake as explorers, although beneath his descriptions of the first man to circumnavigate the globe lies an awareness of Drake's character as a pirate and plunderer that enriches the economic metaphors of the novel. It is more likely that Wolfe based his decision to rename the hotel, however, on a much-publicized con game of the early 1930s in which American swindlers abroad tried to sell shares in the estate of Sir Francis Drake (the plunder that he earned from raiding Spanish galleons) to unsuspecting Americans in the Midwest.

The man responsible for this swindle, Oscar Merrill Hartzell, a former Des Moines sheriff, was first arrested in London, and the *London Times* carried the story of the scandal in its 27 February 1933 issue, an issue that Wolfe would have had no difficulty obtaining even in Brooklyn. The article is titled "Mythical Estates in England" and, given Wolfe's interest in the *real*-estate boom and collapse in Asheville, must have proven particularly interesting. The article runs five paragraphs in length but is perhaps most interesting in the final paragraph, which describes the efforts made by the American consulate to investigate a number of similar real-estate swindles. This paragraph reads: "Some of the alleged estates concerning which this Consulate-General is most frequently consulted are those of Sir Francis Drake, Hyde, Jennings (Janning or Jennens), Patrick Rucker, Hedges, Mosher, Weber (Webber), Duke of Argyll, James Dixon, Helen Sheridan Blake, Lawrence-Townley, (Lawrence Townsend), Walmsely, Jaques, General Richard Winn, Bonnet (Bonet), Page, and Green (or Greene)." The close proximity of the names "Sir Francis Drake," Weber or Webber, and Green in this article, so closely paralleling their proximity in "The Hollow Men" chapter of *You Can't Go Home Again* argues that the Drake scandal in addition to the Cohen suicide served as a subtext for this section.

The widespread economic failure and depression that follows a stock-market crash is an almost perfect metaphor for the exhaustion of the American Dream – for where there is the possibility of infinite success, there is also the possibility of debilitating failure. But Wolfe makes an important point that many of his contemporaries miss. The collapse of the American Dream, its subversion from a spiritual to an economic plane, was no simple matter of an economic failure. It was far more a matter of the pervasive inability of Americans from all walks of life to find the moral resources the dream demanded. All of Wolfe's characters are involved in the depression – on individual, local, and national levels, but they are also responsible for creating the depression. The spiritual and moral vacuum of their lives precedes their economic failure; it is not created by it. Even Nebraska Crane, whose loss is mitigated by his foresight in purchasing three hundred acres of land and his optimistic disposition, has lost his job. In Wolfe's view, the bargain American's have struck with the devil is a poor one in which they have settled for economic rather than spiritual fulfillment.

This spiritual exhaustion permeated even the press, for whom the news was a commodity and writing was more of a business than an art. Wolfe's use of several actual newspaper accounts as subtexts for his narrative suggests how in an extreme situation, such as the suicide of Jack Cohen, direct quotation could by itself be significant parody. In the text, the journalistic voice, despite its "objectivity" is emotionally sterile and presents only the shallowest view of the physical event it describes, whereas the "subjective" voice of the fictional narrative is capable of expressing a human response to human tragedy and is capable of perceiving human activity within a historical and philosophical context. Wolfe's historical tryst with his reviewers and critics over the autobiographical nature of his earlier work, their questions about the "subjective" elements in his fiction, and their loudly voiced preference for "objective" fiction prompted Wolfe to juxtapose subjective fiction and objective journalism in his text. Unlike the critical community that largely believed literature at its best to be monoreferential, Wolfe understood the dark, mythical, and fabulous aspect of fact.

The 1960s and After

The decades following the fifties have been particularly rich in Wolfe scholarship, producing first editions or new scholarly editions of works by Wolfe and books and pamphlets of historical and biographical interest. The proportion of textual and scholarly work to critical work during this period is noteworthy, marking a pivotal moment in Wolfe studies: important attempts by scholars to come to grips with complex textual problems in the Wolfe canon.

Few years in these decades were uneventful; however, the years of *Wolfegate*, 1980–1981, a controversy focusing on John Halberstadt's 1980 *Yale Review* article, "The Making of Thomas Wolfe's Posthumous Novels," were the most turbulent and inglorious. The controversy that found its way, for example, into the pages of *The New York Times Book Review*, *The New York Review of Books*, *The Chronicle of Higher Education*, *The Boston Globe*, and *The San Francisco Chronicle* centered on Halberstadt's misuse of

Wolfe-estate material and on the decision made by the Houghton Library at Harvard (where the materials were housed) that he be barred from the library for a year. Halberstadt did not fabricate the textual problems he saw in the last two novels published in the Wolfe canon, and he actually quoted fewer than ten words from previously unpublished Wolfe material, but his charges of literary fraud and his vociferous insistence that Wolfe had really not written *The Web and the Rock* and *You Can't Go Home Again* sensationalized and distorted material which had been made public nearly two decades earlier by Richard S. Kennedy in *The Window of Memory*. What Kennedy perceived to be "creative editing" on the part of Edward C. Aswell, Wolfe's editor at Harpers and later Wolfe's literary executor, which was made necessary by Wolfe's death in 1938, Halberstadt perceived to be a conspiracy of secrecy designed to disguise the "true author" of Wolfe's posthumous novels. Halberstadt's scenario oversimplified and generalized the complex relationship between editor and writer, presenting sensitive Wolfe estate material to the general reading public in the worst possible light.

John Halberstadt was neither the first nor the last of Wolfe's critics to study the manuscript materials at Harvard in an effort to piece together a picture of what parts of the posthumously published novels had originated in Wolfe's crate of manuscripts left with Harpers in 1938 and which parts were the result of Edward Aswell's editing of Wolfe manuscript material after his death. In his monumental study of Wolfe, *The Window of Memory*, Richard S. Kennedy devotes close to fifty pages to describing Aswell's editing of these texts, printing for the first time on pages 415 to 437 of his text Wolfe's Rough Outline of his last book and presenting two columns of text at another point (pages 404–405) in order to make the nature of Aswell's editorial decisions visually accessible to the readers of *The Window of Memory*. In addition, Kennedy provides in the "Works Cited" list in his text a complete run of access numbers and short descriptive annotations for the manuscript drafts and materials used by him at Harvard. Kennedy concludes in his *The Window of Memory*:

> The hand of the editor intrudes more often in *You Can't Go Home Again* than readers have suspected. By this time, Aswell identified himself with Wolfe to the extent that he felt free to play author with the manuscript. Whereas Aswell's part in *The Web and the Rock* may be likened to that played by Ezra Pound, "the great craftsman," in bringing Eliot's *Waste Land* into final form, his contribution to *You Can't Go Home Again* is like George Kaufman's doctoring of a faulty script for the stage. (405–406)

So, by 1962 the American literary community and the group of Wolfe scholars involved in Wolfe studies had already been advised of the editorial and textual issues involved in the publication of Wolfe's posthumous novels.

Completing his dissertation on Thomas Wolfe at Yale, John Halberstadt received access to the manuscript materials in the Wisdom Collection at Harvard (the same manuscript materials that Kennedy had surveyed there two decades earlier), but Halberstadt never did obtain permission for the publication of that material. As a result, his dissertation though listed in *Dissertation Abstracts*, is not abstracted in it. To a great extent then, Halberstadt was in the same position in the early eighties, at the time his dissertation was completed, that Richard S. Kennedy had been in in the forties when his dissertation was completed. Both needed estate permission to publish Wolfe manuscript material; but neither received that permission at the time they first requested it. Whereas Kennedy, a consummate professional, chose to bear up under what proved to be only a temporary impediment to his work – believing himself to be ethically constrained by the decision of the Wolfe estate, which he perceived as legally owning the publication rights to the manuscript material he had quoted in his dissertation, Halberstadt believed that in the process of writing his Yale dissertation he had stumbled upon a literary conspiracy and decided to publish the manuscript material in his dissertation without the permission of the Estate of Thomas Wolfe. The situation is an interesting turn of events for two reasons: 1) there was no cover-up – the meticulously kept manuscripts edited by Aswell were deposited in the Wisdom Collection, where they are easily accessible to scholars, and 2) the issue of the textual authority of Wolfe's posthumous novels had already been treated at length by Kennedy in his *The Window of Memory* in 1962.

In October 1980, however, Halberstadt decided to publish his "findings" in the pages of *The Yale Review*. Halberstadt concluded his essay by asking several questions: 1) "How is the critic supposed to know who Thomas Wolfe really was if the words and intentions and visions attributed to him are really the work of his editors?" 2) "To what extent is the Thomas Wolfe we know a creation of Edward Aswell?" and 3) "Does an editor or publisher have the right to make such posthumous changes . . . and then represent them to the public as the work of the original author?" The questions were good ones, although it is debatable whether many Wolfeans would have agreed with Halberstadt's conclusion that editors should declare "as precisely as possible" what editorial liberties they have taken with the texts of a dead author.

Halberstadt naively passed a copy of *The Yale Review* article on to Rodney Dennis, the curator of the Houghton Library, who immediately recognized that Halberstadt had used Wisdom Collection material without permission.

The issues involved in the Halberstadt controversy, later dubbed *Wolfegate*, are far more complex than they at first appear. First of all the controversy concerns the issue of literary estates. Are literary estates somehow different from other estates? It is clear that if someone removes money from the trust in which it is held without the permission of the executor of an estate that that is a criminal act. Is the removal of manuscript material (which belongs as clearly to a literary estate as stocks and bonds do to a financial estate) not also a criminal act? Halberstadt argues that literary estates are mythical institutions created to provide some scholars with access to manuscript material that would be denied to other scholars. He fails to recognize that even were this the case (which it generally is not), that documents associated with published works do not on the basis of that association become subject to "fair use" provisions provided by copyright law.

Second, the controversy concerns the power of literary estates to function in a manner that enables them to frame discussion of the literary works in their charge. Is it legal to provide some scholars with access to manuscript material and deny it to others? The situation is much the same as a decision made by a single individual to lend his car to a friend. If he lends his car to one friend, is it necessarily incumbent upon him to lend his car to all of his friends?

Finally at issue is the relationship between literary estates and research libraries. The placing of manuscript material by an estate at a major research institution, which maintains the proper environment for caring for such documents, is often dependent on the agreement of the institution to assert estate policies for access to the documents donated to or deposited with them. The violation of such an agreement, purposely or by accident, can result in a legal violation of trust between the estates and the deposit institutions. That violation could result in estates refusing to place manuscript materials at research centers, and as a result few if any would be able to have access to these materials, and the quality of preservation of the materials would deteriorate dramatically.

One year after the publication of Halberstadt's *Yale Review* article, Richard S. Kennedy responded to Halberstadt's charges in the September/October issue of *Harvard Magazine*. "How does," Kennedy asks at the beginning of his article, "one stop this defamation of a dead author and his work?" (50). Kennedy quotes from an undated letter sent by Aswell to Perkins about the corrected page proof of *The Web and the Rock*:

> Because of the changes we had to make in the names of certain characters, as well as other changes designed to minimize the danger of libel, we have been careful about distributing the uncorrected galley proofs to critics and others who have wanted to see them. In fact, we have al-

lowed none of the uncorrected proofs to go to anyone except the Book-of-the-Month Club. It will obviously be desirable not to have reviewers know about these changes, because some of them no doubt, would jump to the conclusion that, if we could change certain things, we could also change others, and that we probably did, and this might lead to some speculation as to how much of the work was really Tom's and how much the work of some alien hand. All of this, of course, is pretty far-fetched, yet no more far-fetched than some of the guesses which have been published in the papers by some of the literary gossip boys. (52)

Although Aswell labeled the idea that this might happen far-fetched, his editing of Wolfe's novels, as a result of the Halberstadt controversy, had by the 1980s become a subject of "literary gossip" and scholarly attention again.

Because of his misuse of Houghton Library manuscript material, Halberstadt was denied access to the Houghton Library for a year (after which it was stipulated that he would be readmitted upon signing a document agreeing not to quote manuscript material without permission – the same document that all researchers sign when they are given access to materials in the reading room of the Houghton). He was also denied membership in the Thomas Wolfe Society. Instead of accepting the decisions made by the Houghton and the Wolfe Society, Halberstadt decided to take his case to the public, appearing on a succession of talk shows and making out of the issue of Wolfe's posthumous novels a "cause célèbre" which spilled over into a number of major newspapers and popular journals.

In 1987 Leslie A. Field published his study of the Wisdom manuscript material in question in his *Thomas Wolfe and His Editors: Establishing a True Text for the Posthumous Publications*. Field's commonsense approach to the editing process and to the realities of publication, coupled with a wide-ranging familiarity with Wolfe manuscript materials in the Wisdom Collection at Harvard makes his *Thomas Wolfe and His Editors* the authoritative statement on the editing of Wolfe's posthumous manuscripts. Where Halberstadt dwells on "what might have been" (*if* Wolfe had lived though the publication of *The Web and the Rock* and *You Can't Go Home Again*; *if* he had been further along on the manuscript at the time of his death; *if* he had actually participated in editorial decisions with Aswell; *if* he had another editor), Field accurately describes the nature of Wolfe's writing practices, the correspondence between Wolfe and Aswell as it reflects Wolfe's authorial intent, the materials Aswell chose to delete from the novels and the practical reasons for those deletions (65–96) and – in four cameo cases – line-by-line illustrations of Wolfe material edited by Aswell, Perkins, and Elizabeth Nowell (100–165). Field's conclusion is notable:

Whether [Aswell] was always absolutely correct in his deletions, additions, and alterations is a question over which well-meaning and knowledgeable people can differ. Aswell was aware that Wolfe would have changed much in what we now know as the posthumous publications. But one can only speculate endlessly about the direction Wolfe's changes would have taken. Wolfe did not live to make the changes, and Aswell did not have the luxury of endless periods of time or clairvoyance to make his decisions.

He did the best he could, exercising a great deal of sensitivity and judiciousness as he tried to "get Wolfe right." And he left the records of his editing for all to see. (194–195)

As important as Field's conclusions are, of even greater importance is the way in which he reaches them – carefully documenting and structuring his research to make a body of complex manuscript material easily accessible to the reader and, in that way, providing the readers of his text with enough detail to enable them to reach some conclusions of their own on the nature of Aswell's editing. Whereas Halberstadt carefully concealed his cards – making the statement of his conclusions the focus of his study – Field places his cards *face up* on the table, making the manuscript material and the historical facts the focus of the reader's attention.

In 1988 the Thomas Wolfe Society and the Houghton Library again opened their doors to John Halberstadt. The Wolfe Society invited him to address its annual meeting in Cambridge, Massachusetts, in May; the sessions of that meeting were held in the Exhibition Room on the first floor of the Houghton Library. A display of Wolfe/Aswell manuscript material titled "Making Thomas Wolfe's Posthumous Novels: A Small Exhibit Illustrating Mr. Halberstadt's Views" was located in the Amy Lowell Room of the Library.

The media arrived as Halberstadt began his presentation and left when he finished it. Halberstadt's paper titled "Concluding Thomas Wolfe's *The Web and the Rock*" was later printed by the Wolfe Society in its annual publication, *The Proceedings of The Thomas Wolfe Society*, edited by Harold Woodell at Clemson University and distributed to members of the society in 1989.

The decades of the eighties and the nineties in America have been particularly rich in Wolfe scholarship. Of the thirty-six full-length studies produced during this period twenty one are new editions of Wolfe's published writing or editions of previously unpublished Wolfe manuscript material (Aldo Magi's 1980 edition of *The London Tower*; Richard Walser's 1982 edition of *The Streets of Durham*; Richard S. Kennedy's 1983 edition of Wolfe's play *Welcome to Our City*; John Idol's 1983 edition of *Thomas Wolfe K-19: Salvaged Pieces*; Richard S. Kennedy's 1983 edition of the letters of Wolfe and Nowell, *Beyond Love and Loyalty*; Suzanne Stutman's 1983 edition of the letters of Wolfe and Aline Bernstein, *My Other Loneliness*; Leslie Field's 1983 edition of *The Autobiography of An American Novelist*; Richard S. Kennedy's 1984 edition of *The Train and the City*; Louis Rubin and John L. Idol's 1985 edition of *Mannerhouse*; Stutman's 1985 edition of postcards and telegrams, *Holding on for Heaven*; Aldo P. Magi and Richard Walser's 1985 edition of *Thomas Wolfe Interviewed*; John Idol's 1986 edition of *The Hound of Darkness*; Mary Aswell Doll and Clara Stites's 1988 edition of the letters of Aswell and Nowell, *In the Shadow of the Giant: Thomas Wolfe*; Richard S. Kennedy's 1989 edition of *The Starwick Episodes*; Francis Skipp's 1987 *The Complete Short Stories of Thomas Wolfe*; Alice Cotten's 1990 edition of *Thomas Wolfe's Composition Books*; Lucy Conniff and Richard S. Kennedy's 1991 edition of *The Autobiographical Outline for* Look Homeward, Angel; Suzanne Stutman's 1991 edition of *The Good Child's River*; William Grimes Cherry III's 1992 edition of *Thomas Wolfe's Notes on* Macbeth; James W. Clark, Jr.'s 1992 edition of *The Lost Boy*; and Suzanne Stutman and John Idol's 1995 edition of *The Party at Jack's*). All but two of these editions (Skipp's *The Complete Short Stories of Thomas Wolfe*, which was published by Macmillan, and Doll and Stites's *In the Shadow of the Giant*, which was published by Ohio University Press) were published by the University of North Carolina Press, Louisiana State University Press, or the Thomas Wolfe Society. This lengthy list of book-length editions and studies of Wolfe's writing produced over the last fifteen years demonstrates the willingness of responsible Wolfe scholars to come to grips with complex textual problems in the Wolfe canon and the willingness of responsible presses to publish their work.

Of the fifteen full-length studies of Wolfe produced during this period that were not editions, one is Carol Johnston's descriptive primary bibliography, one is David Donald's Pulitzer Prize-winning biography, two are introductions to Wolfe studies, three are full-length studies of Wolfe's themes, five are collections of critical essays, and three are reminiscences. These studies were published by publishers as diverse as Little, Brown; The University of Pittsburgh Press; Frederick Ungar; The University of Oklahoma Press; The Louisiana State University Press; Greenwood Press; The North Caroliniana Society and the North Carolina Collection; the Willamette River Press; Croissant; the Thomas Wolfe Society; and G. K. Hall.

This wealth of Wolfe material published over the last fifteen years may or may not indicate a "renaissance" in Wolfe studies; it does, however, without question, indicate significant renewal of interest in the writings of one of the great twentieth-century American novelists. Throughout this period, Wolfe scholars have made major strides in refining and redefining the Wolfe canon, while successfully defending it against the challenges of fraud leveled by sensationalists. What is left to be said about Wolfe? The answer is *plenty* – especially as the best scholar/critics increasingly avail themselves of the archival material available at Harvard University, at The University of North Carolina at Chapel Hill, and at the Pack Memorial Library in Asheville. Students of Wolfe who resist such careful, demanding work do so at their peril; for as the past two decades of books and articles demonstrate, the study of Thomas Wolfe still has much to tell us about him and his writings, about the nature of literature, and about the complexities of publishing it.

8: *Conclusion*: The Pebble in the Pool

THIS STUDY HAS addressed a central issue in the study of modern literature: the bearing, if any, that the contemporary critical and literary community has on the work of any single author and the bearing, if any, that later critical and literary study has on his literary reputation. It began with a statement of belief in the relationship between literature and criticism as being one of cross-fertilization. In studying the "dialogue" between Wolfe and the critical community over the dozen years of his active literary career and in light of the four novels that form the center of his literary canon, this text also has attempted to demonstrate the special richness of his contribution to American literature and American literary thought. Wolfe's literary productivity could be defined in terms of breadth, but this text has deliberately chosen instead to analyze it in terms of depth – that is in terms of the relationship between the author and the literary environment in which he functioned and in which his works have existed and still exist. The *pebble* (Thomas Wolfe) tossed into the *pool* of American literary history has vanished, but his writings continue to generate critical response.

This book suggests that major works of literature result not from a rejection of the critical context in which they are created, but rather from assimilation and transformation of key images and devices of that context. It also suggests that the work of a literary artist, as rooted as it is in his time and in the literary periods that have preceded him, seems also to be about one decade ahead of the literary critics who – in analyzing what is innovative in his work redefine and revamp their own critical standards. The period under study, the first four decades of the twentieth century, variously referred to by literary historians as *The Age of the Novel* and *The Age of Criticism*, seems a particularly fruitful one for this kind of analysis.

Throughout this volume, critical judgement has been seen both to nurture and to conflict with the work of the literary artist. It is apparent that there is little unanimity in the attitudes taken by Wolfe's reviewers and students as they have dealt with his novels, except for a sense of the importance of these works and a recognition that the reading of Thomas Wolfe's fiction requires some serious critical struggle and reevaluation of standard critical concepts. In responding to Wolfe's "autobiographical fiction" which had been misperceived as "autobiography," for instance, the critics found it necessary to reopen their critical thesaurus to redefine those very issues of form and genre that had biased many of the earliest critics and reviewers against Wolfe's fiction. Later critics may have questioned why so many of the early reviewers called for a "new" Wolfe when the old one had been so good, but in criticizing Wolfe for the lack of "social consciousness" in his first two novels, the critical community did provide him with the kind of leverage necessary to produce the social commentary of his last two novels.

However, Wolfe never *gave in* to the pressures of the critical community. *The Web and The Rock* and *You Can't Go Home Again* are every bit as open-ended and ambiguous in their discussion of life in America as are the two earlier novels. In the process of depicting the state of the disenfranchised in America, Wolfe does not become Marxist or Agrarian or join any other group or "ism"; instead he depicts all of these groups as originating in and perpetuating the interests of a single class, the "upper class." Man's inhumanity to man, as Wolfe is aware, is no simple issue, but a complex web in which all, victims and victimizers, become brutalized. In responding to the critics in his last two novels, Wolfe did not deny the arguments of his earlier work, his discussion and criticism of the undercurrents of life in early-twentieth-century America and his sense of the barrenness of the flawed aesthetic and literary groups he encountered during his career. Instead he continued his criticism of America in a way that moved into a study of the dangers of an increasingly bipolar class structure.

The bifurcated American Dream, treated by so many literary historians, encompassing the spiritual goals of a Jonathan Edwards and the material goals of a Benjamin Franklin, does not adequately account for the writings of someone like Thomas Wolfe. Wolfe, instead, seems to function with a number of other important American authors (Emerson, Whitman, and Melville, for instance) within a third, unrecognized, branch of the American Dream which is based on the belief in the transcendence of art and the artist in the New World. With Emerson and Thoreau, Wolfe believed that the individual artist could function as a kind of "seer" in American life, as not only a depicter – but also as an active critic of the society in which he/she lives. Like Hawthorne's Hester Prynne and Melville's Bartleby, Eugene Gant and George Webber struggle against the emptiness of the American artistic landscape.

Reminiscent of Whitman's verse, Wolfe's prose encompasses "multitudes." Like Emerson and Melville, Wolfe rejects conventional literature, by assimilating almost all of it into his writing. He, then, creates a sense of timelessness and depth in his novels by taking that conventional literature just one step beyond itself, allowing those very conventional forms and echoes of the memorable phrases and passages of earlier literary works to erupt polyphonically in his texts. What often appears to be a chaotic and fragmented text is actually an innovative and rhetorically complex prose style – the reflection of past voices in the present voice (reminiscent in some ways of the manner in which in Boston I. M. Pei's *new* John Hancock Building reflects the *old* John Hancock Building without repeating its now-antiquated structures). Like Emerson's transparent eyeball, Hawthorne's scarlet letter, Melville's white whale, the mixing of the water of the Ganges with Walden Pond, and the spontaneous "yawp" of Whitman, Wolfe's fiction represents an enormous compression and synthesis of literary and cultural voices (as apparently diametrically opposed as the rhetoric of Aeschylus and the folk dialog of Eliza Gant, of Frost's "Road Not Taken" and Cooper's Natty Bumppo, of the voice of the journalist and the voice of the poet); and he uses them in texts which incorporate both the clichéd depictions of the struggle of the artist against a hostile provincial community and a more explosive depiction of that theme as an illustration of the battle between "productivity" and "barrenness" – "good" and "evil" in American culture.

Look Homeward, Angel makes clear Eugene Gant's disillusionment with the aesthetic narrowness of a small provincial community; *Of Time and the River* deals with Eugene Gant's gradual recognition that "provincialism" is not merely the product of small Southern towns, but equally as alive in the educated circles of Boston, New York, and Europe; *The Web and the Rock* and *You Can't Go Home Again* provide Wolfe with the means of chastising an essentially conservative critical community – which recognizes art and the awareness of it only in terms of what has been and is incapable of recognizing art for what it is. In the process, he also critiques the conservatism of the political community – which seems to have become blind to the realities of the disenfranchised in America.

In Wolfe's texts, as in those of Emerson, Thoreau, and Whitman, a sense of mystery (generally embodied in the point of view of the young protagonist) becomes a central issue and forms the basis of an exulted individualism and stylistic potency (as in the phrase "A Stone, a Leaf, an Unfound Door"). When Wolfe's writing is stripped of its merely local and time-specific references, it can be seen to fuse classic references with other and more contemporary textual strategies (the structure of the Oresteia with the internal monologue of Henry James and the stream of consciousness of D. H. Lawrence and James Joyce) in a fashion that creates a sense of timelessness and a new level of universality – a level as transcendent as that reached by Edwards and Emerson as they rediscovered the truth of the natural worlds that surrounded them.

The epiphanies of Wolfe's style come not from rejecting the conventional and the time-worn, but from encircling the knowledge of the past (as Emerson suggested in his essay "Circles") and reaching beyond it to create a new understanding and knowledge. Who but Wolfe could have successfully synthesized the Southern regionalism of the early twentieth century with the voices of Aeschylus's *Oresteia*, Whitman's *Leaves of Grass*, and Goethe's *Faust?* Who but Wolfe could have rejected the focus of a Fitzgerald on the "very rich" and a Hemingway on "the world adventurer" to focus on the commonplace experiences of a young middle-class boy in a small Southern town in a way that makes it apparent that the miracles of American life exist in the common everyday experience of being alive? Who but Wolfe could have at the same time offended the practitioners of the Genteel Tradition, Marxism, Agrarianism, and all the other "isms" of early-twentieth-century America?

Fitzgerald, Hemingway, and Faulkner, like Wolfe, reject the Genteel Tradition of the late nineteenth century, the popular "tameness" of American literature; but only Wolfe uses the barrenness of this tradition as a major theme in his writing. Appending his energies and scathing satires of genteel America, as Whitman and Melville had before him, to a tradition of American Romanticism that can be traced back to the founding of the nation itself, his work also stretches forward through Realism and Naturalism and beyond, into Post-Structuralism with its investigations into the latent chaos and incoherence of language, human consciousness, and living itself.

In depicting the "maturation of the young artist" in America, Wolfe's four novels compose a single novel with four individual chapters, each mirroring an age of critical thought in the new world. There is no indication in either Wolfe's published or private documents that he had this intent. But, somehow, organically, as he dealt with the maturation of the young artist in the new century, his work mirrored the process of maturation of art in the new world. The youthful Romanticism of *Look Homeward, Angel* parallels the early Romantic optimism of Emerson and Thoreau (the much heralded moment in that novel at the end of chapter 19 when time stands still is equally as mystic an experience as anything that Emerson experienced in the Boston Common or Thoreau experienced at Walden Pond); the Manichæism of *Of Time and the River* reflects a theme found in the later romanticism of Hawthorne and Melville (Wolfe's rejection of Starwick and the flawed intellectuals of Esther Jack's circle is similar to the unmasking of Judge Pyncheon in Hawthorne's *House of the Seven Gables* and the maddened striking through the mask of the great white whale in Melville's *Moby-Dick*); the use of experience and detail and the concern with the middle class in *The Web and the Rock* echoes the standards set by realists such as Howells, James, and Steinbeck; and the social consciousness of *You Can't Go Home Again* (in chapters such as "The Hollow Men") suggests the dark, absurd comedies of Ionesco and Beckett.

In another focus, Wolfe's four novels take the American concepts of *optimism* and *individualism* and the *will to power* expressed in works like Emerson's *Nature* and "The Poet" to an agonizing extreme. Emerson's precepts of *will* expressed in the final paragraphs of *Nature,* which urge the reader to "make therefore your own world," stem from the writings of earlier German Transcendentalists whose philosophies also found their way by the late nineteenth century into the writings of Goethe and then Nietzsche. By the twentieth century these philosophies had, in part, become rationalizations for the brutal inhumanities of the Fascist state of Nazi Germany. In his final trip to German in 1936, the historical basis for the last segment of *You Can't Go Home Again,* which originally appeared as the short story, "I Have a Thing to Tell You," Wolfe recognized the disastrous political consequences of the Romantic Emersonian *will* taken to an extreme. In an older, more-populated society, like Germany, the American *will to power* had joined with a generalized and inaccurate perception of the concept of *the survival of the fittest* to yield not democracy but Fascism, not an open but a closed society. As Bella Kussy points out in "The Vitalist Trend," one of the virtues attributed to Nazism by *Mein Kampf* is the reaffirmation of the "value of the individual" as opposed to Democracy's "dead weight of numbers" (317).

In Wolfe's last novels, he renunciates the attempt to capture the greatness of America in the dithyrambs and power of his prose and imagery and instead tries to analyze the dangers that await an America which continues to extrapolate, without reflection, on the Emersonian concept of the "individual" – in the process, ignoring the needs of the many. After his trip to Nazi Germany, Wolfe came to recognize the similarity between his early Romantic Egoism and the Romanticized Ethnocentrism of Nazi Germany. He had met the "enemy" and found him to be much the same as he was. In "turning away" from the Romantic Egoism of his first two novels, he attempts to suggest that America needs to turn away from its flawed Romantic image of itself and come to grips with the economic and social realities of post-Depression America.

Although his criticism of America during the Depression is somewhat obvious and superficial, Wolfe succeeds brilliantly in these works in showcasing the shallowness and unreality of the life and attitudes of sophisticated Americans and New York literati in regards to their fellow man. As such, Wolfe is the first American artist to come to see and record the social dangers of Emersonian *individualism* and *optimism* in the New World. As Kussy suggests, Wolfe's experience in Nazi Germany led him to believe not that democracy needed to be revitalized but that it needed to be "re-humanized."

In the light of this, Wolfe's frequently praised and haunting "Credo" at the end of *You Can't Go Home Again* takes on new meaning. He writes a passage as appropriate for the present decade as it was for the decades of the thirties and the forties:

> I believe that we are lost here in America, but I believe we shall be found. And this belief, which mounts now to the catharsis of knowledge and conviction, is for me – and I think for all of us – not only our own hope, but America's everlasting, living dream. I think the life which we have fashioned in America, and which has fashioned us – the forms we made, the cells that grew, the honeycomb that was created – was self-destructive in its nature, and must be destroyed. I think these forms are dying, and must die, just as I know that America and the people in it are deathless, undiscovered, and immortal, and must live.
>
> I think the true discovery of America is before us. I think the true fulfillment of our spirit, of our people, of our mighty and immortal land, is yet to come. I think the true discovery of our own democracy is still before us. And I think that all these things are certain as the morning, as inevitable as noon. I think I speak for most men living when I say that our America is Here, is Now, and beckons on before us, and that this glorious assurance is not only our living hope, but our dream to be accomplished.
>
> I think the enemy is here before us, too. But I think we know the forms and faces of the enemy, and in the knowledge that we know him, and shall meet him, and eventually must conquer him is also our living hope. I think the enemy is here before us with a thousand faces, but I think we know that all his faces wear one mask. I think the enemy is single selfishness and compulsive greed. I think the enemy is blind, but has the brutal power of his blind grab. I do not think the enemy was born yesterday, or that he grew to manhood forty years ago, or that he suffered sickness and collapse in 1929, or that we began without the enemy, and that our vision faltered, that we lost the way, and suddenly were in his camp. I think the enemy is as old as Time, and evil as Hell, and that he has been here with us from the beginning. (741–742)

Works Consulted

1. Works by Thomas Wolfe

(All references to writings by Thomas Wolfe in this volume are to the first printings of his works; references by critics to later printings of his works have been silently emended.)

Books

The Crisis in Industry. Chapel Hill, North Carolina: The University, 1919.

Look Homeward, Angel. New York: Scribners, 1929; London: Heinemann, 1930; translated by Hans Schiebelhuth as *Schau heimwärts, Engel!*, Berlin: Rowohlt, 1932.

Of Time and the River. New York: Scribners, 1935; London: Heinemann, 1935; translated by Hans Schiebelhuth as *Von Zeit und Strom*, Berlin: Rowohlt, 1936.

From Death to Morning. New York: Scribners, 1935; London: Heinemann, 1936; translated by Hans Schiebelhuth as *Vom Tod zum Morgen*, Berlin: Rowohlt, 1937.

The Story of a Novel. New York and London: Scribners, 1936; London: Heinemann, 1936; translated by Hans Schiebelhuth and H. M. Ledig-Rowohlt and included in the collection *Uns bleibt die Erde: Die "Geschichte eines Romans" mit Briefen und 4 Abbildungen*, Zurich: Verlag der Arche, 1951; reprinted in 1952 as *Uns bleibt die Erde*, Munich: Nymphenburger Verlagshandlung. Newly edited by Leslie Field along with "Writing and Living" in *The Autobiography of An American Novelist: Thomas Wolfe*, Cambridge, Massachusetts, and London: Harvard University Press, 1983.

The Web and the Rock. New York and London: Harper, 1939; London and Toronto: Heinemann, 1947; translated as *Strom des Lebens*, Bern: Alfred Scherz Verlag, 1941; translated by Susanna Rademacher as *Geweb und Fels*, Hamburg: Rowohlt Verlag, 1953.

You Can't Go Home Again. New York and London: Harper, 1940; London and Toronto: Heinemann, 1947; translated as *Es führt kein Weg zurück*, Bern: Alfred Scherz Verlag, 1942; translated by Susanna Rademacher as *Es führt kein Weg zurück*, Hamburg: Rowohlt Verlag, 1950.

The Hills Beyond. New York and London: Harper, 1941; translated as *Hinter jenen Bergen: Erzahlungen*, Hamburg: Rowohlt, 1956.

Thomas Wolfe's Letters to His Mother, edited by John Skally Terry. New York: Scribners, 1943; translated by Ina Seidel as *Thomas Wolfe Briefe an die Mutter*, Munich: Nymphenburger Verlagshandlung, 1949. Newly edited by C. Hugh Holman and Sue Fields Ross as *The Letters of Thomas Wolfe to His Mother*. Chapel Hill, North Carolina: U North Carolina P, 1968.

Mannerhouse: A Play in a Prologue and Three Acts. New York: Harper, 1948; Melbourne, London, and Toronto: Heinemann, 1950; translated by Peter Sandberg as *Herrenhaus: Schauspiel in drei Akten und einem Vorspiel*, Hamburg: Rowohlt Verlag, 1953. Newly edited by Louis D. Rubin, Jr., and John L. Idol, Jr., as *Mannerhouse: A Play in a Prologue and Four Acts*. Baton Rouge and London: Louisiana S U P, 1985.

The Correspondence of Thomas Wolfe and Homer Andrew Watt, edited by Oscar Cargill and Thomas Clark Pollock. New York: New York U P and London: Oxford U P, 1954.

The Letters of Thomas Wolfe, edited by Elizabeth Nowell. New York: Scribners, 1956; edited by Elizabeth Nowell and selected by Daniel George as *Selected Letters of Thomas Wolfe*. London, Melbourne, and Toronto: Heinemann, 1958; translated by Susanna Rademacher as *Thomas Wolfe Briefe*, n.p.: Rowohlt Verlag, 1961.

Thomas Wolfe's Purdue Speech "Writing and Living", edited by William Braswell and Leslie A. Field. Indiana: Purdue U Studies, 1964. Newly edited by Leslie Field along with "The Story of a Novel" in *The Autobiography of An American Novelist: Thomas Wolfe*, Cambridge, Massachusetts, and London: Harvard University Press, 1983.

The Notebooks of Thomas Wolfe, edited by Richard S. Kennedy and Paschal Reeves. Chapel Hill, North Carolina: U of North Carolina P, 1970. Two volumes.

The London Tower, edited by Aldo Magi. N.p.: The Thomas Wolfe Society, 1980.

The Streets of Durham, edited by Richard Walser. Raleigh: Wolfe's Head Press, 1982.

Welcome to Our City, edited by Richard S. Kennedy. Baton Rouge and London: Louisiana State U P, 1983; translated by Peter Sandberg and Susan Rademacher from *Esquire Magazine*, October 1957, as *Willkommen in Altamont! Herrenhaus: Zwei Dramen*, Hamburg: Rowohlt, 1962.

Thomas Wolfe K – 19: Salvaged Pieces, edited by John L. Idol, Jr. N.p.: The Thomas Wolfe Society, 1983.

Beyond Love and Loyalty: The Letters of Thomas Wolfe and Elizabeth Nowell Together with "No More Rivers" A Story by Thomas Wolfe, edited by Richard S. Kennedy. Chapel Hill, North Carolina, and London: U of North Carolina P, 1983.

My Other Loneliness: Letters of Thomas Wolfe and Aline Bernstein, edited by Suzanne Stutman. Chapel Hill, North Carolina, and London: U of North Carolina P, 1983.

The Train and the City, edited by Richard S. Kennedy. N.p.: The Thomas Wolfe Society, 1984.

Holding on for Heaven, edited by Suzanne Stutman. N.p.: The Thomas Wolfe Society, 1985.

The Hound of Darkness, edited by John L. Idol, Jr. N.p.: The Thomas Wolfe Society, 1986.

The Starwick Episodes, edited by Richard S. Kennedy. N.p.: The Thomas Wolfe Society, 1989; reprinted by Louisiana State U P, 1994.

Thomas Wolfe's Composition Books: The North State Fitting School 1912–1915, edited by Alice R. Cotten. N.p.: The Thomas Wolfe Society, 1990.

The Autobiographical Outline for Look Homeward, Angel, edited by Lucy Conniff and Richard S. Kennedy. N.p.: The Thomas Wolfe Society, 1991.

The Good Child's River, edited by Suzanne Stutman. Chapel Hill, North Carolina, and London: U of North Carolina P, 1991.

Thomas Wolfe's Notes on Macbeth: *The University of North Carolina, English 37, Winter Quarter 1919*, edited by William Grimes Cherry III. N.p.: The Thomas Wolfe Society, 1992.

The Lost Boy: A Novella by Thomas Wolfe, edited by James W. Clark, Jr. Chapel Hill, North Carolina, and London: U of North Carolina P, 1992.

The Party At Jack's: A Novella, edited by Suzanne Stutman and John L. Idol, Jr. Chapel Hill, North Carolina, and London: U of North Carolina P, 1995.

Posthumously Published Collections

The Portable Thomas Wolfe, edited by Maxwell Geismar. New York: The Viking Press, 1946; reprinted in 1950 in New York by the Book Society as *The Indispensable Thomas Wolfe*; reprinted in 1952 by Heinemann in Melbourne, London, and Toronto as *Selections from the Works of Thomas Wolfe*.

The Short Novels of Thomas Wolfe, edited by C. Hugh Holman. New York: Scribners, 1961.

The Autobiography of an American Novelist: Thomas Wolfe, edited by Leslie Field. Cambridge, Massachusetts, and London: Harvard University Press, 1983.

Thomas Wolfe Interviewed: 1929–1938, edited by Aldo P. Magi and Richard Walser. Baton Rouge and London: Louisiana State U P, 1985.

The Complete Short Stories of Thomas Wolfe, edited by Francis E. Skipp. New York: Macmillan Publishing; London: Collier Macmillan, 1987.

Miscellaneous

"An Angel on the Porch." *Scribner's Magazine*, 86 (August 1929), 205–210.

"Dark in the Forest, Strange as Time." *Scribner's Magazine*, 96 (November 1934), 273–278.

"I Have a Thing to Tell You: (Nun will ich ihnen 'was sagen)." *The New Republic*, 90 (10 March 1937), 132–136; (17 March 1937), 159–164; and (24 March 1937), 202–207.

"Portrait of a Literary Critic: A Satire." *The American Mercury*, 46 (April 1939), 429–437.

"An American Author's Testament: Unpublished Letter of the Late Thomas Wolfe Reveals a Changed Outlook." *The* (New York) *Daily Worker*, 15 May 1939, p. 7.

"Eleven More Letters of Thomas Wolfe, 1929–1938," edited by Aldo P. Magi. *The South Carolina Review*, 24 (Spring 1992), 5–31.

2. Works about Thomas Wolfe: Books, Reviews, and Critical Assessments

(References to reviews and critical essays published about the writings of Thomas Wolfe refer to the *earliest* printing unless otherwise indicated. Many of these reviews and essays appear as reprints in revised and excerpted format. To locate later versions of these works, see the Phillipson and Johnson bibliographies listed below, as well as the annual updates in *The Thomas Wolfe Review*.)

Books

PRIMARY BIBLIOGRAPHY:

Johnston, Carol. *Thomas Wolfe: A Descriptive Bibliography*. Pittsburgh: U Pittsburgh P, 1987.

SECONDARY BIBLIOGRAPHY:

Johnson, Elmer D. *Thomas Wolfe: A Checklist*. OH: Kent State U P, 1970.

Phillipson, John S. *Thomas Wolfe: A Reference Guide*. Boston: G. K. Hall, 1977; updated to 1981 in "Thomas Wolfe: A Reference Guide Updated," *Resources for American Literary Study*, 11 (Spring 1981), 37–80; and thereafter updated by the bibliographical material published in the fall and spring issues of *The Thomas Wolfe Review*.

BIOGRAPHIES:

Donald, David Herbert. *Look Homeward: A Life of Thomas Wolfe*. Boston and Toronto: Little, Brown, 1987.

Nowell, Elizabeth. *Thomas Wolfe: A Biography*. New York: Doubleday, 1960.

Turnbull, Andrew. *Thomas Wolfe*. New York: Scribners, 1967.

Walser, Richard. *Thomas Wolfe: Undergraduate.* Durham, North Carolina: Duke U P, 1977.

HISTORICAL AND CRITICAL STUDIES:

Berg, A. Scott. *Max Perkins: Editor of Genius.* New York: Dutton, 1978.

Daniels, Jonathan. *Thomas Wolfe: October Recollections.* Columbia, South Carolina: Bostick & Thornley, 1961.

Doll, Mary Aswell, and Clara Stites, ed. *In the Shadow of the Giant: Thomas Wolfe.* Athens, Ohio: Ohio U P, 1988.

Evans, Elizabeth. *Thomas Wolfe.* New York: Ungar, 1984.

Field, Leslie. *Thomas Wolfe and His Editors: Establishing a True Text for the Posthumous Publications.* Norman, Oklahoma, and London: U Oklahoma P, 1987.

Fisher, Vardis. *Thomas Wolfe As I Knew Him.* Denver:Swallow, 1963.

Gurko, Leo. *Thomas Wolfe: Beyond the Romantic Ego.* New York: Crowell, 1975.

Harper, Margaret Mills. *The Aristocracy of Art in Joyce and Wolfe.* Baton Rouge and London: Louisiana S U P, 1990.

Holman, C. Hugh. *Thomas Wolfe.* Minneapolis: U of Minnesota P, 1960.

–––. *The Loneliness at the Core: Studies in Thomas Wolfe.* Baton Rouge: Louisiana S U P, 1975.

Idol, John Lane, Jr. *A Thomas Wolfe Companion.* New York; Westport, Connecticut; London: Greenwood P, 1987.

Johnson, Pamela Hansford. *Hungry Gulliver: An English Critical Appraisal of Thomas Wolfe.* New York: Scribners, 1948. First published as *Thomas Wolfe A Critical Study*, London and Toronto: Heinemann, 1947.

Kennedy, Richard S. *The Window of Memory: The Literary Career of Thomas Wolfe.* Chapel Hill: U North Carolina P, 1962.

Klein, Carole. *Aline.* NY: Harper & Row, 1979.

Magi, Aldo P., and Richard Walser. *Wolfe and Belinda Jelliffe.* N.p.: The Thomas Wolfe Society, 1987.

Muller, Herbert J. *Thomas Wolfe.* Norfolk, Connecticut: New Directions, 1947.

Norwood, Hayden. *The Marble Man's Wife: Thomas Wolfe's Mother.* New York: Scribners, 1947.

Pfister, Karin. *Zeit und Wirklichkeit bei Thomas Wolfe.* Heidelberg: Carl Winter, 1954.

Reeves, Paschal. *Thomas Wolfe's Albatross: Race and Nationality in America.* Athens, GA: U Georgia P, 1968.

Rubin, Louis D., Jr. *Thomas Wolfe: The Weather of His Youth.* Baton Rouge: Louisiana S U P, 1955.

Walser, Richard. *Thomas Wolfe: An Introduction and Interpretation.* New York, Chicago, San Francisco, Toronto, and London: Holt, Rinehart and Winston, 1961.

Watkins, Floyd. *Thomas Wolfe's Characters: Portraits from Life.* Norman: U Oklahoma P, 1957.

Wyatt, David, David Strange, and Phillip Horne. *How I Got Hooked on Thomas Wolfe.* Bloomington, IN: n. pub., 1990.

COLLECTIONS:

(Many of the reviews and articles referred to in the text are reprinted or excerpted in the following collections.)

Bloom, Harold. *Thomas Wolfe.* New York, New Haven, and Philadelphia: Chelsea House, 1987.

Field, Leslie, ed. *Thomas Wolfe: Three Decades of Criticism.* NY: New York U P; London: U of London P, 1968.

Holman, C. Hugh, ed. *The World of Thomas Wolfe.* New York: Scribners, 1962.

Jones, H. G. ed. *Thomas Wolfe of North Carolina.* Chapel Hill: North Caroliniana Society and the North Carolina Collection, 1982.

———. *Thomas Wolfe at Eighty-seven.* Chapel Hill: North Caroliniana Society and the North Carolina Collection, 1988.

Kennedy, Richard S., ed. *Thomas Wolfe: A Harvard Perspective.* Athens, Ohio: Croissant, 1983.

Phillipson, John S., ed. *Critical Essays on Thomas Wolfe.* Boston: G. K. Hall, 1985.

Pollock, Thomas C., and Oscar Cargill, ed. *Thomas Wolfe at Washington Square.* New York: New York University Press, 1954.

Reeves, Paschal, ed. *The Merrill Studies in* Look Homeward, Angel. Columbus, Ohio: Merrill, 1970.

———. *Thomas Wolfe and the Glass of Time.* Athens: U of Georgia P, 1971.

———. *Thomas Wolfe: The Critical Reception.* New York: David Lewis, 1974.

Rubin, Louis D., ed. *Thomas Wolfe: A Collection of Critical Essays.* Englewood Cliffs, New Jersey: Prentice-Hall, 1973.

Walser, Richard, ed. *The Enigma of Thomas Wolfe: Biographical and Critical Selections.* Cambridge: Harvard U P, 1953.

Reviews

F[ranklin]. P. A[dams]. "The Conning Tower." *The New York World,* 6 February 1930. Review of *Look Homeward, Angel.*

Adams, J. Donald. "A New Novel by Thomas Wolfe." *The New York Times Book Review,* 25 June 1939, p. 1. Review of *The Web and the Rock.*

———. "Thomas Wolfe's Last Novel." *The New York Times Book Review*, 22 September 1940, p. 1. Review of *You Can't Go Home Again*.

Adams, Walter S. "Amazing New Novel Is Realistic Story of Asheville People." *The Asheville Times*, 20 October 1929, pp. 1–2. Review of *Look Homeward, Angel*.

Aldington, Richard. "American Novelists." *The* (London) *Sunday Referee*, 6 July 1930, p. 6. English review of *Look Homeward, Angel*.

Alker, Ernst. "Thomas Wolfe und die neue amerikanische Dichtung." *Wort und Wahrheit*, 3 (November 1948), 852–857. German review of *Look Homeward, Angel, Of Time and the River, The Web and the Rock*, and *You Can't Go Home Again*.

Angoff, Charles. "A Promise and a Legend." *The North American Review*, 248 (Autumn 1939), 198–201. Review of *The Web and the Rock*.

Barr, Stringfellow. "The Dandridges and the Gants." *Virginia Quarterly Review*, 6 (Spring 1930), 310–313. Review of *Look Homeward, Angel*.

Basso, Hamilton. "Thomas Wolfe: A Summing Up." *The New Republic*, 103 (23 September 1940), 422–423. Review of *You Can't Go Home Again*.

Benét, Stephen Vincent. "Thomas Wolfe's Torrent of Recollection." *The Saturday Review of Literature*, 22 (21 September 1940), 5. Review of *You Can't Go Home Again*.

"Books of the Day." *London Times*, 20 August 1935, p. 7. English review of *Of Time and the River*.

Bradley, Phillips. "Unselective Bulk." *The Springfield Sunday Union and Republican*, 31 March 1935, p. 7E. Review of *Of Time and the River*.

Brickell, Herschel. "Books on Our Table." *New York Post*, 8 March 1935, p. 7. Review of *Of Time and the River*.

———. "Men, Women, and Books." *Review of Reviews*, 91 (May 1935), 4. Review of *Of Time and the River*.

Butcher, Fanny. "A Posthumous Novel Upholds Wolfe's Genius." *Chicago Daily Tribune*, 24 June 1939. Review of *The Web and the Rock*.

———. "Thomas Wolfe Attains Heights of True Genius." *Chicago Tribune*, 18 September 1940, p. 12. Review of *You Can't Go Home Again*.

Calverton, V. F. "Thomas Wolfe and the Great American Novel." *The Modern Monthly*, 9 (June 1935), 249–250. Review of *Of Time and the River*.

Cameron, May. "Thomas Wolfe's Superb Farewell." *New York Post*, 22 June 1939, p. 13. Review of *The Web and the Rock*.

Canby, Henry Seidel. "The River of Youth." *The Saturday Review of Literature*, 11 (9 March 1935), 529–530. Review of *Of Time and the River*.

Cantwell, Robert. "Books." *New Outlook*, 165 (April 1935), 10, 58. Review of *Of Time and the River*.

Chamberlain, John. Untitled review of *Look Homeward, Angel*. *The Bookman* (December 1929), 449–450.

———. "Books of the Times." *The New York Times*, 8 March 1935, p. L-19. Review of *Of Time and the River*.   p.

———. "Books of the Times." *The New York Times*, 12 March 1935, p. 19. Review of *Of Time and the River*.

Clay, R. T. Untitled review of *The Correspondence of Thomas Wolfe and Homer Andrew Watt* and *Thomas Wolfe at Washington Square*. *Durham Morning Herald*, 14 February 1954, sec. 4:7.

Colum, Mary M. "Spring Books in Review." *The Forum and Century*, 93 (April 1935), 218–219. Review of *Of Time and the River*.

———. "Literature of Today and Tomorrow." *Scribner's Magazine* (December 1936), 98, 100, 102, 104, 106–109.

Cowley, Malcolm. "The Forty Days of Thomas Wolfe." *The New Republic*, 20 March 1935, pp. 163–164. Review of *Of Time and the River*.

———. "Thomas Wolfe's Legacy." *The New Republic*, 99 (19 July 1939), 311–312. Review of *The Web and the Rock*.

Cronin, A. J. "A Book in Which a Man Reveals His Soul and Writes with His Soul." *New York Sun*, 11 March 1935. Review of *Of Time and the River*.

Daniels, Jonathan. "Looking Both Ways." *Raleigh News and Observer*, 18 October 1929, p. 4. Review of *Look Homeward, Angel*.

———. "Wolfe's First Is Novel of Revolt: Former Asheville Writer Turns in Fury upon N.C. and the South." *Raleigh News and Observer*, 20 October 1929, p. 2. Review of *Look Homeward, Angel*.

Davidson, Donald. "Farewell – and Hail!" *Nashville Tennessean*, 16 February 1930. Review of *Look Homeward, Angel*.

DeVoto, Bernard. "A Novel Hammered Out of Experience." *The Saturday Review of Literature*, 12 (27 April 1935), 645. Review of Boyd's *Roll River* that compares it to Wolfe's *Of Time and the River*.

———. "Genius Is Not Enough." *The Saturday Review of Literature*, 13 (25 April 1936), 3–4, 14–15. Review of *The Story of a Novel* that focuses on *Of Time and the River*.

Dewey, Edward Hooker. "The Storm and Stress Period." *Survey Graphic*, 24 (May 1935), 255. Review of *Of Time and the River*.

Effelberger, Hans. "Neue Entwicklungstendenzen in der amerikanishchen Literatur der Gegenwart." *Die Neuren Sprachen*, 44 (1936), 154–161. German review of *Of Time and the River*.

Fadiman, Clifton. "Thomas Wolfe." *The New Yorker* (9 March 1935), 68–70. Some copies of this issue have been located with Fadiman's review appearing on pp. 79–82. Review of *Of Time and the River*.

———. "*The Web and the Rock*." *The New Yorker* (24 June 1939), 69–70.

E[dwin]. F[airley]. Untitled review of *Look Homeward Angel*. *The Christian Register*, 9 January 1930, p. 31.

Fearing, Kenneth. "A First Novel of Vast Scope 'Look Homeward, Angel' an American Saga in Southern Setting." *The New York Evening Post*, 16 November 1929, 12m. Review of *Look Homeward, Angel*.

Fisher, Paul. "Wolfe's Last Look Homeward." *Kansas City Star*, 24 June 1939, p. 14. Review of *The Web and the Rock*.

Franke, Hans. "Unerwünschte Einfuhr." *Die Neue Literatur* (October 1937), 501–508. German review of *Of Time and the River*.

Franzen, Erich. German review of *Look Homeward, Angel*. *Berliner Börsen-Courier*. See Translations 1.

Freeman, Joseph. "Mask, Image, and Truth." *Partisan Review*, 2 (July-August 1935), 3–17. Review of *Of Time and the River*.

Friedrich, Detta. "Thomas Wolfe." *Die Christliche Welt*, 50 (19 December 1936), 1117–1121. Review of *Of Time and the River*.

Gannett, Lewis. "Books and Things." *New York Herald Tribune*, 8 March 1935, p. 17. Review of *Of Time and the River*.

Gould, Gerald. "The Home and the World." *The* (London) *Observer*, 17 August 1930, p. 5. English review of *Look Homeward, Angel*.

Günther, A. E. Untitled, undated German review of *Look Homeward, Angel*. *Deutsches Volkstum* (Hamburg). See Translations 3.

Hansen, Harry. "Ah, Life! Life!" *The New York World*, 26 October 1929, p. 15. Review of *Look Homeward, Angel*.

———. "The First Reader." *The New York World-Telegram*, 8 March 1935. Review of *Of Time and the River*.

Hart, Henry. "*You Can't Go Home Again*." *The New Masses*, 22 October 1940, pp. 25–26.

Hesse, Hermann. Title unknown. *Neue Züricher Zeitung*, undated and unpaginated clipping; reprinted as an enclosure to an advertising brochure sent out by Rowohlt Verlag on 27 April 1933. Review of *Look Homeward, Angel*. See Translations 2.

———. "Notizen zu neuen Büchern." *Die Neue Rundschau*, 46 (December 1935), 664–672. German review of *Look Homeward, Angel*.

Jack, Peter Munro. "Mr. Wolfe's Pilgrim Progresses." *The New York Times Book Review*, 10 March 1935, pp. 1, 14. Review of *Of Time and the River*.

Jones, Howard Mumford. "Social Notes on the South." *Virginia Quarterly Review*, 11 (July 1935), 452–457. Review of *Of Time and the River*.

Jones, Weimar. "Of Time and the River." *The Asheville Citizen*, 21 April 1935, B-6.

Jordan-Smith, Paul. Untitled review of *You Can't Go Home Again*. *The Los Angeles Times*, 22 September 1940.

Karsten, Otto. German review of *Look Homeward, Angel* and *Of Time and the River*. *Die Literatur*, 38 (February/March 1936), 308–311.

———. "Thomas Wolfe und sein großes Epos vom amerikanischen Leben." *Das Deutsche Wort*, 12 (April 1936), 454–457. German review of *Look Homeward, Angel* and *Of Time and the River*.

Koischwitz, Otto. "Echo des Auslands." *Die Literatur*, 43 (February 1941), 240–241. Includes a brief German review of *You Can't Go Home Again*.

Latimer, Margery. "The American Family." *The New York Herald Tribune Books*, 3 November 1929, p. 20. Review of *Look Homeward, Angel*.

Lee, Charles. "Thomas Wolfe in Tempestuous Novel about Art, Love, and Genius." *The Boston Herald*, 24 June 1939, p. 9. Review of *The Web and the Rock*.

Linden, Hermann. Review of *Look Homeward, Angel*. *Frankfurter Nachrichten*. See Translations 2.

"*Look Homeward, Angel*." *The* (London) *Times Literary Supplement*, 24 July 1930, p. 608. English review of *Look Homeward, Angel*.

Love, Lola M. "Stirring First Novel by Local Man Making Big Hit in Literary World." *The Asheville Citizen*, 20 October 1929, p. 8C. Review of *Look Homeward, Angel*.

MacAfee, Helen. "Outstanding Novels." *The Yale Review*, 24 (Summer 1935), vi-viii. Review of *Of Time and the River*.

Mebane, John. "Laughter and Tears." *Carolina Magazine*, 59 (2 February 1930), 4. Review of *Look Homeward Angel*.

Münzer, Kurt. Review of *Look Homeward, Angel*. (Vienna) *Neue Freie Presse*. See Translations 3.

O'Faolain, Seán. "Fiction." *The* (London) *Spectator*, 23 August 1935, p. 300. English review of *Of Time and the River*.

"Of Time and the River." *The* (London) *Times Literary Supplement*, 22 August 1935, p. 522. English review of *Of Time and the River*.

I[sabel]. M. P[aterson]. "Turns with a Bookworm." *The New York Herald Tribune Books*, 24 February 1935, sec. 7:18. Review of *Of Time and the River*.

———. "Turns with a Bookworm." *The New York Herald Tribune Books*, 24 February 1935, sec. 7:18. Review of *Of Time and the River*.

Poore, Charles. "Books of the Times." *The New York Times*, 22 June 1939, p. 21. Review of *The Web and the Rock*.

Porterfield, Allen W. "The Book of the Day." *The New York Sun*, 22 June 1939, p. 15. Review of *The Web and the Rock*.

Powell, Desmond. "Wolfe's Farewells." *Accent*, 1 (Winter 1941), 114–118. Review of *You Can't Go Home Again*.

Quennell, Peter. "New Novels." *The New Statesman and Nation*, 24 August 1935, p. 253. Review of *Of Time and the River*.

[Radecki, Sigismund]. "Thomas Wolfe: Schau Heimwärts, Engel!" *Der Querschnitt*, 13 (October 1933), p. 503. German review of *Look Homeward, Angel*.

Rascoe, Burton. Review of *Look Homeward, Angel*. *Arts and Decoration* (February 1930), 106. Review of *Look Homeward, Angel*.

———. "The Ecstasy, Fury, Pain and Beauty of Life: Thomas Wolfe Sings and Shouts in His Gargantuan New Novel." *The New York Herald Tribune Books*, 10 March 1935, pp. 1–2. Review of *Of Time and the River*.

———. "Of Time and Thomas Wolfe." *Newsweek*, 13 (26 June 1939), p. 36. Review of *The Web and the Rock*.

R[obert]. R[aynolds]. "Gargantuan First Novel." *Scribner's Magazine*, 86 (December 1929), "Literary Signposts," pp. 34, 38. Review of *Look Homeward, Angel*.

R. E. M. "Wolfe Adds Fresh Fuel to His Fire: Posthumous Novel Continues Story of Search for Understanding." *Buffalo Evening News*, 24 June 1939. Review of *The Web and the Rock*.

Rhodes, Arthur. "*The Web and the Rock*: Stormy Struggle for Life's Secret." *Brooklyn Eagle*, 22 June 1939, p. 26.

Robbins, Frances Lamont. "The Leisure Arts." *Outlook and Independent*, 153 (25 December 1929), 669. Review of *Look Homeward, Angel*.

Roberts, Mary-Carter. "Writer and Hero Merge in 'Discovery of Life.'" *Washington Sunday Star*, 25 June 1939, p. F-4. Review of *The Web and the Rock*.

Rugoff, Milton. "Violently, Desperately, Hungeringly Alive." *The New York Herald Tribune Books*, 22 September 1940, p. 5.

"Saga of American Life." *London Times*, 20 August 1935, p. 7. English review of *Of Time and the River*.

Scott, Evelyn. "Colossal Fragment." *Scribner's Magazine*, 97 (June 1935), 2, 4. Review of *Of Time and the River*.

Shaw, Thomas J. "Rare Wine Mixed with Stiff Corn." Duke University *Archive*, 42 (March 1930), 23–24. Review of *Look Homeward, Angel*.

Simpson, Claude. Untitled review of *You Can't Go Home Again*. *Southwest Review*, 26 (Autumn 1940), pp. 132–135.

Slocum, John. Untitled review of *Of Time and the River*. *The North American Review*, 240 (June 1935), 175–177.

Sonnemann, Ullrich. Untitled, undated German review of *Look Homeward, Angel*. *Berliner Tageblatt*. See Translations 1.

Starkey, Marion L. "Along the Course of Time and the River." *The Boston Evening Transcript*, 9 March 1935, Book Section: 1.

Stevens, George. "Always Looking Homeward." *The Saturday Review of Literature*, 20 (24 June 1939), 5–6. Review of *The Web and the Rock*.

Styron, William. "The Shade of Thomas Wolfe." *Harper's Magazine*, 236 (April 1968), 96, 98–102. Review of Turnbull, *Thomas Wolfe*.

Sugarman, Joe. "Thomas Wolfe Hungers On." *Carolina Magazine*, 64 (April 1935), 22–24. Review of *Of Time and the River*.

Swinnerton, Frank. "Where Are the Story-Tellers?" *The* (London) *Evening News*, 8 August 1930, p. 8. English review of *Look Homeward, Angel*.

Sylvester, Harry. Untitled review of *You Can't Go Home Again*. *Commonweal*, 33 (25 October 1940), 29–30.

Theunissen, Gert H. "Thomas Wolfe." *Der Bücherwurm*, 21 (1936), 194–195. German review of *Of Time and the River*.

"Thomas Wolfe Tells Startling Story of North Carolina Life." Unidentified, undated review of *Look Homeward, Angel* (UNC-CH).

Translations of excerpts from the German reviews of *Look Homeward, Angel* by Erich Franzen, Ullrich Sonnemann, Lutz Weltmann, Hermann Hesse, Hermann Linden, Ludwig Winder, Benno Reifenberg, Kurt Münzer, and A. E. Günther. Untitled, three-page document (Houghton Library, Harvard University *AC9.W8327.LZ999g.Box 1).

C[arl]. V[an]. D[oren]. Untitled review of *Look Homeward, Angel*. (Literary Guild) *Wings* (February 1930), 17.

W[olfgang]. v[on]. E[inseidel]. "Romandichtung." *Europäische Umschau* (October 1936), 841–844. German review of *Of Time and the River*.

Wade, John Donald. "Prodigal." *The Southern Review*, 1 (July 1935), 192–198. Review of *Of Time and the River*.

Wagner, Charles A. Untitled review of *You Can't Go Home Again*. *The New York Mirror*, 18 September 1940.

Wallace, Margaret. "A Novel of Provincial American Life." *The New York Times Book Review*, 27 October 1929, p. 7. Review of *Look Homeward, Angel*.

Warren, Robert Penn. "A Note on the Hamlet of Thomas Wolfe." *The American Review*, 5 (May 1935), 191–208. Review of *Of Time and the River*.

Wilson, Elizabeth. "Of Time and the River." Asheville, NC, Biltmore College *Bluets*, 7 (1935), 31–32.

Winder, Ludwig. Review of *Look Homeward, Angel. Deutsche Zeitung*. See Translations 2.

"Wolfe Novel Causes 'Stir' in This Section; Lauded in New York." *The Asheville Times*, 27 October 1929. Review of *Look Homeward, Angel*.

Young, Richard L. "Wolfe Pictures Man and Carolina Scenes." *Charlotte News*, 15 December 1929, p. 5B. Review of *Look Homeward, Angel*.

Critical Assessments and Articles

Albrecht, W. P. "Time as Unity in the Novels of Thomas Wolfe." *New Mexico Quarterly*, 19 (Autumn 1949), 320–329.

Aswell, Edward. "A Note on Thomas Wolfe." In *The Hills Beyond*, pp. 351–386.

———. "Thomas Wolfe Did Not Kill Maxwell Perkins." *The Saturday Review of Literature* (6 October 1951), 16–17, 44–46.

Beach, Joseph Warren. "Thomas Wolfe: Discovery of Brotherhood." In *American Fiction: 1920–1940*. New York: Macmillan, 1941, pp. 197–215.

———. "Thomas Wolfe: The Search for a Father." In *American Fiction, 1920–1940*, pp. 173–193.

Beja, Morris. "Why You Can't Go Home Again: Thomas Wolfe and 'The Escapes of Time and Memory.'" *Modern Fiction Studies*, 11 (Autumn 1965), 297–314.

Benét, William Rose. Untitled. *Book-of-the-Month Club News* (September 1945), 19.

Bishop, John Peale. "The Myth and Modern Literature." *The Saturday Review of Literature* (22 July 1939), 3–4, 14.

———. "The Sorrows of Thomas Wolfe." *The Kenyon Review*, 1 (Winter 1939), 7–17.

Brabham, Lionel. "Wolfean Baby Talk." *American Speech*, 31 (December 1956), 302–303.

Brickell, Herschel. "Thomas Wolfe's Two Books Make Him the Country's Outstanding Literary Figure of Present Year." *New York Post*, 14 December 1935, p. 15.

Budd, Louis J. "The Grotesques of Anderson and Wolfe." *Modern Fiction Studies*, 5 (Winter 1959), 304–310.

Burgum, Edwin Berry. "Thomas Wolfe's Discovery of America." *Virginia Quarterly Review*, 22 (Summer 1946), 421–437.

Burt, Struthers. "Catalyst for Genius." *The Saturday Review of Literature* (9 June 1951), 6–8, 36–39.

———. Responses to Letters to the Editor. *The Saturday Review of Literature* (11 August 1951), 23–24.

Cargill, Oscar. "Gargantua Fills His Skin." *University of Kansas City Review*, 16 (Autumn 1949), 20–30.

Cash, Wilbur J. "Of the Great Blight – and New Quandries." In *The Mind of the South*. New York: Knopf, 1954, pp. 376–379.

Church, Margaret. "Dark Time." *Publications of the Modern Language Association*, 64 (September 1949), 629–638.

Collins, Thomas Lyle. "Thomas Wolfe." *The Sewanee Review*, 50 (October-December 1942), 487–504.

Colum, Mary M. "Literature of Today and Tomorrow." *Scribner's Magazine* (December 1936), 98, 100, 102, 104, 106–109.

Commager, Henry Steele. "The Literature of Revolt." In *The American Mind*. New Haven: Yale U P, 1950, pp. 267–268, 275–276.

Cowley, Malcolm. "Thomas Wolfe." *The Atlantic Monthly* (November 1957), 202, 204, 206, 208, 210, 212.

Cracroft, Richard H. "A Pebble in the Pool: Organic Theme and Structure in Thomas Wolfe's *You Can't Go Home Again*." *Modern Fiction Studies*, 17 (Winter 1971), 533–553.

Cummings, Ridgely. Letter to the Editor. *The Saturday Review of Literature* (11 August 1951), 23–24.

Demming, Charlotte. German review of American literature. *Gral*, 27 (1932-), 203+.

[DeVoto, Bernard]. "On Beginning to Write a Novel." *Harper's Magazine* (July 1936), 179–188.

Dickson, Frank A. A series of articles appearing in the Anderson, South Carolina, *Independent*. Articles in this series include "Thomas Wolfe Started His Hard Work Early," 17 July 1948, p. 5; "Wolfe Play To Be in N.Y.: Will Appear In Book Form," 7 August 1948, p. 5; and "Wyler Will Direct Motion Picture of Famous Novel," 21 August 1948, p. 5.

Fadiman, Clifton. "Of Nothing and the Wolfe." *The American Spectator* (October 1935), 4, 14.

Field, Leslie A. "*You Can't Go Home Again*: Wolfe's Germany and Social Consciousness." In *Critical Essays on Thomas Wolfe*, pp. 99–112. This essay first appeared in H. G. Jones, ed. *Thomas Wolfe of North Carolina*.

Fisher, Vardis. Letter to Elizabeth Nowell, 4 September 1950 (UNC-CH).

----."My Experiences with Thomas Wolfe." *Tomorrow*, 10 (April 1951), 24–30.

----. "Thomas Wolfe and Maxwell Perkins." *Tomorrow*, 10 (July 1951), 20–25.

Foster, Ruel E. "Thomas Wolfe's Mountain Gloom and Glory." *American Literature*, 44 (January 1973), 638–647.

Frenz, Horst. "Bemerkungen über Thomas Wolfe." *Die Neueren Sprachen*, 2 (1953), 371–377.

Frohock, W. M. "Thomas Wolfe: Of Time and Neurosis." *Southwest Review*, 33 (Autumn 1948), 349–360.

Fuchs, Konrad. "Thomas Wolfe der suchende realist." *Die Neuren Sprachen*, 12 (1963), 110–117.

Geismar, Maxwell. "Thomas Wolfe: The Unfound Door." In *Writers in Crisis: The American Novel Between Two Wars*. Boston: Houghton Mifflin, 1942, pp. 187–235.

Gelfant, Blanche Housman. "The City as Symbol." In *The American City Novel*. Norman: U of Oklahoma P, 1954, pp. 119–132.

Green, Charmian. "Wolfe's Stonecutter Once Again: An Unpublished Episode." *Mississippi Quarterly*, 30 (Fall 1977), 611–623.

Hagan, John. "Thomas Wolfe's *Of Time and the River*: The Quest for Transcendence." In *Thomas Wolfe: A Harvard Perspective*, pp. 3–20.

Halberstadt, John. "The Making of Thomas Wolfe's Posthumous Novels." *The Yale Review*, 70 (October 1980), 79–94.

–––. "Concluding Thomas Wolfe's *The Web and the Rock*."In *The Proceedings of The Thomas Wolfe Society: The Tenth Annual Meeting*, edited by Harold Woodell. Clemson, SC: The Thomas Wolfe Society, 1989, pp. 28–44.

Halperin, Irving. "Man Alive." *Delphian Quarterly*, 41 (Winter 1958), 1–3, 31.

Hampson, Carolyn. "The Morels and the Gants: Sexual Conflict as a Universal Theme." *The Thomas Wolfe Review*, 8 (Spring 1984), 27–40.

Hemingway, Ernest. "Green Hills of Africa: Part II." *Scribner's Magazine*, 97 (June 1935), 334–344.

Hill, John S. "Eugene Gant and the Ghost of Ben." *Modern Fiction Studies*, 11 (Autumn 1965), 245–249.

Hoagland, Kathleen, and Clayton Hoagland. "Terry, Wolfe, and the Biography That Never Was." *The Thomas Wolfe Newsletter*, 1 (Spring 1977), 9–14.

Holman, C. Hugh. "The Loneliness at the Core." *The New Republic*, 133 (10 October 1955), 16–17.

–––. "Thomas Wolfe: A Bibliographical Study." *Texas Studies in Literature and Language*, 1 (Autumn 1959), 427–445.

–––. "'The Dark, Ruined Helen of His Blood': Thomas Wolfe and the South." In *South: Modern Southern Literature in its Cultural Setting*, edited by Louis D. Rubin, Jr., and Robert Jacobs. Garden City, New York: Doubleday-Dolphin, 1961, pp. 177 – 197.

–––. "Thomas Wolfe's Berlin." *The Saturday Review of Literature* (11 March 1967), 66, 69, 90.

———. "Thomas Wolfe: Rhetorical Hope and Dramatic Despair." In *Thomas Wolfe and the Glass of Time*, pp. 78–96.

Idol, John L., Jr. "Thomas Wolfe and T. S. Eliot: The Hippopotamus and the Old Possum." *The Southern Literary Journal* (Spring 1981), 15–26.

———. "Fame and the Athlete in Wolfe's Fiction." In *Critical Essays on Thomas Wolfe*, pp. 112–118.

———. "Richard S. Kennedy." In *Dictionary of Literary Biography: American Literary Biographers (Second Series)*, edited by Steven Serafin. Detroit: Gale Research, 1991, pp. 117–127.

———. "Thomas Wolfe and Marjorie Kinnan Rawlings." In *Thomas Wolfe at Eighty-seven*, pp. 20–27.

Jenkins, Elaine P. "The Gants in a Bottle." In *Thomas Wolfe at Eighty-seven*, pp. 71–81.

Johnson, Edgar. "Thomas Wolfe and the American Dream." In *A Treasury of Satire*. New York: Simon & Schuster, 1945, pp. 741–745.

Johnson, Pamela Hansford. "Thomas Wolfe and the Kicking Season." *Encounter*, 12 (April 1959), 77–80.

Kazin, Alfred. "The Rhetoric and the Agony." In *On Native Grounds: An Interpretation of Modern American Prose Literature*. New York: Harcourt Brace, 1942; reissued 1970, pp. 470–484.

Kennedy, Richard S. "Wolfe's *Look Homeward, Angel* as a Novel of Development." *South Atlantic Quarterly*, 63 (Spring 1964), 218–226.

———. "Thomas Wolfe and the American Experience." *Modern Fiction Studies*, 11 (Autumn 1965), 219–233.

———. "Thomas Wolfe's Fiction: The Question of Genre." In *Thomas Wolfe and the Glass of Time*, pp. 1–30.

———. "Thomas Wolfe's 'Last Manuscript.'" *Harvard Library Bulletin*, 23 (April 1975), 203–211.

———. "The 'Wolfegate' Affair." *Harvard Magazine*, 84 (September/October 1981), 48–62.

Kennedy, William F. "Economic Ideas in Contemporary Literature – The Novels of Thomas Wolfe." *The Southern Economic Journal*, 20 (July 1953), 35–50.

Klein, Carole. "Thomas Wolfe: The Aggrieved and Greedy Lover." In *Thomas Wolfe at Eighty-seven*, pp. 82–85.

Kussy, Bella. "The Vitalist Trend and Thomas Wolfe." *The Sewanee Review*, 50 (July-September 1942), 306–324.

Lanzinger, Klaus. "Thomas Wolfe's Modern Hero: Goethe's Faust." In *Thomas Wolfe: A Harvard Perspective*, edited by Richard S. Kennedy. Athens, OH: Croissant, 1983, pp. 21–30.

"Laurels to an Editor." *Publisher's Weekly*, 127 (23 March 1935), 1230–1231.

Ledig-Rowohlt, H. M. "Thomas Wolfe in Berlin." *The American Scholar*, 22 (Spring 1953), 185–201.

Letters to the Editor. *The Saturday Review of Literature* (23 May 1936), 9. See De-Voto's review of *The Story of a Novel*, "Genius Is Not Enough."

Letters to the Editor. *The Saturday Review of Literature* (11 August 1951), 22–25.

Lewis, Sinclair. From Sinclair Lewis's press conference on winning the Nobel Prize. *The New York Times*, 6 November 1930, p. 27.

———. Address on receiving the Nobel Prize in Literature, 12 December 1930. In *The Man from Main Street*, edited by Harry E. Maule and Melville Cane. New York, 1953, p. 17.

Macauley, Thurston. "Thomas Wolfe: A Writer's Problems." *Publisher's Weekly* 134 (24 December 1938), 2150–2152.

McElderry, Bruce R., Jr. "The Durable Humor of *Look Homeward, Angel*." *Arizona Quarterly*, 11 (Summer 1955), 123–128.

Maloney, Martin. "A Study of Semantic States: Thomas Wolfe and the Faustian Sickness." *General Semantics Bulletin*, nos. 16–17 (1955), 15–25.

Meyerhoff, Hans. "Death of a Genius: The Last Days of Thomas Wolfe." *Commentary*, 13 (January 1952), 44–51.

Miehe, Patrick. "The Outline of Thomas Wolfe's Last Book." *Harvard Library Bulletin*, 21 (1973), 400–401.

Natanson, Maurice. "The Privileged Moment: A Study in the Rhetoric of Thomas Wolfe." *Quarterly Journal of Speech*, 43 (April 1957), 143–150.

Nowell, Elizabeth. Letter to Edward Aswell, 29 August 1950 (UNC-CH).

Owen, Guy. " 'An Angel on the Porch' and *Look Homeward, Angel*." *The Thomas Wolfe Newsletter*, 4 (Fall 1980), 21–24.

Perkins, Maxwell E. "Scribner's and Thomas Wolfe." *Carolina Magazine*, 68 (October 1938), 15–17.

———. "Thomas Wolfe." *Harvard Library Bulletin*, 1 (Autumn 1947), 269–277.

Phelps, William Lyon. "As I Like It." *Scribner's Magazine*, 97 (June 1935), 379–382.

Priestley, J. B. "The Moderns: Between the Wars." In *Literature and Western Man*. New York: Harper; London: Heinemann, 1960, pp. 438–440.

Pusey, William. "The German Vogue of Thomas Wolfe." *The Germanic Review*, 23 (April 1948), 131–148.

Reaver, J. Russell, and Robert I. Strozier. "Thomas Wolfe and Death." *Georgia Review*, 16 (Fall 1962), 330–350.

Reeves, Paschal. "Thomas Wolfe: Notes on Three Characters." *Modern Fiction Studies*, 11 (Autumn 1965), 275–285.

"The Results If Any." *The Saturday Review of Literature* (7 December 1935).

Rothman, Nathan L. "Thomas Wolfe and James Joyce: A Study in Literary Influence." In *A Southern Vanguard*, ed. Alan Tate. Englewood Cliffs, New Jersey: Prentice-Hall, 1947, pp. 52–77.

Rubin, Louis D., Jr. "The Historical Image of Modern Southern Writing." *Journal of Southern History*, 22 (1956), 147–166.

———. "Thomas Wolfe: Time and the South." In *The Faraway Country: Writers of the Modern South*. U of Washington P, 1963, pp. 72–104.

———. "The Sense of Being Young." Introduction to *Thomas Wolfe: A Collection of Critical Essays*, pp. 1–30.

Schneider, Duane. "Thomas Wolfe, England, and *Look Homeward Angel*." In *Thomas Wolfe: A Harvard Perspective*, pp. 55–72.

Seib, Kenneth. "Thomas Wolfe in Miniature." *The Thomas Wolfe Newsletter*, 2 (Fall 1978), 10–15.

Senior, Nanette. Postcard to Myra Champion, 10 August 1953 (Pack Memorial Library, Asheville, North Carolina).

Skinner, James L. "Hugh Holman: From Goldville to Clinton." *The South Carolina Review*, 16 (Spring 1984), 35–49.

Skipp, Francis E. "*Of Time and the River*: The Final Editing." *Papers of the Bibliographical Society of America*, 64 (1970), 313–322.

Slack, Robert C. "Thomas Wolfe: The Second Cycle." In *Lectures on Modern Novelists*, ed. Arthur T. Broes et al. Pittsburgh: Carnegie Institute of Technology, 1963, pp. 41–53.

Snyder, William U. "Thomas Wolfe, Women, Narcissism and Dependency." In *Thomas Wolfe at Eighty-seven*, pp. 93–99.

Stearns, Monroe M. "The Metaphysics of Thomas Wolfe." *College English*, 6 (January 1945), 193–199.

Taylor, Walter Fuller. "Thomas Wolfe and the Middle-Class Tradition." *The South Atlantic Quarterly*, 52 (October 1953), 543–554.

Thompson, Betty. "Thomas Wolfe: Two Decades of Criticism." *The South Atlantic Quarterly*, 49 (July 1950), 378–392.

Underwood, Thomas A. "Thomas Wolfe's Trip to Richmond: Détente at the 1936 MLA Meeting." *The Virginia Magazine of History and Biography*, 95 (July 1987), 353–362.

Unrue, Darlene. "The Gothic Matrix of *Look Homeward, Angel*." In *Critical Essays on Thomas Wolfe*, pp.48–56.

Van Doren, Mark. "The Art of American Fiction." *The Nation*, 138 (25 April 1934), 471–474.

Wagenknecht, Edward. "Gargantua as Novelist." In *Cavalcade of the American Novel*. New York: Holt, Rinehart, and Winston, 1952, pp. 409–415.

Walser, Richard. "Look Homeward Angel." In *Thomas Wolfe: An Introduction and Interpretation*. New York, Chicago, San Francisco, Toronto, and London: Holt, Rinehart and Winston, 1961, pp. 53–71.

———. "The Angel and the Ghost." In *Thomas Wolfe and the Glass of Time*, pp. 45–67.

———. "The Angel in North Carolina." *The Thomas Wolfe Newsletter*, 3 (Fall 1979), 19–25.

Watkins, Floyd C. "Rhetoric in Southern Writing: Wolfe." *The Georgia Review*, 12 (Spring 1958), 79–82.

Wolfe, Fred. Letter to the Editor. *The Saturday Review of Literature*, 34 (11 August 1951), 23–24.

Miscellaneous

"Bank Examiner Blames Boom." *The New York Times*, 21 November 1930, 43:1.

"Brooklyn Man Falls to Death." *The New York Times*, 30 April 1938, p. 16.

"8 Carolina Banks Fail as Boom Ends." *The New York Times*, 21 November 1930, sec. 43:1.

"Mythical Estates in England: Bait to Defraud Americans." *London Times*, 27 February 1933, p. 6E.

"Two Die As Blast Rocks the Marguery and Routs Guests." *The New York Times*, 4 January 1930, pp. 1–2.

"Wallace B. Davis Points With Pride to Asheville and Her Splendid Growth." *The* (Asheville) *Sunday Citizen*, 31 July, 1927.

Index